Streets, Railroads, and the Great Strike of 1877

HISTORICAL STUDIES OF URBAN AMERICA
A series edited by James R. Grossman and Kathleen N. Conzen

David O. Stowell

Streets, Railroads, *and the* Great Strike *of* 1877

The University of Chicago Press • Chicago & London

David Stowell is assistant professor of history at Keene State College, where he has taught since 1994. He received his Ph.D. in history from the State University of New York at Buffalo.

The University of Chicago Press, Chicago 60637
The University of Chicago Press, Ltd., London

© 1999 by The University of Chicago
All rights reserved. Published 1999

08   07   06   05   04   03   02   01   00   99   1   2   3   4   5

ISBN 0-226-77668-9 (cloth)
ISBN 0-226-77669-7 (paper)

Library of Congress Cataloging-in-Publication Data

Stowell, David O. (David Omar)
    Streets, railroads, and the Great Strike of 1877 / David O.
Stowell.
        p.   cm. — (Historical studies of urban America)
    Based on the author's Ph.D. thesis.
    Includes bibliographical references and index.
    ISBN 0-226-77668-9 (alk. paper) — ISBN 0-226-77669-7 (pbk. :
alk. paper)
    1. Railroad Strike, U.S., 1877. 2. Strikes and lockouts—Rail-
roads—United States—History—19th century. 3. Railroads—
United States—Employees—History—19th century. 4. Working
class—United States—History—19th century. I. Title. II. Series.
HD5325.R2 1877.S76   1999
331.89′281385′097309034—dc21   98-50941
                                                          CIP

To Sabine

Contents

Illustrations

Acknowledgements

This study began its life on a hot summer day in the research library of the Buffalo and Erie County Historical Society, when I first encountered notations of petitions against some of the injurious consequences of the railroad's intersection with streets. As a dissertation, it won the Urban History Association's "best dissertation" award for 1992. Winning that award pushed me to turn a dissertation into a book; so too did the critical encouragement of James Grossman, coeditor of the University of Chicago's series on Historical Studies of Urban America. Other colleagues and friends provided invaluable aid and support as well. In particular, I am indebted to the following people for reading and offering written critiques of the manuscript at various points in its development: William W. Freehling, David A. Gerber, Paul Hehn, Bruce Laurie, Sabine Nicole Merz, and Nick Salvatore. Bill Freehling, David Gerber, and Nick Salvatore have been steadfast personal and professional supporters of my work; I cannot thank them enough. David Gerber has been both critic and friend for over a decade now. Bruce Laurie volunteered to read the dissertation of an unemployed history Ph.D. he happened to encounter working as a clerk in an Amherst video store. Matt Howard, my editor at Chicago, has been great to work with. I also want to thank my manuscript editor, Lila Weinberg, and managing editor, Anita Samen. Each and every one of the people noted above share in the merits of this work; any deficiencies are the sole intellectual property of the author. I also want to thank one of my colleagues at Keene State College, Andy Wilson, for his friendship and support.

The staff of the following institutions deserve thanks for the assistance they offered during the course of the research for this book: the Buffalo and Erie County Historical Society, the Lockwood Library of the State University of New York at Buffalo, the Buffalo and Erie County Public Library, the Albany Public Library, the McKinney Library of the Albany

Institute of History & Art, the New York State Library and Archives, the Onondaga County Public Library, the Onondaga Historical Association, the Buffalo, Albany, and Syracuse City Halls, the William Allen Neilson Library of Smith College, the W.E.B. Du Bois Library of the University of Massachusetts at Amherst, and the Jones Library of the Town of Amherst, Massachusetts. I especially want to thank Mary Bell and Catherine Mason of the Buffalo and Erie County Historical Society; John Valenti, formerly of the City Clerk's Office, City of Syracuse, and Patrick Driscoll, Deputy City Clerk, readily provided access to the original common council proceedings; Scott McCloud, reference librarian at the McKinney Library of the Albany Institute of History & Art, professionally and expeditiously handled my requests for photographic reproductions from the Library's collections; Judy Haven, of the Onondaga Historical Association, was always of great help. Funding from the Keene State College Professional Development Fund made possible the purchase of many of the illustrations.

Last, I thank Sabine for her encouragement and her love. Her perseverance in the face of duplicity is testimony to her fortitude. I dedicate this book to her.

David Omar Stowell
Amherst, Massachusetts
June 1998

Introduction

The year 1877 looms large in the panorama of mid-to-late nineteenth-century America. The inauguration of the Republican Rutherford B. Hayes as U.S. president ended the dangerous political crisis of 1876–77; white rule was restored throughout the South as Reconstruction died; and a nationwide strike of railroad workers triggered the Great Strike, "one of the bitterest explosions of class warfare in American history." With Reconstruction at an end, a new era of increasing conflict between labor and capital commenced.[1]

The Great Strike sealed the demise of Reconstruction by presenting the federal government, dominated by a bourgeoisie and Republican party based in the North, with a grave and immediate crisis. Federal troops, which only weeks earlier guarded the Louisiana statehouse, massed in northern cities to help suppress rioting free white laborers and other urban residents. As Eric Foner writes, the Great Strike "marked a fundamental shift in the nation's political agenda," for the Strike "propelled to the forefront of politics 'the question of labor and capital, work and wages.'"[2] Reconstruction and the issues that had arisen from the Civil War as well as the abolition of slavery receded from the national spotlight. This book is a comparative study of the Great Strike in three upstate New York cities—Buffalo, Albany, and Syracuse. It argues that a powerful *current* of the uprisings consisted of a spontaneous rebellion of urban residents against one of the most direct and damaging ways they experienced capitalist industrialization outside of the workplace, namely, the use of city streets by railroads. Such a perspective, however, is not shared by other historians of the Strike. Historians generally portray the Great Strike of 1877 as a "strike"—a job action of labor—albeit, a strike with insurrectionary overtones.[3] On July 25, 1877, as the Great Strike climaxed in the United States, the German historian and philosopher Karl Marx wrote a letter to his friend and colleague Friedrich Engels. "What do you say to the workers of the United States," he queried. "This first outbreak against the associated capital oligarchy that has arisen since the Civil War, will of course be smashed but it could serve as the beginning of the establishment of a serious labor party."[4] The Strike, in Marx's view, was the first national uprising of the working class against "associated capital," and stemmed from conflicts between labor and capital in the workplaces of industrializing America. Marx's passing commentary on the Strike, including his hope that the event would stimulate the political organization of labor, encompasses the perspectives of most, if not all, of the scholarly studies of the Strike by twentieth-century historians.

Within the broad consensus of viewing the Great Strike as a labor uprising, there are differences in perspective and emphasis. For example, Alan Trachtenberg writes that the Great Strike was "the first instance of machine smashing and class violence on a national scale," which, he suggests, arose largely as a result of "the trauma inflicted on American society by unexpectedly rapid mechanization." Shelton Stromquist views the Strike as not only a dramatic expression of class violence but "the clarion call of a new class," specifically "a broader, urban working class not bound by differences of trade or skill." And Robert V. Bruce's seminal *1877: Year of Violence* views the Strike as an event triggered by the railroad workers' walkout, but predicated on the explosive living conditions of the urban lower classes—"the mob-in-being"—which "brooded on the oppression of labor, the arrogance of capital, the wild inequality of fortune, the misery of tenement life, the fear and hunger and degradation of hard times."[5] The overriding theme in the historiography regarding 1877, however, is to view the Strike as a struggle between employers and employees set in the context of the nation's first industrial depression.

It follows from the prevailing view of the Great Strike as a "strike" that the most common portrayal of the 1877 "crowds"[6] contains two elements: railroad workers on strike due to pay cuts and other grievances, and workers who bore no wage relation to the railroad striking in solidarity with railroad workers and/or striking over their own workplace issues. In part, the depiction of the crowd is a function of the urban setting being studied and the specific intracity location of crowd activity. In Terre Haute, Indiana—a small city of 26,000—the strike and its crowds were an affair of railroad workers and few, if any, nonrailroad workers. In St. Louis, for a short while at least, a "general strike" of the working classes was underway, while in Chicago the composition of a working-class crowd could vary significantly from ward to ward and day to day.[7] The presence of "others" or "sympathizers"—women, the unemployed, boys, and even middle-class people—is acknowledged, but the "crowd" is cast for the most part as a heterogeneous collection of workers. It is as if the city street of 1877—the focal point of most crowds—is but an extension of the point of production and the crowd composed solely of proletarians holding and acting upon workplace grievances. At the same time, portraying the Great Strike as an affair of workers (employed and unemployed) puts men in the forefront and women—who by many accounts played prominent roles in crowds—in the background, given the fact that men overwhelmingly dominated the paid work force.

Few propositions, and even less evidence, have been put forward as to why workers with no wage relation to the railroad would join striking railroad workers in stopping trains—or, over the strenuous objections of railroad workers, destroy railroad property and equipment. Supposedly, working-class consciousness bound together both groups, who were expressing their opposition to the capitalist terms of industrialization by attacking the nation's preeminent symbol of that process, the railroad. It has been asserted, for example, that "as soon as the strike began other workers spontaneously associated their own grievances against employers with those of the trainmen." Similarly, Marianne Debouzy states that the "community of claims of the different sections of the working class" led a diversity of wage earners—railroad strikers and other laborers—to join together during the Strike.[8]

In addition, while historians have acknowledged nonworking-class support for the striking railwaymen, they espouse equally vague statements as to why portions of the community supported the Strike and even, for example, joined crowds to stop a train in a city street. Most historians agree with the proposition of the labor historian Walter Licht that "community supporters rallied to the cause of railroad workers to protest against economic conditions and hard times, and more important, to challenge the growing, encroaching political and economic powers of concentrated capital, a power destructive of cherished republican ideals and a power best symbolized by the nation's first and largest corporations, the railroads."[9] Other studies point to "anti-monopoly" sentiments which cut across class lines and naturally targeted railroads for their monopolistic business practices. And it is suggested, as noted above, that the widespread "trauma inflicted on American society by unexpectedly rapid mechanization" produced widespread "anger and wrath against the railroad companies."[10] Terms such as "economic conditions and hard times," "the arrogance of capital," "anger and wrath," and "republican ideals," however, are vague and imprecise—they reveal little about specific and concrete grievances involving railroad corporations, and the role these grievances played in the Great Strike.[11]

A number of other general themes stand out in the historiography of the Great Strike of 1877. First, as Philip Foner criticizes in *The Great Labor Uprising of 1877,* there is a tendency to see the Strike as "born out of the frustrations of a depression"—the Depression of 1873, from which the country did not recover until 1878–79.[12] This tendency is most evident in the studies of Bruce, David T. Burbank, Philip English Mackey, and Bill L. Weaver, for whom the depression is an indispensable factor in the development of the Strike.[13] Second, as Nick Salvatore observes in his article on the Great Strike in Terre Haute, most historians treating the Strike remain "chronologically locked within the time frame of the last two weeks of July 1877."[14] This chronological near-sightedness leads to an overemphasis on the class anger evident in the Strikes, and precludes in-depth studies of the communities in which the Strikes occurred. Third, as Salvatore also points out, most studies of the Strike treat the event as delineating the end of one historical era and the start of another. The Strike is viewed as a "watershed" event in U.S. history. The Strike as turning point involves the concept that it helped to mark the end of the Civil War and the Reconstruction period and the full-fledged commencement of the era of the Industrial Revolution with its epic battles between labor and capital. This perspective entails assertions that the Strike was both the expression of a growing class consciousness among urban workers and a factor stimulating the development of that consciousness. In short, the Strike is seen as marking a sharp break with the past. Indeed, it is as if the Strike has more in common with strikes in 1886 and 1892 (or even strikes in the early twentieth century) than with, for example, popular actions against track laying in city streets in the 1840s.[15] Last, if there is a single idea historians use to synthesize the 1877 strikes, it is the concept that they spurred the formation of trade and industrial unions and the political organization of the working classes. Particularly on the level of politics, it is routinely asserted (and rarely empirically examined) that the Strike translated into votes for the nascent workingmen's and Greenback-Labor parties or, as Alexander Saxton writes, a "political revolt against the two-party establishment."[16]

Two final observations must be made about the historiography of the Great Strike. Much is attributed to the thousands of urban residents who took to the streets in July of 1877. But the plain fact is that we do not have direct evidence concerning their motivations and intentions. What little direct evidence we have takes the form of a handful of "interviews" in the press about why the Strike was occurring—usually an interview with a striking railroad worker or excerpts of speeches given to crowds by individuals like Albert Parsons, the famous anarchist (during the Strike in Chicago). The research, however, indicates that striking railroad workers, with few exceptions, were a minority in most crowds,[17] and leaders frequently do not speak for the rank and file. Methodologically speaking, in other words, all studies of the Great Strike, including this one, draw inferences about the nature and meaning of the Strike from one or more of the following: the behavior of crowds; information on some of the rank-and-file crowd participants (those arrested by the police and/or wounded and killed in clashes with armed forces) and Strike leaders; information on those who actively opposed the Strike; and the social, political, economic, and cultural contexts (local and national) surrounding the Strike. It is also difficult to avoid the conclusion that the nature of the Great Strike has been judged in large measure in the light of events occurring in the years and decades after the Strike (usually the development of the labor movement in the 1880s and 1890s), as if historians were unconsciously trying to make up for the relative dearth of information on the Great Strike's participants and their motivations by reading the history of the 1880s and 1890s backward into 1877.

The last observation is a critical one and central to the thesis of this book. The towns and cities where the Strikes occurred are treated by nearly all historians as inert containers within which the uprisings took place. In 1959, Bruce seemed to set the Strike in the context of the socioeconomic processes underway and intensifying in post–Civil War, urban America. Bruce wrote that "whenever quitting time poured thousands into the streets, whenever warm weather emptied the tenements onto sidewalks and front stoops, there stood the mob, ready-made." What was on the minds of these lower-class peoples of the manufactories and tenements that would incline them toward "mob" behavior? According to Bruce, they "brooded" on the "dishonesty and cynicism of politics, the injustice of law and courts, the weakness of law enforcement . . . the oppression of labor, the arrogance of capital, the wild inequality of fortune, the misery of tenement life, the fear and hunger and degradation of hard times." The railroads played a key role in the intense transformations so evident after the war, primarily industrialization and urbanization. "Within the memory of living men," Bruce points out, the railroads had and still were creating "the map of the new urban age."[18] On that map could be found some of the key causal factors underlying the Great Strike. When railroad management decided to cut wages in July of 1877 and portions of the railroad work force went out on strike in response, the explosive elements found in the urban social structure detonated.

Bruce's suggestion that there was something specifically urban about the Great Strike, other than the fact that it took place in cities, was left largely undeveloped in his own and later work. David Roediger observed in his 1985 *Journal of Social History* article that the Great Strike in St. Louis had yet to be situated in the urban history of the period. His observation is equally applicable today for nearly all studies of the Great Strike. Urban forces and processes have little to do with the nature and scope of the Strike, according to most historians. The urban environment is but "a passive backdrop" to the Great Strike. This study argues that the epic uprisings known as the "Great Strike" of 1877 cannot be comprehended apart from the urban environments within which the uprisings originated and developed. Indeed, these strikes, beginning as a job action of segments of the railroad work force, became the "Great Strike" by virtue of their interaction with aspects of the urban environment. To borrow a term from Sam Bass Warner, Jr., if we are to erect an interpretive "scaffolding" for the Great Strike of 1877, and other strikes as well, they must be situated in their urban milieus. The Great Strike's relationship to the city extends beyond the city as site—the Strike was also *of* the city. The city— especially, the physical relationship between railroads and streets—is an independent variable of the first order.[19]

The widely accepted but narrowly conceived view of the Great Strike as a labor rebellion has inhibited further inquiry into the Strike and the differing concerns and identities of people in the 1877 crowds. As many studies illustrate, the working classes defined themselves in ways besides that of worker or laborer.[20] Workers also saw themselves as, for example, Democrats or Republicans, Irishmen or Germans, Protestants or Catholics, men or women, or the residents of Main or Elk Streets. Whether these identities were mutually exclusive, overlapping, competing, or reinforcing is not at issue here. The point is that the Great Strike involved processes and sentiments in addition to those emanating from workshops and factories. The Great Strike of 1877 must also be treated as an urban phenomenon, not just as a narrowly drawn component of labor history.

Given the centrality of the railroads in both the U.S. economy of the mid- to late-nineteenth century and the Great Strike, it is remarkable that the Strike has not been viewed in the context of conflicts between railroads and communities in post–Civil War America. Railroads—"the nation's first big business" and a harbinger of capitalist corporations—

were "one of the most revolutionary forces of the nineteenth century," yet we have few critical studies of their impact on American cities.[21] Railroads created, sustained, and symbolized the new industrial order; indeed, they were "the most important single sector of the American industrial revolution." The railroads were the most visible and culpable component of "the disorderly processes of capitalist development and urbanization," for there was no greater sower of disorder in an urban area than a steam locomotive running down a crowded street.[22] Furthermore, a study of the impact of railroads on urban areas and the ensuing conflicts illustrates and enlarges upon Ira Katznelson's assertion that "capitalist industrialization was experienced directly as conflict over the use of scarce space at the community level."[23] Katznelson's proposition is derived from his analysis of class and politics in antebellum urban America, and refers to residential or territorial conflicts between different ethno-religious groups. I apply his concept to the post–Civil War period in which, regardless of ethnicity or religion, capitalist industrialization was experienced by a wide array of urban residents as railroad encroachment on scarce urban space.

One of the most contested spaces in the nineteenth century was the city street, and there many people—workers, women and children, middle-class people—daily experienced capitalist industrialization as railroad "encroachment." A powerful current of the Great Strike was a spontaneous rebellion against that invasion of people's streets. Thus viewed, the Great Strike becomes more an element of urban history, less one of labor history. The Strike was explosive and the crowds socially heterogeneous precisely because the railroads' invasion of scarce urban space fused workplace with neighborhood and community concerns over industrialization.[24]

In an article published in 1980, labor historian David Montgomery wrote that in the mid-nineteenth century there was a "gradual transition from neighborhood to workplace as the locus of mobilization in popular protest and the replacement of community grievances by wage demands as the cause of confrontation." Indeed, the Great Strike of 1877 was for Montgomery a prime example of the changed foundation for popular urban struggles.[25] Urban life outside of the workplace, however, continued over many decades to generate tensions and conflicts. In fact, no such transition ever occurred.[26] Grievances generated outside of the workplace never lost their capacity to mobilize people or provide the foundation for popular protest, whether the setting is the late-nineteeth century and railroad use of crowded urban space, or the mid- to late-twentieth century and conflicts over busing to achieve racial integration or the location of waste dumps.

Conflicts over the use of urban space were numerous and intense. Railroad use of particular city streets, for example, pitted railroad corporations against neighborhoods, against nonindustrial property owners, and against any users of avenues occupied by railroad tracks. Streets were vital arteries of economic and social life, and people from throughout the social structure opposed their use by railroads and the critical consequences of such use: death and injury, obstruction of specific forms of commerce and travel, loss of business, noise, and, on occasion, fires. These concrete issues fostered "resentment" and "anger" at railroads in the 1870s, and in the Great Strike more than labor history came to a climax. Particularly for people who did not work for the railroad, the great majority of most crowds, a powerful current of the Great Strike was the product of the development of a capitalist, industrializing infrastructure and the resistance it engendered in urban areas. For years before July 1877, opponents of the railroads' intersection with streets and neighborhoods tried traditional and legal forms of protest: petitions and litigation. These methods were largely ineffectual in dealing with the injurious consequences of railroad encroachment.

As Herbert Gutman wrote with respect to a series of strikes in 1873–74 that foreshadowed the Great Strike, "[T]he significance of the strikes lay not in their success or failure but rather in the readiness of the strikers to express their grievances in a dramatic, direct, and frequently telling manner."[27] During the Great Strike, urban residents of streets and neighborhoods traversed by railroads attacked railroad property, spiked switches, and stopped trains from moving down their streets—past retail stores, saloons, churches, schools, and residences. By such "direct" and "telling" acts, people confronted a force hazardous to their lives and well-being. For one week, few trains thundered down city streets, and no locomotives crushed residents "caught on the track" or smashed wagons to pieces. For those who suffered the presence of the railroad, July 1877 provided an excellent opportunity to enter streets lined with railroad tracks and strike a blow (however ineffectual) against the railroad's deadly use of a vital urban space.

On the evening of July 23, 1877, in the midst of Buffalo's "Great Strike," a crowd gathered at the railroad crossing on Hamburgh Street. Striking railroad workers were present in this crowd. Also present, apparently, were many people, workers and nonworkers, with no wage relationship to railroad corporations. The crowd intercepted a train. After striking railroadmen boarded the stopped train, they learned that the wages of the Buffalo and Jamestown railroadmen operating the train had not been cut, as theirs had. Consequently, the trainmen had no desire to strike. Respecting the wishes of their fellow railroad workers, the striking railwaymen proceeded to tell the Hamburgh Street crowd that the train would continue. But other members of this crowd had a different agenda. As the train crept ahead, a number of people from the crowd jumped forward and removed the pins connecting one car to another. The train stopped again. The railroad strikers recognized the opposition of many in the crowd to any trains being allowed to travel across Hamburgh Street and through the city. Hence, the strikers positioned themselves along either side of the train, carefully guarding the coupling pins. In doing so, they took on the role performed by police and militia in similar incidents. Ever so slowly, the train moved through and away from the crowd. Once through, the railroadmen told the passengers on the train that "they owed their safe passage to the strikers."[28]

On the evening of July 25, 1877, a crowd of men and boys gathered at the Van Woert Street railroad crossing in Albany. They waited for a train to approach the crossing, and as one did, they subjected the train to a barrage of stones and other "missiles." Militiamen sent to the crossing immediately after the incident were treated to the same; the crowd "assailed [the soldiers] with stones" before retreating. The following night, another train was attacked at the Van Woert Street crossing. After the second episode of antirailroad violence at this crossing, the mayor of Albany specifically requested that no troops be sent to "that locality." Instead, local police would protect the crossing and any trains passing through the street. The military obliged.[29]

In the absence of statements from the actors themselves, why did a group of men and boys stone trains at the Van Woert Street crossing in Albany? And why did some people in the Hamburgh Street crowd oppose the passage of any trains? What I call the traditional labor interpretation of the Great Strike would answer essentially as follows: At the Van Woert Street crossing in Albany, people stoned trains because the railroads were the "symbol" of the harsh terms of industrial capitalism in the 1870s. The traditional interpretation of 1877 does not provide a ready answer for the different agendas of those in the Hamburgh Street crowd; the reply probably would be that those who uncoupled the train and wanted to see all train traffic stopped were either striking railroad workers themselves (evincing a split over tactics), or were workers on strike from other industries who sought to create a general strike. Yet, there are other possibilities every bit as plausible, persuasive, and compatible with the limited evidence as those offered by labor historians. The explanations posed in the traditional interpretation of 1877 largely ignore the urban environment within which—and from which—such behavior occurred. What was there about railroads and cities that may have generated antipathy toward railroads? Besides failing to ask this, the widely accepted labor interpretation views the workers in the 1877 crowds one-dimensionally; in accounts of the Great Strike, workers are disconnected from their city. For example, they are seen as employees of a particular firm or industrial sector but not as people who maintain residences on certain streets, frequent neighborhood saloons and groceries, or walk to work each day.

At the Van Woert and Hamburgh Street crossings, I argue, people stoned trains and tried to stop trains, respectively, because for years they were subjected daily to the noise, disorder, and dangers consequent upon the railroads' intersection with streets and neighborhoods. Everyone risked life and limb to pass over dangerous grade crossings; dozens lost their lives and limbs. Urban inhabitants were required to negotiate such hazards while on their way to work, to the grocer, to the saloon, to a friend's, to church. The chances were good that more than one person in the Van Woert and Hamburgh Street crowds lost a family member, friend, or neighbor to the railroads in the years prior to 1877. There are other reasons evident from an examination of the urban milieu of the Great Strike and the relationship between railroads and cities in the years leading up to the Great Strike. Small nonindustrial property owners, such as grocers and saloonkeepers, opposed the railroads' intersection with streets given the consequences. Not only were they appalled by the human costs attendant upon the railroads' use of streets, but those same streets contained their customers and property. Streets were vital arteries of local commerce, pedestrian and horsepowered. The sight and sound of passing locomotives created periodic havoc in streets, prompting countless "runaways"—horsepowered wagons and carriages careening down streets with or without their drivers. In short, tracks and trains sowed disorder, killed and injured people with stunning regularity, and injured specific forms of local commerce. There were many concrete reasons for a wide variety of people, workers and nonworkers, to hate the railroads in the 1870s and to participate in crowd behavior that injured the interests of railroad corporations. These reasons include those offered in the traditional labor interpretation of 1877. Walter Licht perceptively writes that the "labor struggles of the nineteenth and early twentieth centuries have to be understood as community uprisings as well."[30] This book emphasizes the urban roots of the Great Strike overlooked by previous studies; combined with the insights of the traditional labor approach to 1877, they together explain the widespread series of working-class strikes and popular attacks against railroads known as the "Great Strike" of 1877. The Great Strikes were indeed community uprisings.

1 The "Industrial Revolution Incarnate"

You walk down the main street of a large town: and, slap-dash, headlong, pell-mell, down the middle of the street; with pigs burrowing and boys flying kites and playing marbles, and men smoking, and women talking, and children crawling, close to the very rails; there comes tearing along a mad locomotive with its train of cars. . . [1]

Charles Dickens, *American Notes for General Circulation,* 1842

Had Charles Dickens visited America again three decades later, his observation would have been equally valid: railroads ran their tracks and trains right through the densely packed streets and neighborhoods of cities throughout the United States. Leo Marx refers to steam locomotives and railroads in general as the "industrial revolution incarnate."[2] Indeed, the railroads embodied capitalist industrialization in a number of ways, not the least of which was the massive, seemingly unstoppable nature of the steam locomotive itself. Until the 1880s, the most widely used steam locomotive in the United States was an eight-wheel engine known as the 4-4-0 or "American type."[3] This particular version of the Iron Horse was an imposing creature weighing on average about thirty-five tons or 70,000 pounds. The driving wheels of the New York Central Railroad's 1874 4-4-0 were slightly over six feet in diameter—in other words, taller than most adult men and women. Perhaps the most widely recognized feature of the nineteenth-century steam locomotive, next to the smoke-spewing funnel, was the euphemistically named "cowcatcher" which jutted out in front of the locomotive (see fig. 1). Cowcatchers were typically iron cantilevers and often weighed 1,000 pounds or more; earlier cowcatchers made of wood proved inadequate to their task. Cowcatchers did not "catch" hapless cows caught on the tracks, of course; they smashed them off the tracks. Their function was to hurl any object—cows, horses, wagons, anything and everything—off

Fig. 1. A typical steam locomotive poised for a run through city streets, Albany, c. 1870.

the tracks and out of the path of the locomotive. In doing so, the probability of any "obstruction" getting underneath the locomotive and derailing the train was greatly lowered, if not entirely eliminated.[4]

Buffalo, Albany, and Syracuse were located along the Erie Canal in upstate New York. Buffalo lay at the western end of the canal, next to Lake Erie, and some twenty miles south of Niagara Falls. Albany, the state's capitol, lay 260 miles to the east. Albany was the eastern terminus of the canal—the point at which the canal joined the Hudson River; New York City lay about 130 miles downriver. Roughly midway between the two cities lay Syracuse. By the 1840s, the cities were also connected by railroad tracks. All three cities were industrializing in the period 1860–80, although the levels and intensity of that complex and uneven process differed significantly. Using the mean level of capitalization recorded in the 1880 census for "manufactures" as a rough index of industrialization, Buffalo was clearly the most industrialized of the cities. The mean level of capitalization for all manufactures in Buffalo was $22,695, for Albany $18,264, and for Syracuse $11,308. Buffalo's mean level of capitalization was 24% greater than Albany's; Albany's was 62% greater than that of Syracuse. Indicative of the accelerated development of industrialization, the population of the three cities grew dramatically during the period 1860–80. Buffalo's population increased 91% during the period; Albany's increased 46%; Syracuse's population increased 84%. Buffalo had a population of 155,134, Albany a population of 90,758, Syracuse a population of 51,792 in 1880. They ranked thirteenth, twenty-first, and thirty-second, respectively, in the United States.[5]

The Iron Horse came to Buffalo, Albany, and Syracuse in the 1830s. Indeed, the first railroad in New York State was the Mohawk and Hudson Railroad that traveled between Albany and Schenectady. That line began operation with the famous "De Witt Clinton" in 1831. Two years later, the Saratoga and Schenectady Railroad was running two trains every day from Albany to the fashionable resort community of Saratoga. The first railroad in Buffalo was the Buffalo and Niagara Railroad which started operations in 1836. In Syracuse, the Syracuse and Utica Railroad began to run trains in 1839.[6]

Railroad construction proceeded rapidly. By 1842, one could travel by rail from Albany to Buffalo (via Syracuse and other cities), albeit with irregular schedules and numerous transfers. This route became the New York Central Railroad in 1853 when Erastus Corning, an Albany merchant, consolidated the various lines stretching between the two cities. The Central quickly became the largest corporate entity in the State of New York. Some 2,682 miles of track were laid by 1860, and virtually all parts of the state had at least some service.[7]

During the 1830s, many villages, towns, and cities became enthusiastic solicitors and promoters of railroads. The commencement of a railroad was frequently the cause for celebration; in Syracuse, for example, the running of the first train down Washington Street was the occasion for a festive dinner organized by the city and the railroad company and attended by 500 people.[8] Competition for railroads was frequently intense, and municipalities jousted with one another over railroad routes. The route to Saratoga was particularly coveted in the Albany area. When businessmen and civic boosters in the neighboring city of Troy managed to take control of the Saratoga and Schenectady railroad in an effort to control travel to Saratoga, Albany businessmen were furious. The advantages of traveling and shipping by rail were readily apparent, and local businessmen and municipal boosters equated railroad connections with economic growth, progress, and prosperity. Conversely, isolation and economic loss would result from failing to get a rail connection.[9] Few communities wanted to miss out on what appeared to be, and frequently was, the engine of economic growth.

In the rush to have a railroad connection, more than 300 villages, towns, and cities in New York State provided $37 million dollars in cash or bonds to eighty-five railroad corporations. By the mid-to-late 1870s, though, particularly after the 1873 depression, many communities regretted this largesse. Indeed, "the enthusiasm for railroads so evident in pre–Civil War years gave way to indifference and in many instances to open hostility." Railroad rate "wars" were legendary, with devastating consequences for local businessmen, shippers, farmers, and others. Cutthroat competition between railroads in a context of rapid expansion led to numerous bankruptcies and reorganizations—frequently at the expense of the investments of scores of communities. Much of the tax burden shouldered by municipalities and taxpayers was due to investments, soured or otherwise, in railroad corporations.[10] The 1870s were also years marked by conflict between urban residents and railroads over the railroads' injurious intersection with a vital urban space.

Railroads and Streets

Railroads laid tracks and ran locomotives through city streets from their inception. For example, the first steam locomotive ran through Syracuse in June 1839. Two years earlier, the village's government had formally consented to having the Syracuse and Utica Railroad lay a track down Washington Street, one of the village's major thoroughfares. But even at that time, village leaders were concerned over the impact the railroad would have on the streets through which it was to travel. Reflecting this concern was the stipulation in the original grant that the railroad company would have to plant a row of "shade trees" on either side of the tracks to be laid on Washington Street. In 1852, when the railroad began to lay a second track on Washington Street, the street's property owners protested, but in the end they were apparently satisfied with having the railroad lay flagstone sidewalks on both sides of the entire street. And besides, many thought "there were not enough trains to be really bothersome." Nevertheless, conflicts erupted periodically over the presence of the railroad in Washington Street (see fig. 2) and other streets in the city, especially as train traffic escalated.[11]

During and especially after the Civil War, the processes of capitalist industrialization gathered speed. Although these processes and transfor-

Fig. 2. Railroad tracks on East Washington Street, Syracuse, c. 1869–1876.

mations clearly manifested themselves in the antebellum period, the war eliminated major obstacles to the advance of industrial capitalism. Southern secession not only removed from national power a slaveowning class at odds with key elements of capitalism, it also allowed the representatives of an ascendant capitalism to pass through Congress a number of measures deemed imperative for continued economic expansion. The Homestead Act of 1862, the Pacific Railroad Act (culminating in the completion of the transcontinental railroad in 1869), increased tariffs, and legislation modernizing the nation's fiscal structures were all passed courtesy of the South's absence from the U.S. Congress. With the abolition of slavery and the defeat of the slaveowning planter class, industrial capitalism faced no serious structural obstacles to expansion and development after 1865, notwithstanding the continued resistance of American Indians to the expropriation of their land and the wholesale destruction of their way of life. The Civil War was, as John Ashworth writes, a "bourgeois revolution."[12]

Railroad encroachment on urban space was for most cities a process that intensified greatly after the start of the Civil War: more tracks were laid in streets, and those tracks carried increasing numbers of trains. Philadelphia and Baltimore, for example, were cities marked by the discontinuous nature of the railroads entering the area of the city. In 1861, the tracks of various railroads did enter the city limits of Philadelphia, but none of them ran through the city and connected with other roads. In fact, "the only means of moving goods" between the various railroads terminating or starting in Philadelphia "was by drays or horse cars drawn through congested city streets." It was only under the pressure of the Civil War and the need for an expeditious movement of troops and supplies, along with the competitive threat posed by a railroad to be built from Washington, D.C., to New York City, that the various railroads in the Philadelphia area were connected. Even so, the lines were connected by a route that ran largely around the city, not through it.[13] Similar situations prevailed on the eve of the Civil War in Baltimore and other southern cities, particularly port cities. Indeed, in Petersburg and Richmond, opposition to railroad use of city streets was located primarily among those with a vested interest in maintaining the transfer business consequent upon breaks in railroad routes. According to George Rogers Taylor and Irene D. Neu, "tavern keepers, teamsters, porters, forwarding agents, retail merchants, and others" opposed the tracks. These groups had the support of the Virginia legislature. But in both cities, the exigencies of the Civil War led to track laying. Yet the opposition, based largely on business calculations, according to Taylor and Neu, was so intense, it was stipulated the tracks could only be used for military purposes and that after the war was over the tracks were to be removed.[14] In Chicago in the 1870s, railroad encroachment on urban space was especially intense as a result of the rebuilding of major portions of the city in the aftermath of the 1871 fire. The railroad companies' demand that the city government "create new railroad rights of way" to facilitate both the rebuilding and expansion of railroad routes through and around the city met with intense opposition from property owners and other residents. People wanted to limit or end the obstruction of traffic and the killing and injuring of people caused by grade level street crossings, in addition to the pollution, dirt,[15] and noise generated by trains. William Cronon estimates that, by the early 1890s, railroads were killing nearly 600 people a year at grade crossings in Chicago.[16]

Railroad encroachment on urban space increased as part and parcel of the accelerating growth of capitalist industrialization. Railroads were central actors in both the process of industrialization and capital accumulation. They were simultaneously the nation's "first big business" and a transportation network linking various sectors of the economy. Railroads commanded hundreds of millions of dollars in capital as industrial enterprises in their own right; with extensive vertical and horizontal links to the economy, as well as being a transportation network, railroads were for a time the prime agents of industrialization and "the major single source of investment" in the latter half of the nineteenth century.[17] Not surprisingly, the period from 1860 to 1890 witnessed the "most rapid construction of new track" in U.S. history; no other period of time witnessed such a quick increase in track mileage. In 1865 the nation had 35,000 miles of track; by 1880 there were 93,000 miles of track. Track mileage also increased relative to the population of the country. In 1860 there were 985 miles of track per million inhabitants; in 1880 there were 1,858 miles of track per million people. In New York State, 5,400 miles of track were laid between 1860 and 1900, an increase of nearly 50%.[18]

The railroads were one of the most visible and culpable components of "the disorderly processes of capitalist development and urbanization."[19] There was no greater manifestation of the disorder capitalist development entailed in urban areas than a steam locomotive running down a crowded city street. In fact, the conflicts that ensued between railroads and portions of the urban social structure over use of the streets are evidence that "capitalist industrialization was experienced directly as conflict over the use of scarce space at the community level."[20] The "space" of the street was the focal point of conflict between cities and the prime mover (and symbol) of capitalist industrialization: the railroads. Industrialization was experienced not only in workplaces but also in the streets and neighborhoods adjoining workplaces. In addition to experiencing increases in train traffic consequent upon the general intensification of industrialization, the cities of Buffalo, Albany, and Syracuse were specifically affected by the New York Central's new four-track freight line built in 1874.[21] The new line meant not only the quicker movement of goods shipped by rail but, more important, an increase in the number of trains traveling through Buffalo and Albany; Syracuse was spared rising levels of freight train traffic due to a bypass built around the city in 1874.[22] The volume of traffic on all the railroads in New York State increased in the post–Civil War period as industrialization intensified and the economy expanded. Given its intersection with streets and neighborhoods, the Iron Horse had a direct impact on key facets of urban life.

The Life of the Streets

City streets in nineteenth-century America served a variety of social and economic functions. Indeed, streets were central to the social and economic life of a city.[23] Clay McShane observes that "for most urban

Americans at the close of the Civil War, streets served vital neighborhood and family social uses." By the start of the twentieth century, however, streets were primarily used and viewed by many, if not most, urban residents as "arteries for transportation." But different forms of traveling through streets clashed. And as McShane demonstrates, this change was "slow, incomplete and uneven." The traditional social, economic, and recreational uses of streets persisted for many years after 1865. In the 1870s, for example, Milwaukee residents fought against the use of steam-powered, intracity transportation vehicles on the grounds that the "noise, smoke, fear of explosion, and high speed destroyed the enjoyment of the street space in front of their homes."[24] The sentiments of many Milwaukee residents were not unique.

Although people from throughout the social structure had occasion to use city streets, both the nature and frequency of that use varied according to social class, gender, and age, along with the specific circumstances groups and individuals experienced at any given time. A city's elite did not use the street with the same frequency and purpose as did the laboring poor, nor did a fully employed, skilled workingman use the streets in the same manner as the woman to whom he was married, their children, or an irregularly employed day laborer.

In areas of a city containing manufacturing establishments and the tenements and residences of the working classes, the average day commenced with crowds of men—and those women and children employed outside of the home for wages—walking through the streets on their way to work. As "Rambler"—an anonymous writer who took walks in different parts of Buffalo and wrote about their sights and sounds—observed, each sunrise witnessed a "disorderly mass of orderly men" walking to work through the streets. Rambler mused that it was no doubt a surprise to many of his readers that "daily, between the hours of five and seven o'clock, an army of twenty thousand men, all armed with a tin pail, march through the avenues." This daily occurrence in various streets marked the morning routine of most of the working classes throughout the mid- to late nineteenth century.[25]

Throughout the day, streets were characterized by a variety of social and economic activities, particularly those of the poor and working classes. In fact, as Christine Stansell illustrates, "[F]or the working poor, street life was bound up not only with economic exigency, but also with childrearing, family morality, sociability, and neighborhood ties." Poor women and children were some of the most frequent users of streets in poor neighborhoods. The many and varied uses they made of streets blurred the lines between public and private, the street and the household. The street, as Stansell persuasively argues, was a "sphere of domestic life" among the urban poor.[26]

For poor and working-class women, "tenement neighborhoods" allowed for "a female form of association and mutual aid" that served to act as "a crucial buffer against the shocks of uprootedness and poverty." Neighbors and neighborhoods (native and foreign born) involved themselves in a number of "domestic" matters—from childrearing to marital discord between husbands and wives. While kinship networks and ethnic loyalties formed an important part of the cooperation that characterized poor neighborhoods, "the interchange between households and the streets," Stansell argues, also facilitated cooperative bonds. The incessant striving to come up with the necessities of life "generated its own intricate network of exchange among neighbors and between parents and children and created the material basis for a dense neighborhood life."[27] Streets were a central arena in this "moral economy of the tenements" (which also generated conflict in addition to cooperation and mutuality). Streets in and around tenements were witness to many forms of behavior involving female (and male) "sociability and neighborhood ties." They were the arena for conflicts over, and expressions of, differing conceptions of what constituted proper sexual behavior, for example. Behavior that violated the sexual mores of the neighborhood was not infrequently brought to people's attention in and via the streets; a physically abusive husband might be publicly tongue-lashed in the street by neighborhood women, for example. Conversely, behavior that did not violate neighborhood mores, such as "public drunkenness," might also involve streets and the surrounding residences. For example, the arrest of a person for public drunkenness in Albany in 1877 prompted the formation of a crowd that unsuccessfully tried to prevent the arrest and consequently stoned the arresting police officers. Arguments initiated inside of the household or involving two or more households could spill out into the streets, whereby the arguments were advertised to the neighborhood and sometimes reconciled, or at least ended in some manner through third-party interventions.[28]

Household work among the poor was by its very nature an activity that linked household members with the street. Women and children spent much of the day trying to acquire the necessities of life, and in doing so, they spent a great deal of time in the streets. In Buffalo, for example, many women who were unemployed needleworkers continued their work at home on an individual basis and peddled their goods from door to door—an economic activity requiring frequent travel in the streets.[29] Children hunted for pieces of wood or coal to use as fuel (particularly in the winter), or scraps and bits of just about anything that might be of use in the household or could be sold to generate money for household expenses. Railroad tracks were commonly scoured for bits of wood and coal left by passing locomotives. "Street scavenging" by children was of vital importance to the existence of the poor household, and there was no better place to scavenge than in or around streets. Routine errands also took children out into the streets, whether a trip to a nearby grocer for food or a neighboring tenement in order to borrow an item from a friend or relative. The very structure or lack of structures such as indoor plumbing, storage spaces, and refrigeration units, Perry Duis explains, sent household members into the streets on a variety of missions required by the lack of such facilities. The lack of storage spaces in cramped tenements, or the lack of refrigeration units, necessitated multiple trips to obtain needed items and, consequently, greater use of the streets. Even weather patterns accounted for greater use of the streets by the poor: hot summers witnessed people spending as much time as they could outside of their dwellings, in the relatively cooler air of the street.[30]

Particularly in lower-class sections of cities, the relative lack of public ground for recreation and amusement led to the streets being an important arena for such behavior. Children of the lower classes, in particular, used streets as their playgrounds. In the space of the street, they played various ball games and engaged in other recreational activities. Boys seemed to spend a significant amount of time in the streets and on street corners, amusing themselves in various ways or simply "lounging." "Coasting" on the snow and ice in the streets was a popular winter pastime. As Clay McShane points out, surviving lithographs and photos from the 1860s "show great herds of children playing in the streets." And Roy Rosenzweig's study of workers and leisure in industrializing Worcester, Massachusetts, notes that in the early 1880s the police routinely had to drive boys out of one of their most important playgrounds—the streets.[31]

Besides the variety of social, economic, and recreational functions played by the streets in lower-class neighborhoods, the street was a major artery of business and commerce in the mid-to-late nineteenth-century American city. A number of streets were primarily commercial in nature. Thoroughfares like Quay Street in Albany, for example, were centers of commercial activity, not only in the fact the street was lined with warehouses, wholesale and retail stores, and shipping offices but also in the activities carried out in the street proper.[32] Quay Street and others like it in Buffalo and Syracuse were crowded with people and vehicles of all kinds—hacks, travelers, teamsters, customers and suppliers of the streets' businesses. The very survival of relatively small businesses, particularly retail and wholesale enterprises, depended on location and accessibility. First and foremost in that equation was the street on which the business was located, and how easily customers and products could move through the street, to and from the entrances of the business.[33]

Wholesale ice dealers, for example, had to have a relatively straightforward transportation route from the sources of their ice—a nearby lake or pond in many cases—to their ice warehouses. The streets between their businesses and ice source were key ingredients in the success and health of their enterprises. The horse teams that transported the product had to make good time through the streets, particularly at the close of winter so that adequate supplies could be laid in for the summer season. Similarly, ice transported by horse-drawn wagon teams from ice dealers to retail customers or private homes could not brook delays in the streets during warm weather; profits literally melted away in obstructed streets.[34] Saloons, to cite another example, were very "dependent on the street traffic that moved by outside." Saloon owners sought streets crowded with people during the day and a location making it easy for would-be patrons to go in and out of the saloon. If the flow of traffic outside a saloon was altered or obstructed for any reason, a saloon's business could be adversely effected. At times, the street outside of a saloon might serve as an extension of the saloon itself: a performance by a musical group, for example, could attract so many people that the street outside would be packed with people listening to the sounds of the band.[35]

The flour and feed stores on Genesee Street in Buffalo near the Washington Street Market were very dependent upon the patronage of the city's surrounding farming population. In particular, these stores and places of business required "an unobstructed space for backing up, loading and unloading wagons" in the street. Obstructed streets interfered directly and fundamentally with the economic activities of both visiting farmers and small businessmen in this particular area of the city.[36] However crowded and chaotic that traffic might be at times, relatively small and medium-sized businesses were dependent on the free flow of traffic in streets leading to and from the location of the enterprise (see fig. 3).

While a variety of small and medium-sized businesses (and judged within the context of a specific community, large businesses) were dependent upon the nature of the streets surrounding them, a number of individual occupations were largely carried out in city streets and were there-

Fig. 3. J. W. Stevens & Co. tobacco shop on Broadway, Albany, 1869. Small, nonindustrial businesses of this sort, dependent upon pedestrian and horse-drawn wagon traffic, took the lead in remonstrances to common councils over the railroads' presence in streets.

fore linked to other activities taking place in the streets. Streets were the principal workplace for draymen, truckmen, hackmen, teamsters, and many peddlers. These occupations were conducted in the street—teamsters driving their wagons; draymen and hackmen driving or pulling their carts, trucks, and hacks; peddlers moving through the street by foot or wagon, traveling from home to home, neighborhood to neighborhood, or business to business, showcasing their goods for sale. For people in these occupations, the city street was a workplace; it was an environment in which they spent much of the workday. A number of these occupations expanded during the latter decades of the nineteenth century. The number of teamsters and their horsepowered vehicles in Buffalo and other cities, for example, grew rapidly from 1870 to 1900, far surpassing population growth. And the *Albany Morning Express* remarked in 1874 that "the number of street vendors and peddlers appears to be increasing."[37]

In sum, streets were vital arenas for social and economic life. Streets served vital social roles in the life of the poor in particular, whose children spent a great deal of time in the streets, both at work and at play. Streets were important parts of the "moral economy" of poor neighborhoods and were as much a part of the lives of the urban poor, it can be argued, as their households. Streets also served as crucial avenues for the movement of goods and people within the urban economy, whether that economy was the family economy of the working poor, or the economy of retail and wholesale businesses. Concerns about what transpired in the streets, then, were of the utmost importance to a variety of people—from working-class women concerned over what their children and neighbors encountered in the streets around their residences, to specific working-class occupations based in the streets, and proprietors whose retail businesses or small-scale manufactories depended heavily on the free— and relatively safe—flow of people and property outside their place of business.

"Caught on the Tracks": The Toll in Lives

The consequences of railroad use of city streets were frequently disastrous and grew worse as industrialization, population growth, and the increasing density of urban life magnified the impact of having railroads run through streets and neighborhoods. In Albany during a routine twenty-four-hour period, for example, 132 trains departed and arrived; in other words, a train traveled into or out of Albany every eleven minutes. Most of these were passenger trains; freight trains added greatly to the number and frequency.[38] Undoubtedly, the most appalling result of having locomotives and freight and passenger trains run through crowded streets and neighborhoods was the many people killed or injured by trains.

Evidence for the high toll in human lives comes from a variety of sources. Railroad corporations and state authorities collected data on the number of deaths and injuries caused by railroads in New York State in the mid-to-late nineteenth century. The data indicates the 1870s were years in which deaths and injuries steadily increased; most of these deaths and injuries resulted from railroad use of crowded urban space. In 1868, 150 people (neither railroad passengers nor employees) were killed by railroads, and eighty-six were injured. In 1880, 238 people were killed; 239 were injured. Over the span of those twelve years, deaths increased by 59%; injuries increased by 178%! The year of the Great Strike was firmly situated on a steepening slope of death and injury caused by railroads.[39] The data for the 1880s illustrate the same trend: deaths and injuries continued to escalate. In 1883, 280 people died in railroad accidents; 250 were injured. Six years later, in 1889, 370 were killed, and 258 were injured. Deaths had increased in 1889 by 32% over 1883; injuries had increased by 3%.[40]

A closer look at the numbers provides a fuller picture of the enormous human toll exacted by railroads in the 1870s. The Erie Railroad's accident report for the year ending September 30, 1876, lists sixty-one people killed and fifty-three injured. Twenty-three of the deaths are listed under two categories: "from walking on the track" and "from standing, sitting, lying or playing on track." Fourteen deaths occurred when people tried to cross the track on foot or in vehicles. And another fourteen people were simply "found dead on [the] track."[41] The statistics from the report of the New York Central and Hudson River Railroad for the same year are similar in nature. That report tabulates the deaths of eighty-nine people and the injuries to sixty-four people. The greatest number—twenty-nine—were killed when "walking, lying, sitting or being on [the] track." Twenty-two people were killed when "crossing [the] track in front of trains." The third category with the greatest number of deaths was "found dead on track."[42] Ten years later, the nature of the deaths and injuries from railroad use of populated space had not changed significantly. The third annual report of the Board of Railroad Commissioners, submitted in 1886 and typical of the commissioners' annual reports with respect to the listed "cause of accident," cited 261 deaths to "others" for the year 1885. Of these deaths, 189 or 72% were attributed to "walking or being on [the] track." The second highest number of deaths (twenty-four or 9%) had as the cause of the accident "not protected with gates or flagmen"—a reference to the state of the crossing. The third highest number of deaths (twenty-two or 8%) was attributed to "getting on or off trains in motion," a favorite and deadly pastime of young urban males in both decades.[43]

The accident reports submitted to the State of New York allow a reasonable determination of the ages and gender of those killed and injured by railroads. The Erie Railroad's accident report for the year ending in September 1876, as was the case for most accident reports, listed the names and ages of those killed and injured when available, along with the location, date, and description of the accident. The Erie's 1876 report included the names and ages of fifty people killed or injured. Six (12%) of those casualties were female; forty-four (88%) were male. Approximately two-thirds of the deaths and injuries occurred to people between the ages of twenty and sixty. The ages ranged from two to seventy-three, with a mean and median age of forty. The typical person killed or injured by railroads in the 1870s, then, was a forty-year-old man.[44] Although the Board was primarily concerned with examining the deaths and injuries to railroad passengers and employees, the large numbers of people killed due to "being" on a railroad track cry out for attention. Working for the railroad was an extremely dangerous occupation in the nineteenth century, one with a "high probability of injury and death."[45] Coupling and uncoupling trains, riding atop or astride cars, and working in crowded and busy switching yards killed thousands of railroad workers over the years. Yet, city streets lined with railroad tracks and railroad crossings on the outskirts of a village, town, or city could and did claim more lives. In 1877, for example, the State Engineers and Surveyors reported eighty-seven railroad employees killed, while during the same period of time 212 people, neither employees nor passengers, were killed. Over a decade later, in 1889, nationwide statistics compiled by the newly created Interstate Commerce Commission revealed that 61% of all railroad accident fatalities happened to people who were not railroad workers or passengers.[46]

These grim statistics are supported by some anecdotal accounts of foreign visitors. Foreign visitors to the United States commented upon the intersection of railroads with urban space and the consequent toll in human lives. A Frenchman who visited New York City in 1868 viewed the city, or at least parts of it, as having streets "covered with tracks and engines constantly in motion—as if they were in the open country."[47] Auguste Foubert, a Frenchman born around 1840, traveled throughout North and South America during the years 1864–74. In 1875, he published an account of his travels entitled *La Vie d'Emigrant en Amerique.* In it he related a conversation he had with a fellow countryman while in New York City. Foubert's countryman, a peddler who traveled in some of the small villages and towns surrounding New York City, spoke at some length about the frequency of fatal railroad accidents in New York. In nearby Port Chester, he had personally witnessed a man being run over by a passing train. What had shocked the peddler almost as much as seeing the accident was learning from the residents of the small town "that he was the sixteenth person killed by the railroad, in the village in the last four months." The peddler added that, in his view, "I cannot think of a single country where human life is more scorned than in this one. Every day throughout the whole territory, the numbers of victims are appalling."[48] Foubert's peddler was not alone in his shock or surprise at the presence of railroads in urban centers and the numbers of people killed or injured as a result. Frenchmen were not the only foreign visitors to the United States to comment upon the fact that railroads killed people unfortunate enough to be in the way of a locomotive. English travelers made similar observations.[49]

Statistics compiled by railroad corporations and the state government, as well as accounts from foreign visitors, reveal the fact that railroad use of urban space killed and maimed hundreds of people every year in New York State during the 1870s. Daily newspapers provide an even closer look at what transpired in city streets used by railroad locomotives and their passenger and freight cars (see fig. 4). Railroad use of the streets resulted in a wide variety of deadly encounters between locomotives and people engaged in routine, everyday activities. In the streets, each day presented a contest of sorts—"THE IRON HORSE VS. HUMANITY"—as a Syracuse newspaper termed it on a day when a railroad switchman was killed, and a teamster traveling through the streets narrowly escaped death at the wheels of a passing train.[50] "Runaways"—horse-drawn carriages and wagons careening wildly out of control, with or without their drivers—were a common occurrence in city streets. Many of these episodes were the result of horses becoming frightened at the sight and sound of a locomotive. The noise of a locomotive, particularly the steam whistle, was very unsettling to both horses and people. Locomotive whistles grew larger and louder with time, until the journal *Engineering* described them as "a howling reservoir of sound, with an unearthly roar instead of a shriek."[51] The *Albany Morning Express,* for example, sympathized with "those unfortunate people who reside within hearing distance of the railroads." Such residents, the editors wrote, "must find at times

Railroad Accident.

Jacob Seabert, a German, and glazier by trade, living at the corner of Broadway and Madison avenue, came out of a saloon on Lawrence street about noon yesterday, and stepping on the track was struck by the engine of the Troy local and thrown down, his feet being under the wheels. The train was stopped as soon as possible. He was carried to St. Peter's Hospital, where it was found that his feet were crushed so badly that amputation was necessary. Both were amputated, one at the ankle joint, the other a little above. The operation was performed by Dr. Balch. The injured man's recovery is very doubtful.

Runaway Accident.

At 4 30 o'clock yesterday afternoon a farmer from Bethlehem, named Robert King, stopped his team at the foot of Hamilton street to allow a train of cars to pass. The horses became frightened at the locomotive, when they started on a run down Quay street. Mr. King was thrown out, injuring his hand severely. The team continued down Quay street to the Steamboat Landing and turned into Broadway, where they collided with a horse car. This somewhat stopped their progress, when a citizen caught them by the head, stopping them. The horses were not injured, but the wagon was broken to pieces. Officer Apple rendered valuable assistance to Mr. King.

Fig. 4. Common railroad "accidents": *Albany Express*, November 18, 1876 (*top*), and July 3, 1877 (*bottom*).

that the unearthly shriek of the steam whistle is an appalling nuisance." The locomotives' whistles were "especially disturbing to sick people, and a sad disturber of nervous horses." The paper mused that in some New England towns "the use of the locomotive whistle has been entirely discontinued, except as a danger or distress signal," a fact which made the "whistle-ridden communities . . . profoundly grateful."[52] Albany could

have looked west to Syracuse, however, for guidance. In that city, the
common council unanimously passed an ordinance—in 1877—stating
that "no steam or other whistle attached to any locomotive shall be blown
on the New York Central and Hudson River Railroad or any of its
branches" within the city.[53] Whether shriek or roar, the steam whistles
of locomotives were unsettling to people and horses and caused many
an accident.

Rarely a week passed in larger urban centers like Buffalo without a
runaway through crowded city streets. Examples of such dangerous mis-
haps abound. In Buffalo a wagon drawn by a team of horses "became
frightened at a train of cars at the Michigan street crossing and ran away."
While the drivers fought to bring the panicked horses under control, the
wagon raced down the street until it "struck a lamp-post," hurling both
drivers out of the wagon and onto the ground. Two weeks later, two married women "were driving across the Genesee street crossing" of the New
York Central Railroad when their "horse became frightened" at the approaching train "and ran away." Worse, the animal "dashed down the railroad track, throwing out both ladies." As one of the women "was arising
from the ground she was struck" by the passing train "about the head
and right shoulder and side."[54] Even though the lower classes were more
frequently in the streets, steam locomotives did not discriminate on the
basis of class—anyone in a street with a railroad was at risk. In Buffalo,
for example, the owner of a manufactory was riding in his carriage in
Ohio Street when a train passed over the grade crossing he was approaching. The horses panicked at the sound and sight of the locomotive
and bolted, overturning the carriage and throwing the capitalist onto the
street. The factory owner was injured, although not seriously. One of the
two frantic horses, however, proceeded to impale itself on a New York
Central railroad wagon. But neither the noise nor the damage from locomotives was confined to streets. In Albany, for example, a team of horses
drawing a boat along the Erie Canal became frightened by the noise of a
train "and started on a run." As the panicked animals dashed off, the tow
rope stretching between them and the boat snapped taut. The force of the
snapping rope caught two men behind the horses and knocked them into
the canal. They were quickly rescued, but the snapping rope had "severely injured" one of the men.[55]

The presence of railroad tracks in streets could seriously aggravate
those runaway accidents not caused by railroad locomotives. In Syracuse,
for example, a gentleman out for a ride in his sleigh had the misfortune
of losing control of his horses, who proceeded to run down the street.

Before the gentleman could regain control, however, they turned onto a street with tracks. When the horses and cutter ran over the tracks, the cutter broke apart "throwing Mr. Snow out, injuring him quite severely."[56] Railroad tracks also posed a danger to wagons not out of control. A twelve-year-old employee of a coal dealer died when the wheels of his wagon were momentarily caught in a railroad track. The resulting jolt or bump was enough to cause the boy to fall from the wagon, after which the heavily laden vehicle passed over him, killing him on the spot.[57] Nor were runaway accidents limited to city folk. Farmers' markets in urban locales meant among other things that farmers and their produce-laden wagons traveled from country to town on market day. As less frequent users of city streets, they also had to contend with locomotives and tracks. In Albany, for example, a farmer on his way to the market stopped his team at a railroad crossing "to allow a train of cars to pass." Unfortunately, the horses "became frightened at the locomotive" and bolted down an adjacent street—one of the busiest in Albany. The farmer "was thrown out, injuring his hand severely." His horses and wagon continued on down the street to Steamboat Square, where they turned onto another street—and "collided with a horse car." Luckily, no one else was hurt. The farmer was left with a crippled hand and a wagon "broken to pieces."[58]

Walking in a street lined with railroad tracks was dangerous. One was not at risk simply because of easily frightened animals. Many pedestrians were killed and injured because they misjudged the speed of an approaching train or failed to see it and ended up being "caught on the track." A momentary lapse in attention could cost a life or limb. In Buffalo, a boy simply trying to cross the railroad crossing on Perry Street "was struck by an approaching engine and knocked down . . . one of the wheels passed over his left arm, badly crushing it."[59] A German glazier fell victim to a locomotive in Albany when he carelessly walked in front of an onrushing train. Moments before, he had walked out of a neighborhood saloon, into the street and onto the railroad track. "Struck by the engine" of the train, the man's feet were caught by the wheels and severely mangled. He died in the hospital four days after having both feet amputated. A coroner's inquest, which frequently followed such accidents, ruled the death accidental and exonerated the railroad company of any legal wrongdoing.[60]

The Broadway crossing in Albany was notorious for the number of accidents that took place there, as suggested by a newspaper's comment that "scarcely a day passes but some citizen narrowly escapes accident." The *Evening Times* noted the "great dissatisfaction" of "citizens residing in the northern part of the city" over the accidents at the crossing and the New York Central's apparent indifference to the problem. One week after the newspaper's notice of the problem, James Campbell, a wagon driver for a tile manufacturer, was at work on the company wagon when he traveled over the Broadway crossing. Campbell made it across. The company wagon did not; it was "completely demolished" by the passing locomotive.[61] By 1881, the Broadway crossing killed "on average, a man a month." When the New York Central Railroad in the early 1880s finally constructed a viaduct to eliminate the grade crossing, the company, and the popular pressure that resulted in the building of the viaduct, finally put an end to what was labeled "the terror."[62] Similar sentiments about railroad use of city streets were voiced in Buffalo. In fact, one contemporary compared the carnage resulting from railroad accidents in the city to that suffered in war and the railroad to wartime enemies. In the War of 1812, Buffalo was virtually destroyed by British forces, yet "the deadly grade crossing" resulted in greater "loss of life" and represented a greater "menace" to the well-being of Buffalo residents.[63] Even crossings guarded by flagmen were the scenes of many accidents.

Coroners' inquests sometimes resulted in the jury returning verdicts indicting the railroad company, and victims of the railroads' intersection with streets and neighborhoods on occasion sued railroad companies in the courts in an effort to gain financial compensation for injuries or deaths. In Albany, a young boy was struck and killed by "a locomotive as it was passing McCarthy avenue." As required, the coroner convened a jury of Albany residents to investigate the death. The jury concluded that the boy, Michael Roach, was killed as a result of the locomotive "running at a rate of speed not allowed within the city limits." Hence, the railroad company was "responsible for the death" of the boy.[64] Nathan Pakalnisky, the ten-year-old son of a family of Syracuse peddlers, had the misfortune of tripping and falling down while trying to cross the Clinton Street railroad crossing on a rainy night. An oncoming locomotive hit the lad, crushing his leg so badly that it had to be amputated. Sixteen months later, the boy and his family were in court suing the railroad.[65] In Syracuse, a woman's brother, in the city for a visit, was killed by a locomotive "at the Mulberry street crossing." In spite of the fact that the man may have been intoxicated at the time of his death, the deceased's family argued at the coroner's inquest that he was killed by a train "running at too high a rate of speed." The verdict of the coroner's jury was apparently noncommittal on the issue of culpability; the family announced it would sue the railroad company in court for damages.[66] As Roger Lane demonstrates with respect to Philadelphia, coroners' juries rarely censured anyone. But when they did, railroads were usually the target of the censure.[67] Speeding locomotives aggravated the problem of trains intersecting streets and neighborhoods. Consequently, residents tried to have their local government exert a measure of control. In Syracuse, residents protested to the common council in 1876 on behalf of an ordinance "providing that locomotives shall not run in the city at a speed to exceed eight miles per hour."[68] Such ordinances passed on occasion, but enforcement was another matter. There was little that a municipality could do to force powerful railroad corporations to obey local speed regulations.

If one judges by the tone of newspaper headlines, then what probably upset city residents the most about the death and injury toll from railroad use of urban space was the number of young boys killed. One of the favorite pastimes of young urban males seemed to be jumping trains for a ride. This was both illegal and extremely dangerous. These particular deaths seemed to prompt a greater level of outrage in the press, most of which was seemingly directed at the deadly foolishness of many boys. Under the headlines "KILLED BY THE CARS," "THE SAME OLD STORY," a Syracuse paper lamented the fact that "time after time we have been called upon to chronicle the killing, or maiming for life, of adventurous boys who jump upon railroad trains while passing through the streets."[69] Its lament was not a singular one, for the problem of youths jumping trains plagued urban areas. Despite the regularity of such accidents, they were still "shocking" to many urbanites, and they never failed to make the headlines. "A SHOCKING RAILROAD ACCIDENT—A LITTLE BOY RUN OVER AND INSTANTLY KILLED," reported the *Albany Express* in late 1876 when an eleven-year-old boy fell off the train on which he and other youths had stolen a ride. As the paper observed, "[A]lmost every day the police are obliged to arrest boys for stealing rides on the cars." The editors also lamented that such "shocking accident[s]" did not seem to deter the popularity of train hopping.[70] Not unexpectedly, the problem was greater in larger, more densely populated urban areas like Buffalo. The Buffalo *Express* in early 1877 featured a short news article entitled "BEHEADED," which related the last moments of a twelve-year-old boy as he attempted to board a train running down a street. While arguing that the boy should have been in school and thus was a "truant" at the time of his death, the paper hoped the fact the boy's head was "completely severed from [his] body" would serve as a gruesome warning "to those youths who are continually stealing rides on the cars." It did not. Two days later, the headline read "ANOTHER BOY KILLED" as a fifteen-year-old, after successfully hopping on the front of a train, "attempted to change his position." Unfortunately, "a sudden jar of the engine precipitated him to the track."[71] While these episodes are evidence of a male youth culture that valued demonstrations of risk taking, they were also occurrences that both saddened and angered portions of the community—at the very least, the friends, family, and acquaintances of the dead and injured. The problem of boys being killed by hopping on and off trains reached common councils on occasion. In Albany, the killing or injuring of a number of youths during the course of one year prompted that common council to pass a resolution. Noting the casualties, the aldermen formally asked the police to make greater efforts to arrest offending youths.[72] Dead and maimed boys were another entry in the list of injuries suffered by residents of urban areas traversed by railroads.

Undoubtedly, the most spectacular form of the railroad presence in city streets was seen in railroad accidents involving colliding locomotives and trains. Buffalo was the scene of two serious railroad collisions in the space of twenty-four hours—accidents which prompted a relatively prolonged outburst against railroad accidents in general. Both wrecks involved a train running into stationary railroad cars and happened at railroad crossings inside the city. The first wreck, which killed at least one railroad employee and injured a number of others, resulted in railroad cars being thrown from the track onto the street. The wreck prompted the *Daily Courier* to declare that the accident resulted from "a criminal negligence somewhere that should meet with the promptest punishment." Yet, before the city could further contemplate the ramifications of the accident, another wreck occurred, due apparently to a mis-set switch. As the *Daily Courier* observed, the trains collided with such force that many of the cars "were so utterly demolished as to lose nearly all semblance of railroad cars." This collision killed a neighborhood boy, a thirteen-year-old who just happened to be near the crossing when the trains collided. Both of the boy's legs were "severed from his body." He died within minutes of the accident. The two "frightful collision[s]," the paper cried, had been "manifestly occasioned . . . by criminal negligence."[73]

The *Courier*'s assertion that "the entire community" was interested in the accidents and who or what was to blame was no doubt accurate, for the deadly wrecks occupied the city's attention for the next three weeks. The railroads conducted their own investigation of the accidents, and two coroner's juries met to examine the deaths. The railroads excluded newspaper reporters from its hearing on what had caused the collisions—a move giving the appearance of a cover-up. The coroner's jury investigating the death of the boy concluded that he died "through and by the culpable negligence of the New York Central and Hudson River Railroad Company, and its employees," for the railroad was responsible for the improperly set switch. The coroner's jury investigating the death of a railroad employee in the first wreck also concluded that the railroad was at fault. In addition, both railroads (the other railroad company was not identified) were condemned "for running at too high a rate of speed" and "for not requiring the trains to come to a stop before [the] crossing."[74]

A few days after the matter of the Buffalo wrecks had been apparently put to rest, a major railroad accident occurred on the Chicago and Alton Railroad, killing eleven people and injuring many more. That accident, coupled with the two Buffalo train wrecks, prompted a major editorial in the *Courier* entitled "THE LAST RAILROAD SLAUGHTER." The editorial acknowledged that "there always will be railroad accidents," but asserted there could be fewer and less costly accidents "if the law should hold railroad employees and railroad corporations to account for actual murder committed." But until the time when "popular sentiment" decided to do something about "railway homicide," the editors cried, "the American public must expect to be occasionally smashed, scalded or burned to death."[75]

2 The Contested Terrain of the Streets

ailroad corporations ran their tracks and trains right through some of the most densely inhabited areas of Buffalo, Albany, and Syracuse via the streets, as they did in cities throughout the United States in the post–Civil War period (see fig. 5). Railroad use of streets killed hundreds of people each year in New York State. The high toll in human lives, and the even greater number injured and maimed, generated dismay and animosity at the railroads' deadly intersection with crowded streets and neighborhoods. Railroad use of the streets also obstructed and delayed travel and injured specific forms of commerce, particularly for relatively small, nonindustrial businesses (retail and wholesale) dependent upon the relatively unobstructed movement of pedestrians and horse-drawn vehicles. Businesses and residents, for varying but dovetailing reasons, repeatedly petitioned their common councils for various forms of relief. Such relief, for example, might be viewed as the stationing of flagmen at particularly dangerous railroad crossings, or it might be seen as the removal of the tracks themselves. Although most of the petitioning was led by small business owners, the significance of the legal opposition to railroad encroachment extended beyond the struggles of small business owners to keep tracks and trains out of the streets through which goods and customers traveled by foot and horse. As Alexander Hoffman argues, many retail shops functioned as community centers, and local shopkeepers—grocers and saloonkeepers, for example—commonly articulated and represented the interests of the surrounding neighborhood.[1] Common council petitions submitted by some small businessmen signaled not only their opposition but also the concern of their customers, the neighborhood residents. Neighborhood residents are probably the ubiquitous, but unidentified "others," referred to in many of the petitions noted in common council records. Some petitions were rejected outright; others were approved, although the approved

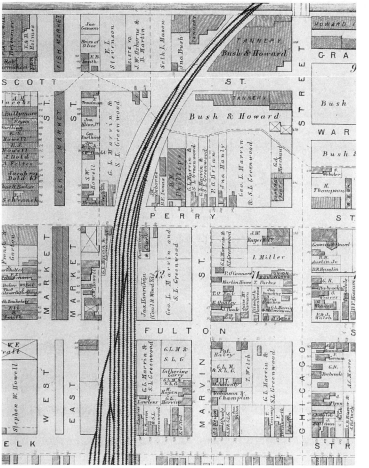

Fig. 5. One of many sections of Buffalo laced with railroad tracks, 1872.

petitions were far from a guarantee of railroad compliance. Common councils also dealt with the disruptive and injurious consequences of the railroads' intersection with streets and neighborhoods in the absence of formal petitions. The efforts of varied residents and their municipal governments met with some success (approved petitions) and some notable failures.

Buffalo

Buffalo was a city whose economic life originated largely on the basis of waterborne commerce from the Great Lakes and, in the 1820s, the Erie Canal. Not surprisingly, the city had grown out from the waterfront. Most of the city's streets ran north/south or east/west. Main Street was in general one of Buffalo's major commercial streets, and the street was a dividing line of sorts—the area east of Main was referred to as East Buffalo (see fig. 6). Most of the city's working-class neighborhoods and much of the city's industry lay in East Buffalo. The eastern portion of the city was also home to most, but not all, of the city's railroad depots, yards, freight houses, and tracks. Indeed, it was in the eastern half of Buffalo that the consequences of the railroads' use of city streets were most directly felt, for tracks sliced through the centers of the First Ward, the Second Ward, and the Third Ward. Railroad facilities east of Main were enveloped by, and their tracks made use of, some of the city's major streets. Louisiana, Alabama, Hamburgh, Michigan, and Chicago Streets were major north-south thoroughfares; Seneca, Exchange, Carroll, Elk, Fulton, and Perry Streets were major east-west avenues. Ohio Street ran along Buffalo's waterfront; William and Spring Streets were major arteries in the northern part of East Buffalo. Most of these streets, including the foot of Main Street, were crossed by railroad tracks in at least one place. Relative to the eastern side of the city, the western part of Buffalo was largely unmarked by railroad tracks prior to 1877; tracks west of Main Street skirted the edge of the city.

In the 1870s property owners and other residents legally contested the expansion and sometimes the very presence of railroads through city streets. Small, nonindustrial property owners frequently spearheaded the opposition. But the prospect of successfully fighting the railroads was daunting. Railroad corporations wielded tremendous economic and political power on the national, state, and local levels. The political influence of railroad corporations in the New York State legislature was legendary, although not exceptional among the states. Their capacity to persuade, cajole, or bribe common councilmen and mayors far surpassed the re-

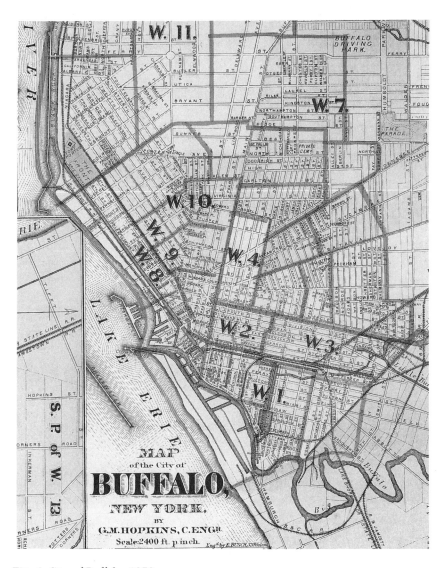

Fig. 6. City of Buffalo, 1872.

sources available to neighborhood residents and small property owners. Former abolitionist Wendell Phillips's remark about Tom Scott, the president of the Pennsylvania Railroad, was overstated but not far off the mark in describing the political power of railroad corporations: "[W]e have thirty-eight one-horse legislatures in this country and we have a man like Tom Scott with three hundred and fifty millions in his hands, and if he walks through the States they have no power. Why, he need not move at all; if he smokes, as Grant does, a puff of the waste smoke out of his mouth upsets the legislatures."[2] Horse-powered legislatures, let alone common councils, were no match for the steam locomotives of wealthy railroad corporations. The forces contesting the uses of the streets were anything but equal.

The decade of the Great Strike presents numerous instances of small businesses and various residents petitioning their common councils for relief from some of the problems consequent upon the railroads' intersection with streets and neighborhoods. For example, when the Buffalo, New York, and Philadelphia Railroad Company began to lay tracks in Carroll Street in April 1875, Alpheus Reynolds, of Reynolds & Wessel, a wholesale dealer of drugs, paints, oils, and glass, immediately protested. Reynolds's wholesale store was located on Main Street, about one block from the western end of Carroll (see fig. 7). Reynolds—and anonymous "others," property owners or those without property—remonstrated against what they defined as the "encroachment" of the railroad on Carroll, a major east-west thoroughfare in central Buffalo. Carroll Street had a diversity of occupants fronting the street. At its western end at Washington Street (one block from Main), Carroll contained insurance offices, boarding houses, a livery, a chapel, and a number of residences. As one moved east along the street it became decidedly more industrial: along with other manufacturing establishments, the street contained the Union Planing Mill and Buffalo Scale Works—two major industrial enterprises. Within a block or two of this manufacturing area of the street was a major railroad grade crossing at the intersection of Carroll and Hamburgh Streets, and near that crossing were facilities of some of the city's railroads.[3]

The council referred the petition to committee. The railroad replied to Reynolds's petition with its own petition to the council. The railroad company, not surprisingly, was against any action that might attempt to force it to remove tracks from the street.[4] In May, the council returned to the opposition of the firm of Reynolds & Wessel and others to the laying of additional railroad tracks in Carroll Street. The committee reported that it would be unwarranted to repeal the 1871 grant to the Buffalo, New York and Philadelphia Railroad Company that originally sanctioned track laying in Carroll Street. Those opposed to the additional tracks in Carroll Street, however, had obtained legal counsel, and their attorney managed to postpone a full council vote on the committee's recommendations. The entire matter was returned to the committee for further consideration.[5]

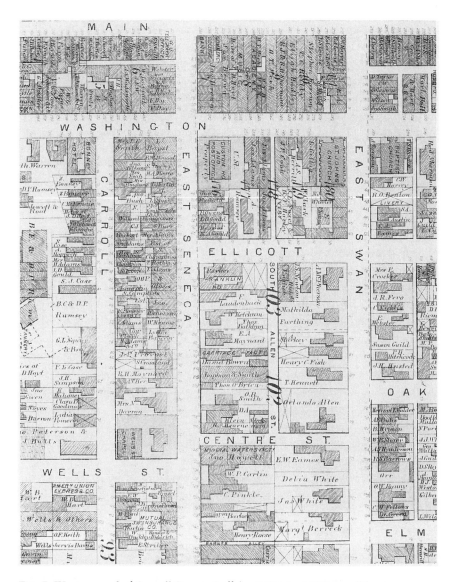

Fig. 7. Western end of Carroll Street, Buffalo, 1872. In 1875, small businessmen and other residents protested against railroad "encroachment" on the street.

In June the city attorney delivered his opinion on the relative rights of the two parties contesting the uses of Carroll Street. The city attorney stated the original grant was legitimate, but he noted "this was not a permanent right, it was in the nature of a license or permission and may be revoked." He also advised the council it "would certainly have the right to regulate or even prohibit the use of steam engines on said tracks." Whatever the council decided, though, "it could not give the railway company the right to occupy Carroll Street with its track and run its cars thereon, as against the right of adjoining owners of land."[6]

As was frequently the case with such conflicts that reached the common council, the matter lay untended for months. The railroad, of course, laid its tracks and was running locomotives and cars on Carroll Street. The obstruction of and disruption to the many nonrailroad uses of the street was even more aggravated when the company left cars "standing" on the track so they could be loaded and unloaded. Finally, in October, six months after Reynolds and others first protested the "encroachment" of the railroad on Carroll Street, the common council ordered the street commissioner to serve notice on the Buffalo, New York and Philadelphia Railroad Company that it must not allow cars to remain standing on the street. At the same time, the council decided it had no authority to order the railroad company to remove the tracks. As for the property owners and others who opposed the railroad's increased use of the street, the council noted only that they were free to pursue whatever options they might have in the courts.[7]

As property owners and other residents on or near Carroll Street fought against intensified railroad use of that street, a conflict arose on Scott Street—another east-west avenue. The Lake Shore and Michigan Southern Railroad Company sought permission from the council to lay a single track on the street from its existing crossing on Scott to Alabama Street (a distance of about two blocks). The socioeconomic nature of Scott Street was decidedly different from Carroll Street. In general, Scott Street ran through, and was occupied by, some of Buffalo's biggest manufacturing establishments; there were few residences along Scott Street and few small businesses or stores, as was the case on much of Carroll Street. Yet, the portion of Scott Street which the Lake Shore and Michigan Southern Railroad proposed to lay track on was characterized by residences and small businesses.[8] Two months after the railroad's request, the council unanimously granted permission to the Lake Shore to lay its track.[9] One month later, however, Elizabeth Bale "and others" protested to the council "against laying railroad track" in Scott Street. Their petition was referred to committee, but the council also decided to reconsider the grant to the Lake Shore. In June of 1875 the council voted unanimously to approve the remonstrance of Elizabeth Bale and others; the grant to the Lake Shore was revoked.[10] They had managed to at least temporarily stave off further encroachment by the railroads.

Babcock and Ganson Streets also witnessed conflicts over railroad use of city streets in 1875. In August, the Erie Railroad asked the council for permission to lay track on part of Babcock Street; the street already had two railroad lines crossing it in a relatively uncongested part of eastern Buffalo near the city limits. As usual, the request was referred to committee. During the same week, however, the council ordered the street commissioner to "direct" the Buffalo, New York and Philadelphia Railroad "to place a flagman on their crossing on Babcock street, and that said R. R. keep the roadway cleared, to give free passage to teams." Although this directive involved a different railroad company, it is clear that the railroads' intersection with Babcock Street was already obstructing the travel of horse-drawn wagons and other users of the street. The council, shortly thereafter, voted to reject the Erie Railroad's petition, and the matter was referred back to committee.[11]

The council's action denying the Erie Railroad access to Babcock Street prompted Lemuel C. Crocker "and others" in September to petition the aldermen for permission to be granted to a different railroad corporation, the New York Central Railroad, "to lay tracks on Babcock street." Crocker sought to have a direct rail link with "his factory," the Buffalo Fertilizer Factory. In order to construct this rail link, tracks had to be laid on part of Babcock Street. Crocker also wanted to see the Central, not the Erie, construct the link, due primarily to the fact that Crocker was also the superintendent of the New York Central's stockyards. But a week later the council granted permission to the Erie Railroad, not the New York Central, to lay track on the street.[12]

Two months later the matter erupted in council again. This time, however, as contending parties fought over use of the street, four separate remonstrances were presented to the aldermen. Most important of all, however, was the fact that the struggle between the Erie and Central Railroads pricked the sentiments of people who did not want *any* more tracks laid in Babcock Street. Joseph D. Dentinger "and others" took an unrecorded position toward "the matter of the N.C.Y. & H.R.R. Co. to construct and operate its tracks along the east side of Babcock street." Opposed to the desire of the Central (and some affiliated businesses) to lay tracks in Babcock Street was the petition of the Erie Railroad "against

laying railroad tracks on [the] east side of Babcock street." These petitions clearly involved disputes between railroad companies over which
company would lay track on certain streets, and conflicts among large
shippers over the railroad company with which they would do (or have to
do) business. This contest, however, prompted people opposed to any
track laying in Babcock Street to enter the fray. George R. Babcock, one
of the city's most prominent attorneys and elder citizens, and Edward
Boldt, the owner of a saloon at the intersection of Babcock and Clinton
Streets—"and others"—presented two remonstrances "against laying
railroad tracks in Babcock street" regardless of what company did the
track laying.[13] But Crocker's desire to have a direct link from his fertilizer
factory to a railroad eventually won council approval, notwithstanding
continued disputes over which railroad company would lay track on Babcock Street and with which company Crocker would do business. The
legal opposition of Babcock, Boldt's saloon, and anonymous "others" to
more railroad tracks in Babcock Street failed to stop the laying of new
tracks.[14]

A similar situation developed in 1875 on Ganson Street, a street starting and ending on the Buffalo waterfront, specifically along the island-like
pier containing many of the city's grain elevators and loading docks. As
was the case on Babcock Street, the conflict over track laying on Ganson
Street derived in part from the desires of shippers and other large businesses for a direct link to the railroads. The dispute arose when S. S.
Guthrie, a commission merchant located on the Central Wharf, sought
permission to lay track connecting the Sturges Elevator to the terminus
of a nearby railroad. In order to make the connection, however, it would
be necessary to lay track in Ganson Street. Guthrie's petition to the council for permission to do so prompted a remonstrance from H. H. H. Hale—
"and others." Hale was of Hale & Shaw, a maker of shooks and staves
located at the foot of Main Street adjacent to one end of Ganson Street.
All of the petitioners were "against laying railroad tracks in Ganson
street." One month after the request, the council voted to deny the petition of the Sturges Elevator Co. and Guthrie—no railroad tracks would
be laid in Ganson Street, at least not for the time being.[15] The Ganson
Street conflict, on the surface at least, pitted two capitalists against one
another. As the Babcock Street case also illustrated, the issue could and
did separate some capitalists, specifically large shippers and manufacturers, from others. Part of the conflict over track laying in Babcock Street
stemmed from disputes among large companies over with which railroad
corporation they would have to ship freight. Yet, in the Babcock Street

conflict, the desire of large shippers for direct rail connections elicited opposition from residents and small, nonindustrial enterprises that did not want any additional tracks in their streets.

Railroad encroachment on streets continued in 1876. In February, the New York Central Railroad sought permission from the council to lay two tracks across Genesee Street. The council quickly approved the request, noting that the railroad would lay its new tracks "adjacent to and parallel with the tracks of said road as now laid" on Genesee Street. In other words, the tracks would be added to an already existing railroad crossing on that street. Likewise, the Erie Railroad sought and obtained permission to lay additional tracks across Hamburgh and Louisiana Streets; both projects entailed adding track to already existing grade crossings. The consequently increased volume of train traffic at these crossings made them even more dangerous, but, for whatever reason, area property owners and residents did not petition the council.[16] Perhaps they felt it was hopeless to contest the addition of tracks to existing grade crossings.

Nevertheless, existing grade crossings were a continual source of conflict between residents and railroad companies. Around the same time as the Central was adding tracks to its Genesee Street crossing in 1876, a grade crossing in the northwestern part of the city was the object of a protest to the council. Christopher Laible "and others" complained to the aldermen over the disruption that the crossing caused to anyone needing to move through the street. Laible, who ran a grocery store on Tonawanda Street, undoubtedly objected to the delays and dangers faced by customers and suppliers of his store who had to travel over the crossing; such concerns plagued store owners unfortunate enough to be in the vicinity of railroad crossings. The "others" were probably neighboring small businesses and other users of the street, such as teamsters, who also suffered from obstructed streets. In fact, Tonawanda Street was crossed by railroads in two places. The council concurred with the grocer and adopted a resolution stating that if the railroads "do not keep the streets open" in order "that people can pass without more than five minutes detention," the city attorney would file suit in court. Whether the store owners in the vicinity of the crossing were satisfied with the council's action is not known, although it is unlikely the resolution significantly altered the number or frequency of trains using the crossing.[17] Railroad corporations did not construct their freight and passenger train schedules according to the wishes of local common councils.

In September 1876, another grocer and his neighbors reached the point where they sought council action to relieve them of the disruptions and injuries railroads could cause to small businesses. James Cosgriff, a grocer—"and others"—petitioned the council "to have [the] railroad track removed from Washington square." The petitioners waited two months before the council denied their petition. In fact, the council reaffirmed the grant to the Tifft Fire-Proof Elevating Company to have tracks running from the elevator, through the square (located at the foot of Chicago Street near the waterfront), to a nearby rail line. Cosgriff and others on or near the square would continue to suffer the presence of the tracks and the consequent disruption and threat they posed to local commerce, life and limb.[18]

For most of 1877, various businesses and residents of streets or areas traversed by railroads continued to confront an unpleasant fact of urban life: railroad corporations ran their tracks and trains through city streets, and the railroads continually attempted to expand. Yet for most of 1877 prior to the Great Strike in late July, little railroad expansion took place. The only track laying noted in the proceedings occurred in May, when the New York Central sought and obtained permission to lay a track across the intersection of Carroll and Hamburgh Streets—where a major grade crossing had been in existence for some time.[19] As noted above, Carroll Street was the scene of conflict in 1875 over track laying in the street. Those who opposed the tracks then were most likely even more disgruntled with additional tracks and train traffic at the Hamburgh and Carroll Streets crossing.

Other grade crossings and tracks in various parts of the city were the object of continued concern by residents and businesses. In January, James Wilson "and others" petitioned the council to have a flagman stationed "at [the] crossing of [the] N.Y.C. & H.R.R.R. Co. on Walden avenue"—a thoroughfare on the outskirts of the city—and the council adopted a resolution directing the Central to do so.[20] The following month, Simon Colligon and other "residents of Fulton street" petitioned the council to order the railroad to place a flagman at one of the crossings on that street. Fulton Street was an east-west avenue running through central Buffalo. It was crossed in three places by railroad tracks. Fulton was home to a number of saloons, retail grocery and provision stores, and at least one retail meat market, among other relatively small businesses. These businesses had good reason to want flagmen at the railroad crossings to warn customers and wagons carrying goods to and from the stores of approaching trains. Other residents of Fulton Street probably supported the petition. Indeed, the Catholic Church and school (of nearly

1,000 students) at the corner of Fulton and Louisiana Streets was sand-wiched between two of the railroad crossings. Certainly the members of that Catholic community would have welcomed a safer crossing. Fulton Street residents received at least part of what they sought from the city government when the council ordered the Erie Railroad to place a flag-man at its crossing. The flagman, it was hoped, would "warn and notify pedestrians of all approaching trains."[21]

Similar resolutions ordering flagmen to be posted at various crossings in the city were also passed in April 1877. These resolutions, however, may have been little more than wishful expressions of the common coun-cil, for they were resolutions that sought to force railroad corporations to add to their payroll. They carried little if any legal weight, and railroad corporations were able to ignore them with virtual impunity. In fact, there is evidence suggesting that such resolutions were ineffective in dealing with the problems posed by railroad use of city streets. In December 1877, the council created a new city ordinance requiring railroads to sta-tion flagmen at crossings within ten days after being notified to do so by the city. The ordinance specified a schedule of fines that increased over time if railroads failed to comply with council resolutions. The time schedule of fines suggests that railroad companies tended to ignore coun-cil resolutions or, at the very least, take a great deal of time to act.[22]

Getting safely over crossings and tracks was problematic in more ways than one. Crossings at grade level—the level of the street—often became obstacles even without trains crossing over them. Crossings could, through repeated use, sink lower than street level, or be raised above street level as the result of railroad repairs and maintenance of the cross-ing and track bed. Whenever tracks were at a level other than that of the street, crossing over the tracks became even more difficult and precari-ous, especially for wagon teams, carriages, and other horse-drawn ve-hicles. Wagon wheels could become lodged or stuck in the tracks or ties; cargoes could be thrown out of wagons and drays if the crossing was un-even and bumpy. If moving quickly over a bumpy crossing, drivers could be tossed off their vehicles and seriously injured, or even killed, as hap-pened to the twelve-year-old coal wagon driver in Buffalo. The Clinton Street crossing of the Erie Railroad caused such problems, and in May 1877 the council directed the company to repair the crossing so that it might present less of an obstacle to vehicles. Likewise, the crossing of the New York Central at Fillmore Avenue was particularly difficult to negoti-ate given the condition of the crossing between the rails; in June the council ordered the company to "lay planks between their rails" at the crossing so that a smoother surface would ease travel over the tracks.[23]

The Crosstown Railroad

By far the gravest struggle between the railroads and Buffalo residents over the use of city streets involved the Crosstown railroad. Although this conflict becomes most visible to the historian in the year after the Great Strike, the threat of this large, intracity freight railroad surfaced in early 1875. While various residents were already struggling to confront the threats posed by the railroads' intersection with streets and neighborhoods, a group of local capitalists organized a company—the Buffalo Crosstown Railway—for the purpose of building an intracity rail route. Many residents could only have been alarmed, if not overwhelmed, by the prospect of a new, major rail line being constructed in the midst of the city. The proposed line would "connect the railroads with most of the large working [grain] elevators of the city," provide direct rail links with many of the city's largest factories, and connect the New York Central's two depots. Originally envisioned and sanctioned by the common council as a project controlled by local capital, the Crosstown railroad was quickly subsumed by the Central before any construction began. Although the entire route of the project was not publicized, a number of the streets through which the railroad would run appeared in the *Express*. In addition to running through many of central Buffalo's streets, the projected railway was "rumored" to include the building of a large depot on the Terrace—a historic promenade with an elevated view of the river and Lake Erie. The Terrace was an important space for some abutting businesses; residences also fronted the Terrace. Work on the intracity route was scheduled to "begin at once."[24]

Some of the major issues surrounding the proposed Crosstown railroad were explicitly politicized by the *Express* during Buffalo's fall mayoral elections. A. P. Laning was the Democratic nominee for mayor. He was also an attorney for the New York Central Railroad. His Republican opponent was Philip Becker, the German-born owner of a prosperous grocery and bakery concern. The election was notable for the intensity of the partisan attacks on the opposing candidates made in and by the press, largely due to the fact that Becker was German-born. But the *Express*, the organ of the Republican party in Buffalo, also chose to attack Laning on the issue of the Crosstown railroad and the deadly consequences of railroad use of city streets.[25] The day before the election, the *Express* wrote that "readers will remember that the city has given great grants to the Crosstown Railroad enterprise." Indeed, the grant would allow the railroad "to drive the iron horse plumb through the heart of the city, in its busiest, most populous part," where consequently it would be "most dangerous to life and property." The paper stated that "provisos, safeguards and requirements" would mitigate the dangers, although "perhaps not enough of these safeguards were put into the contract." In fact, the paper reported that perhaps there could never be enough safeguards written into a railroad contract "to secure the rights of the people against railroad encroachment." The specific and immediate issue as it related to the mayoral election was city enforcement of the existing contractual safeguards. The paper posed the following question: Would Laning, the paid attorney of the New York Central Railroad, be more likely than Becker "to enforce the people's rights as against the Central railroad?" The paper responded:

> [A]re not the ordinances daily violated by the Central Railroad as to running fast in populous parts of the city and endangering the lives of men, women and children? Are our street crossings and the switches of this railroad guarded as required by law for the safety of the people? Are the crossings not regularly obstructed by trains ten, fifteen, twenty minutes, in spite of all the city authorities can do? How then will it be when the head and commanding officer of the city authorities is a paid attorney of the Central Railroad?

The "only hope" for the people of Buffalo lay in rigorous enforcement of the law. The only candidate who would enforce city ordinances dealing with railroads, specifically the New York Central, was Republican Philip Becker.[26] It is impossible to gauge the extent to which the issue of the railroads' injurious intersection with streets impacted upon the election. Clearly, the newspaper hoped the hazards and disorder stemming from railroad use of the streets would translate into anti-Laning votes, if not pro-Becker votes. Becker defeated Laning in the election, although traditional party allegiances and Becker's ethnicity were perhaps a greater determinant of voting behavior than the issue of railroad use of city streets.[27] For a variety of reasons, the attorney of a powerful railroad corporation would not be Buffalo's next mayor.

Construction on the Crosstown railroad did not start in 1875. The joint project, now under the control of the Central, the state's largest corporate entity, required an amendment of the original common council grant made earlier to the Crosstown when it was primarily a local enterprise. The project also required the consent in writing of the property owners along the streets to be used by the railroad. In addition, the common council and the Crosstown had to "take the fee" of portions of certain streets, so they could be appropriated by the city for use by the railroad. Last, at some point in time between 1875 and 1877, the coalition between the Central Railroad and local capitalists broke apart. D. S. Bennett became the Crosstown president, and he sought to build the line independent of the New York Central.[28]

Two years after Laning's defeat and Becker's election, the Crosstown railroad project started to move forward again, this time as a venture of local capitalists. On June 25, 1877—less than four weeks before the Great Strike exploded in Buffalo—the common council granted permission to the Buffalo City Railway Company (the Crosstown project now headed by D. S. Bennett) to build and operate the projected railroad. The June grant, however, pointed to the problems created by railroad use of the streets. The council's grant specified the company could not begin to lay track on any street without "the consent in writing of a majority of the owners of property fronting on the street." Furthermore, the railroad was to employ flagmen at all of its crossings. These flagmen had to be "constantly present during all hours when trains are being run." Not only did pedestrians have to be protected but also the interests of local businessmen dependent upon the movement of property and people through the streets. The crossings, "at all times," were to be "kept in such condition that they will be accessible to public travel."[29] The Buffalo City Railway Company stated that it had already obtained the consent in writing of a majority of property owners on the streets through which the railroad was to run, and the council took note of that fact. Yet the aldermen also gave those same property owners thirty days to withdraw their consent, should they decide to oppose the project. In spite of the apparent consent of property owners, three aldermen voted against the grant. Perhaps they agreed with their colleague who argued in council that while the "heavy taxpayers" or large businesses and shippers might favor the proposed route, "the residents" along the proposed line "should also be considered." Indeed, it was doubtful, one alderman asserted, that "people residing along the proposed route would like to have locomotives pass by their doors."[30] The alderman's comments acknowledged the existing division among the "public" concerning the use of city streets by railroads; while "heavy taxpayers" such as shippers and large manufacturers might desire the intracity railway with its direct rail links to regional and national markets, a variety of residents and small and medium sized, nonindustrial businesses opposed the tracks and trains.

When the common council met once again to approve the construction of a large intracity railroad, it did so in the midst of the city's Great Strike. On July 23, 1877, the aldermen once again sanctioned the building of the Crosstown railroad. The vote was unanimous.[31] The July grant significantly differed from the one passed the previous month. The June grant stated "the consent of property owners heretofore obtained in behalf of the Buffalo Crosstown Railway for laying tracks . . . shall be deemed a consent . . . unless the said property owners shall, within thirty days" withdraw their consent in writing. That provision, which implicitly supported the company's claim that property owners along the proposed route consented to having tracks and locomotives run down their streets, was dropped from the July grant.[32] The omission of that provision can be read as a veiled acknowledgment of opposition to the Crosstown railroad. By eliminating that segment of the June grant, the council effectively reopened the question of consent. In short, the sentiments of property owners along the route, not to mention propertyless residents, would be revisited. Perhaps the modified grant was the result of the sentiments dramatically on display in the streets of the city, for, during the day of July 23, hundreds of people joined in crowds and struck blows against the interests of the railroads.[33]

Buffalonians were not alone in their efforts to prevent railroad encroachment on city streets. The same concerns and issues revolving around the uses of streets were present in Albany and Syracuse in the years preceding the Great Strike.

Albany

Railroad encroachment on areas of vital social and economic importance in the daily lives and economic pursuits of many people was particularly intense in two locations in Albany in the 1870s: Quay Street and Steamboat Square, alongside the Albany docks, and Broadway (one of Albany's major thoroughfares) near Colonie Street.

Quay Street was notable for its historic role in Albany's commerce. Quay fronted the Hudson River or, more precisely, the Albany docks. From Steamboat Square (a landing for river craft and an important space for all kinds of transport activities), the street ran northward for eight blocks along the waterfront, ending at Quackenbush Street. As the name suggests, Quay Street was the focal point of shipping and closely related economic activities in Albany. The Albany basin ran alongside much of the street and was also the eastern terminus of the Erie Canal, the point at which the canal joined the Hudson River. The outer or river edge of the basin was formed by a long pier or wharf which was as long as Quay Street itself; three piers linked the wharf to the street.[34] Prior to the Civil War, Quay Street and the basin were the center of the city's bustling, waterborne commercial activity. Based upon its location on the Hudson River (130 miles north of New York City) and the eastern end of the Erie Canal, Albany was an important transshipment point for goods traveling between Buffalo, Rochester, Syracuse, and New York. The activities of Albany's chief shipping merchants centered on Quay Street and the piers. The offices and warehouses of commission and forwarding merchants jammed the waterfront along Quay. Property on the street had been among the most highly valued in the city. Goods and products of all kinds were piled high on the wharves and parts of the street itself during the peak of the shipping season. Tow-boat lines on the canal had offices and warehouses along the street; and a variety of auxiliary wholesale, retail, and manufacturing establishments dependent on or closely linked to commerce and shipping were located on Quay Street: restaurants, hotels, ship chandlers, and machine shops, to name a few.[35]

The competition posed by the railroads to the Erie Canal and waterborne transport in general had altered the appearance and function of Quay Street by the 1870s. The railroads not only usurped commerce previously handled by waterborne systems of transport, they also encroached physically onto the domain of merchants, and many others, by laying tracks on Quay Street. Railroads drove many commission and forwarding merchants into early retirement or bankruptcy. Some merchants diversified their interests and moved into other economic ventures, much as their counterparts had in Buffalo in earlier years under similar pressures. As railroad competition came to include encroachment on Quay itself, merchants also relocated to other streets. The flight from Quay Street, driven by the presence of the railroad on that street, is evident in the number of commission merchants able or willing to do business there. In 1869, the city directory listed nineteen commission merchants on Quay. A little over a decade later, there were but five left. Symbolic of the retreat of the merchants in the face of the competition posed by the railroads was the disbanding in 1873 of the institutional expression of the merchants on Quay Street and the wharves—the Wharf Association—after a life of nearly eighty years.[36]

While the 1870s witnessed a sharp decline in merchants doing business on Quay Street, however, the street was still of major commercial importance. The withdrawal of the merchants, therefore, was marked by conflict with the forces disrupting their street and dock-centered economic enterprises. The New York Central Railroad first laid tracks in Quay Street in 1867. The merchants were not alone in being adversely impacted by the railroad. Other occupations and social groups which used and were dependent on the relatively unobstructed movement of people and goods on Quay Street also contested the railroad's use of that street. Quay contained a variety of wholesale, retail, and manufacturing establishments dependent on the flow of people and property through the streets. Quay was home to wholesale grocers who received deliveries from the docks and also needed the street as an avenue to distribute and sell goods to others in the city; iron manufacturers and dealers, maltsters and distillers, hotels, restaurants, seed and salt stores—all were dependent on a relatively unobstructed flow of pedestrians and man and horsepowered vehicles through Quay Street.

Railroad use of the same street caused lengthy delays that cost time and money and posed a danger to life and limb. Various occupations—cartmen, draymen, truckmen, and teamsters—spent much of their work-day in the street, hauling and carting goods from ship to store, warehouse to warehouse, and so on. These occupations were based in the streets, so to speak, and always sought and desired relatively unobstructed and safe travel. The more obstacles around or through which to drive a team of horses or pull a hack, the harder, longer, and more dangerous the job. These trades had been previously and negatively affected by the railroads when the first railroad bridge across the Hudson was built in 1866. Prior to that time, particularly in the winter when the river was covered with ice, railroad freight was unloaded and transported across the river. This transfer business "kept swarms of drays, carts and porters busy." In 1866, and in 1872 when a second railroad bridge was completed, these trades suffered an enormous loss in their ranks.[37]

The conflict over the scarce space of Quay Street erupted in 1874, when "merchants, property owners, boatmen, truckmen and cartmen" presented a petition to the Albany Common Council. The petition im-plored the aldermen "to take some action immediately" to stop the rail-roads "from using and running trains of cars on Quay street."[38] The appeal of these groups was prompted by the action of the railroads using Quay Street. Days before the presentation of the remonstrance to the council, the railroads, upset "by the persistency with which cartmen and truck-men on Quay street impede the passage of trains," had U.S. marshals arrest two cartmen. They were charged with having "impeded and obstructed" mail trains, a federal offense. Both sides in the conflict over Quay Street appeared quite willing to finally decide the issue, as mer-

chants, cartmen, and others "doing business on that thoroughfare" welcomed the legal showdown. At a hearing before a federal commissioner,
prominent residents of the city (including the mayor and the school superintendent) argued that "the property owners along the line of the
streets through which the tracks passed had the primal right to the use
of the thoroughfare." Property owners abutting the street, not the railroads, had the first right to unobstructed use of the street.[39] The legal
showdown, however, did not take place. What the property owners abutting Quay Street—and specific working-class occupations such as teamsters, cartmen, and truckmen—hoped would be the "test question," failed
to materialize when the federal commissioner simply dismissed the
charges against the cartmen. As the *Argus* noted, the dismissal failed to
"finally dispose of the question as to who has the primal right of way
through the streets." "Regrets" were expressed by "truckmen and others
that the question was not finally determined."[40]

The petition of the merchants and workers who labored in the street
to take action against the railroads running on Quay was referred to the
railroad committee. In October of 1874, the committee recommended
that the council adopt a resolution directing the mayor to take "legal or
other measures" to rectify the problem posed by the running of trains on
Quay Street. Specifically, the committee found that "the railroad tracks"
in Quay Street and on Steamboat Square were "a public nuisance." Indeed, the committee threatened their removal. The resolution passed the
council with but one dissenting vote.[41] Two months later, however, the
mayor had apparently not acted on the resolution. In December, the
council requested that the mayor report "what action, if any, [had] been
taken" to "abate the nuisance with regard to the railroad tracks on Quay
street." One week later, the council tabled a motion made by a single
alderman; the motion asked the mayor to work for "the removal" of the
tracks.[42]

The conflict over "who has the primal right of way through the
streets," particularly Quay Street, continued in 1875 and 1876. The city's
legal department was also involved in assessing the conflict over Quay
Street and the respective rights of the parties contesting the uses of the
street. In early 1875, a law department report noted one particularly dangerous aspect of having railroads run through Quay. "The merchants"
along Quay complained that a fire at a large elevator was seriously aggravated by railroad cars standing upon the tracks in the street. The obstruction posed by the cars made it difficult for the fire fighters to get water
from the basin to use in extinguishing the fire. The elevator fire was not

a singular episode linking railroads and fires in the city. The early spring of 1877, in fact, happened to be a particularly bad time for railroad-caused fires. In April "the roof of a house . . . caught fire [Saturday afternoon] from the sparks of a passing locomotive." Fortunately, the fire was spotted by residents and extinguished before causing serious damage. The next month, there was another roof fire caused by "sparks from a passing locomotive." And just a few days later, yet another roof fire was attributed to the hot cinders and ashes emitted from a passing locomotive. The latter fire hit a house near the Van Woert Street railroad crossing, the scene of a number of antirailroad crowd incidents during the Great Strike.[43] Albany was not alone in this respect. In Buffalo, the extensive ice warehouses of Briggs & Company, located near railroad tracks, burned down in late 1872. The company went to court alleging that the New York Central Railroad was responsible "for setting them on fire." Such fires were a problem throughout the country. The *Master Mechanics Report* estimated in 1883 that railroad corporations nationwide paid hundreds of thousands of dollars annually for damage done as a result of fires started by passing locomotives.[44]

The situation on Quay Street worsened in 1875 when a railroad corporation began to lay additional tracks on Steamboat Square (see fig. 8). The track laying was the object of frequent debate in the council, vacillating council actions to stop the track laying and sanction the work, mayoral vetoes, and continued demonstrations of opposition to railroad tracks on Quay Street and Steamboat Square from merchants and other users of Quay and the square. For its part, the council wavered on the issue before definitively prohibiting the building of more tracks on Quay Street. In April the council voted to stop further track laying on Steamboat Square. The mayor, however, refused to sign the resolution, claiming that the issue needed further examination and reconsideration so that all parties in the conflict could be heard. The mayor's delay came despite the fact that he had held a meeting in his office wherein the merchants along the street had "insisted" that "their interests would be greatly prejudiced by the laying of the proposed track." In the face of the mayor's refusal to sign the resolution, the council referred the entire matter back to committee "so that the parties interested may have a hearing."[45]

In May the council voted again to prohibit the railroad from laying more tracks on Steamboat Square. Two weeks later, however, the council reversed itself and granted the right to lay tracks on Steamboat Square to the Delaware and Hudson Canal Company, the railroad seeking the additional tracks. One week later, as if to emphasize the vacillating nature

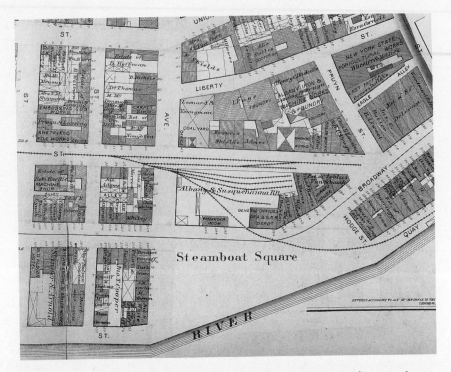

Fig. 8. Steamboat Square, Albany, 1876. The square was the site of repeated conflict between residents and railroads. In 1876, neighborhood residents angrily confronted a railroad construction crew that was attempting to lay track.

of the aldermen, the council, following the turnabout of the mayor who now was recommending more hearings instead of track laying, rescinded its grant to the railroad. The issue, for the year 1875 at least, was decided in June, when the council voted again to prohibit track laying on the square. And in spite of the council's vacillations and contradictory actions, it issued a lengthy statement as to why the railroad should not be permitted to lay more tracks on the Square.[46]

Steamboat Square, the aldermen observed, had been for many years a space for "the use and convenience of the residents, tax-payers, merchants and traders." The primary use of the square, of course, had been economic, primarily "the transaction of legitimate transportation business." The aldermen now regretted the fact that in 1867 they allowed "monopoly and foreign railroad interests" to mar "the appearance of the square, as well as its usefulness for business purposes, by permitting a railroad track" to be laid on the square. "Most of the citizens of the vicinity" of the square opposed the presence of the track and did not want to see further tracks laid. The council concluded that "however much the interests of gigantic corporations should be fostered and protected and their patronage solicited," the city government was responsible primarily "to the residents of the city." Through the expenditures of their government, residents "already helped, to the extent of hundreds of thousands of dollars, corporations." Enough was enough, the aldermen claimed: the city's residents could "not be compelled yearly to make sacrifices of their property and the[ir] interests" in order to "merely reduce the expenses of these corporations."[47]

The aldermen's statement tied together a number of issues involving urban residents and railroads, not only in Albany but also Buffalo and Syracuse. First, of course, was the conflict over uses of the streets, and from the point of view of many small businesses and working-class people, such as teamsters and draymen, the negative economic consequences of the railroads' intersection with streets. In the aldermen's statement, that conflict was framed in broader political terms. The threat to the economic and social activities carried out in Quay Street and Steamboat Square was a "foreign" one originating from outside of Albany. It was also one entailing the danger of "monopoly." In addition, it was not only local business interests that had a right to oppose railroad use of the street and square, but also the "residents" in the "vicinity," some of whom might rightly be concerned simply with the "appearance of the square" (similar antimonopoly and aesthetic concerns motivated some who opposed the laying of tracks by the New York Central in Buffalo's Terrace). Finally, the aldermen obliquely made reference to taxes, one of the great and growing concerns of propertied elements in Albany, Buffalo, and Syracuse. Taxes were in turn part and parcel of the ongoing movement for municipal "reform" in all three cities. A large part of the indebtedness of Albany, Buffalo, and Syracuse was accounted for by investments in railroads, largely through the issuing of bonds to help finance construction. And the indebtedness of local government was identified by municipal and tax reform movements as a major cause of unnecessary and burdensome rates of taxation.[48]

The conflict over Quay Street and Steamboat Square erupted once again in the year preceding the Great Strike. In the summer of 1876, the Delaware and Hudson Canal Company decided to try to lay track on Steamboat Square. This time, however, opposition to track laying took a new and more confrontational form: neighborhood residents gathered and directly challenged the railroad's presence in the square. Early in the morning of June 6, a crew of about forty railroad laborers commenced "tearing up the pavement" on the square in order to lay track. News of the construction crew quickly spread to nearby residents, who "were at once aroused" and marched down to the square. The residents confronted the workers and "protested against the work being proceeded with." The railroad laborers, however, continued to work as angry residents surrounded them. Hearing of the track laying and the confrontation, a number of prominent property owners in the area, including an ex-alderman, hurried to the mayor's office. With the mayor and the city attorney at their sides, this group went to Police Court, filed a formal complaint, and procured arrest warrants. Armed with the warrants and a squad of policemen, they rushed to the square. The entire construction gang was arrested and marched to the city jail. All but the foreman of the gang were then released. The charges? "Tearing up the pavement" and, hence, "obstructing the street."[49] In June 1877, four weeks before the start of the Great Strike, the conflicts consequent upon railroad use of Quay Street and Steamboat Square resurfaced when the council noted that a petition had been presented by "citizens and property owners" in the area remonstrating against the railroads. Once again, the railroads were "blocking up the streets."[50]

The railroad crossing at Broadway near Colonie was the other major focal point of conflict between the railroads and various residents of Albany during the years leading up to 1877. The railroad crossing on Broadway—about three-quarters of a mile north of the center of town—ripped through Albany's most important north-south thoroughfare. In fact, the same New York Central Railroad tracks intersected Colonie, Van Woert, and North Pearl Streets within the space of about two blocks. Once past the crossing, Broadway continued on to north Albany and eventually became the Watervliet Turnpike, the main road to nearby Troy.[51] The Broadway crossing was the site of many accidents and obstructions to users of the avenue. Indeed, by the early 1880s, the crossing was responsible for killing an average of one person a month. Its reputation as "the terror" was well deserved.[52] The crossing had become more dangerous in 1874 when the Central laid additional tracks across the street as part of its new and improved freight service across upstate New York.

The additional tracks the Central added to the Broadway crossing were initially contested by the common council in October of 1874. At that time, the aldermen adopted a resolution ordering the city attorney to initiate litigation to prevent the railroad "from laying any new railroad tracks across Broadway, within the city." Over the next few weeks, however, the council and the New York Central managed to fashion a compromise of sorts. In exchange for a pledge by the railroad to start constructing a bridge over Broadway by the spring of 1875, and to "pay all damages to property owners by reason of the laying of such additional tracks," the council voted in November to sanction the new tracks.[53] In addition to crossing Broadway, the additional tracks crossed Van Woert Street—the site of significant crowd disturbances during the Great Strike.

The plan to eliminate the Broadway crossing by means of a railroad bridge over the street quickly went awry. Instead of the railroad commencing the construction of a bridge in the spring of 1875, the spring and summer passed with no construction taking place. A consequent exchange of letters between the city's legal department and lawyers for the New York Central accomplished little. In the fall of 1875, the aldermen's patience apparently ended. A resolution passed ordering the city attorney to "take the necessary proceedings against the New York Central and Hudson River Railroad Company, so as to compel them to carry out their agreement" to obviate the crossing by way of a bridge.[54] The resolution initiating litigation acknowledged that the crossing now created even greater problems for pedestrians and vehicles. But it was more a prod to spur the Central than a genuine move to sue the company; at the next meeting of the council, the order to the city attorney was "recalled" for reconsideration.[55]

The increased danger posed by the larger and busier railroad crossing on Broadway was indeed of concern to people having to travel over the crossing, to those residing close to the tracks, and to local commercial interests dependent upon Broadway travel. Shortly after the council threatened litigation against the company, the *Evening Times* observed in an editorial that "great dissatisfaction" with the crossing was voiced, not only by members of the council but also "by citizens residing in the northern part of the city." Noting that the crossing had been a serious problem since 1872, the editorial lambasted the "empty promises" of the Central and called for more "pressure" on the railroad. A railroad bridge had to be constructed, the paper asserted, in order to eliminate a situation where "scarcely a day passes but some citizen narrowly escapes accident." Such was the editors' backhanded acknowledgment that the crossing took a high toll in lives.[56]

What kinds of "citizens" in the area opposed the crossing and sought its removal? Public school no. 13 and St. Peter's Hospital were on Broadway, quite close to the crossing. Those institutions and the people they served no doubt would have welcomed the elimination of the dangerous crossing. Within just a two-to-three-block radius of the crossing, there were at least four bakers, eight "refreshment" saloons, and twenty retail grocers, in addition to other small businesses and residents. And for many of the small nonindustrial enterprises located in the vicinity of the crossing, the railroad crossing affected more than their business endeavors. The saloons of Thomas Maher, John Cantwell, and James Judge, for example, at 835 and 869 Broadway and 16 Van Woert Street, respectively, were also the homes of these men—and their families.[57] In November the law department issued a recommendation against litigation; the council concurred. A compromise, it appeared, had again been worked out with the Central. A bridge over Broadway would be built, but the construction would include a significant lowering of the grade of Broadway at the site.[58]

The conflict over the Broadway crossing continued into 1876 and 1877. For most of 1876, the city—especially the residents in the northern part of the city—awaited the start of construction. But by year's end, no construction had begun. In November, the council requested that the Central "place crosswalks in Broadway" at the crossing to ease pedestrian travel near, but not over, the tracks. Finally, as 1876 ended, the council asked the city's lawyers to ascertain why the New York Central had again failed to comply "with [its] agreement to construct a bridge across Broadway."[59] In April 1877, the council asked once again why the New York Central had yet to fulfill its promise of "bridging Broadway at [the] railroad crossing." If the railroad answered the aldermen's query, it went unrecorded in the minutes of the council. No doubt, the state's largest and most powerful corporate entity did not feel pressured to respond. Indeed, construction of the bridge had not begun by the time of the Great Strike.[60] The New York Central Railroad had once again demonstrated its indifference and arrogance. The council had demonstrated its inability to force the railroad to live up to its promises and provide residents with measures of relief.

Across the Hudson River from Albany, Greenbush and East Albany had similar conflicts with railroad corporations in the years preceding the Great Strike. Similar types of problems existed between railroads and residents over use of the streets. In late 1875, the Boston, Hoosic Tunnel and Albany Railroad Company finally obtained permission from the village of Greenbush to lay tracks in various streets. Attempts to gain such permission in 1874 had failed, despite alleged bribes to unspecified village leaders. Construction of the tracks was sanctioned in October 1875, with but one stipulation—the railroad was "to be liable for any damages to private property."[61] The residents of Greenbush could not have been particularly pleased to see that railroad expand within the city limits. The Boston, Hoosic Tunnel and Albany Railroad had a major crossing at the Rensselaer and Columbia turnpike in Greenbush which was the the site of many accidents. In fact, in early 1876, the residents of the village were reportedly "very much exercised over the crossing." People asserted that the crossing was "dangerous; that many accidents . . . occurred there." Exacerbating the situation was the fact the railroad company "refuse[d] to remedy the evil."[62] A committee of "citizens" was formed to try and force the railroad to comply with an 1874 law mandating a bridge over the turnpike—a situation not unlike that in Albany with respect to the Broadway crossing. The committee wasted little time in acting. "The persons residing in the vicinity" of the crossing held meetings, and the committee obtained an indictment against the railroad "for maintaining a nuisance." In the words of the *Express*, residents were "determined" to eliminate the grade crossing.[63] Their determination was tested, however, as litigation dragged on into 1877. In March 1877, stockholders of the turnpike company obtained a separate legal decision ordering the railroad to build the bridge. At that hearing, the plaintiffs noted that "fatal accidents" were not uncommon at the crossing. Furthermore, the turnpike was frequently "blocked by trains for hours at a time." The railroad, of course, appealed the decision, ensuring further legal maneuverings, not to mention continued accidents and obstruction of travel at the crossing.[64] The interests of the turnpike company and residents intersected: both would benefit from eliminating the crossing.

Syracuse

Similar conflicts between railroads and urban residents, retail businesses, and other users of the streets occurred in the city of Syracuse prior to the Great Strike. Syracuse, however, was unique among the three cities in that the escalating level of train traffic was mitigated after 1874. In that year, the New York Central Railroad built its new four-track freight line around the city of Syracuse rather than through the city. The new tracks converged with the intracity tracks three-to-four miles east of Syracuse, thereby creating the community of East Syracuse virtually overnight.[65] As a result of this decision, the city of Syracuse was spared the effects of having greater numbers of locomotives and freight trains running down Washington Street. In fact, most of the freight trains used the bypass rather than Washington Street, as was previously the case.[66] The 1874 bypass and the removal of most freight trains from the central city occasioned relief, if not joy. The "vexatious freight trains" had for many

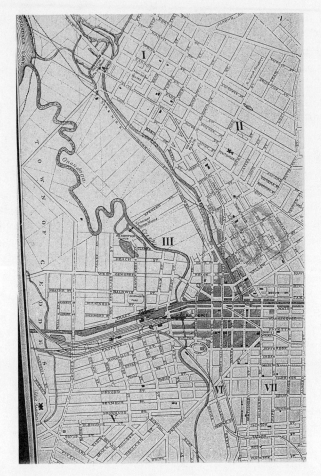

Fig. 9. City of Syracuse, 1873.

years "thundered along through Washington street, constantly blockading the cross streets and public thoroughfares." Obstruction of the streets would now be much less frequent. The bypass also meant the residents of Washington Street and vicinity could "sleep without having their chimneys tumbling down about their ears, and stove pipes rattling down at the dead of night." In addition, a "prolific source of accidents" was gone. As a result, the city would see fewer "amputations of limbs."[67]

Nevertheless, trains operated by a number of railroads, including the Central, still ran through the city and caused a variety of conflicts (see fig. 9). The bypass itself, although built largely around the central city, passed through the northern part of the sparsely populated first ward, and the residents of that ward would now have to deal with increased freight train traffic. There were also problems in the center of Syracuse as well. In early 1875, C. H. Baker and Company, a lumber dealer located on James Street, petitioned the Syracuse Common Council. He asked the aldermen to direct the Syracuse and Chenango railroad to plank its "railroad track between James and Canal streets." Such planking, when present and properly maintained, facilitated the movement of both pedestrians and wagon teams over railroad tracks. As a lumber dealer, Baker's business was dependent on the ability to transport lumber and other supplies to and from the lumber yard and various customers. Most of this transporting was accomplished by horse-drawn wagon teams, and the condition of the streets adjacent to the business's location was an important factor in the flow of goods and customers. If railroad tracks had to be on James Street, then planking in-between the rails and on either side of the tracks was essential if impediment to travel would be lessened. The council agreed and approved Baker's petition.[68]

While a number of streets and areas in the city had to deal with the problems caused by railroads, conflict in the years 1875–77 focused on Washington, Salina, and Jefferson Streets. Salina Street contained many of the city's retail businesses, yet the street was intersected in four places by railroad crossings.[69] North Salina Street, near Onondaga Lake, was also the spot where the New York Central's major new freight lines crossed after 1874 in order to bypass the central city. The crossings presented a dangerous obstacle to wagon teams, carriages, and pedestrians.[70] Little time passed before the common council received complaints. At a council meeting in May 1875, E. Hiscock "and others" asked the council "that something be done towards filling up the road on each side of the Northern railroad" crossing on North Salina Street "so that it may be crossed by teams, etc."[71] Those who petitioned with Hiscock could have come from the long list of retail enterprises on North Salina Street. Among the businesses located on the street were thirty-eight saloons, eighteen grocers, seventeen tailors/clothing stores, twelve shoe stores, as well as bakers, booksellers, tobacco shops, druggists, and dry goods stores.[72] North Salina Street residents who were not business owners were likely supporters of this petition as well.

Conflicts continued throughout 1875 and into 1876. In November of 1875 the common council ordered the Syracuse and Chenango Railroad "to plank between their tracks" running on a portion of Salina Street. Two months later the conflict still continued. A group of property owners, in particular retail store owners, petitioned the council to take action to ensure the unobstructed movement of wagon teams and goods through the streets. Charles Listman and Frederick Yehling, ice dealers, "and others," asked the council to order the New York Central "to repair the approaches at each side of their tracks on Salina street . . . as great difficulty is now experienced by parties going to and from the lake." Salina Street ran right up to the southeast side of Onondaga Lake; the Central's grade crossing was just a short distance down the street from the edge of the lake. For Listman and Yehling, Salina offered direct access to and from the lake, their primary source of ice. But the grade crossings presented serious and costly obstructions. At the close of the ice harvesting season in late spring, profits melted away as ice-laden wagons waited for trains to clear the street. The crossings also posed a danger to company drivers, teams, and wagons. The Salina Street crossing hindered noncommercial access to the lake as well, whether for ice skating in winter or swimming in summer. Similarly, Philip Ackerman, a grocer at 139 North Salina Street, "and other property owners on North Salina street," requested that the council prohibit the Syracuse and Chenango Railroad from using tracks on a nearby street "for the purpose of storing cars" and also "from making up trains at the Salina street crossing." These practices by railroads hindered and threatened the movement of pedestrians and horse-drawn vehicles in those streets, besides adversely impacting the business of neighboring stores like Ackerman's grocery. The council approved a resolution ordering the Central to improve the approaches to its tracks in Salina Street, but the Ackerman petition was not approved. Even an approved petition, however, may not have meant much, for a little over a year later the *Journal* sarcastically observed that the new council had yet to pass "that stereotyped resolution directing Vanderbilt to plank the railroad tracks."[73]

Washington Street, another focal point of conflict between railroads and people, was the major east-west thoroughfare in the city. Washington paralleled and ran south of the Erie Canal; both transportation routes effectively bisected the city (as did the railroad tracks on Washington). Although secondary to Salina Street in importance for retail trade, the street contained a variety of retail and wholesale businesses: five "segar" and tobacco stores, five grocers, seven shoe businesses (two wholesale and four retail), and sixteen restaurants and saloons, among others.[74] The railroad was an early, if slightly ambiguous, presence on the street. Virtually the entire length of Washington had been occupied by a railroad track since the late 1830s; since the 1850s, a double track ran the length of the street.[75] In the early 1870s, there was a court challenge to the continued presence of the railroad in Washington Street. The tracks had become a "source of annoyance" for the users and residents of the street for a variety of reasons: obstruction of commerce and travel, noise, and accidents.[76] Washington Street was the chief rail avenue into and out of Syracuse for the New York Central Railroad, and, not surprisingly, the court challenge seeking the removal of the tracks failed.

But friction between users of the street and property owners abutting the avenue and the Central continued. Toward the western end of Washington Street, the New York Central altered the grade of the street in June 1875 in order to change the grade of its tracks. The result was that "the curb on the south side . . . is covered with gravel and the sidewalks lower than the roadbed." The raised level of the tracks relative to the sidewalk, not to mention the stores, homes, and businesses abutting the street, meant that gravel, coal, wood, and other flotsam from the trains collected on the lower grade (along the sidewalk and building fronts). The raised grade of the trackbed also funneled rainwater in the same direction. The common council immediately adopted a resolution ordering the Central to adjust the level of the curb and sidewalk so that it would conform to the elevated grade of the tracks.[77] Five months later, the city was still having problems with the railroad's presence on Washington Street. Indeed, in November the council adopted a resolution to initiate legal proceedings against the Central. Specifically, the city sought to compel the railroad "to properly grade, fill in and place in good order East Washington street from Mulberry street to Almond street at once. Also to remove therefrom the piles of dirt and rubbish which now encumber the same." The Central agreed to clean up the street in January 1876, and the city dropped its suit.[78] The issue of the railroad's disruption of Washington Street would not go away, however, even with railroad promises of action. In July 1876, the common council once again adopted a resolution requesting that the mayor initiate appropriate measures to ensure that the Central would place East Washington Street in "good order." The resolution was necessary, the aldermen noted, because the Central did not keep its promise.[79] As was the case at the Broadway crossing in Albany, local government resolutions frequently failed to address the adverse impact of railroad use of the streets; railroad promises to rectify the situation rang hollow.

In June 1877, less than a month before the start of the Great Strike, the conflict caused by the Central's use of Washington Street erupted again. The Central, once again, was in the process of raising the level of its tracks relative to the grade of the street. In effect, the Central was placing the tracks in a position that heightened their obstruction of the many and varied nonrailroad uses of the street. Consequently, crossing the tracks was even more hazardous. A number of the property owners on Washington Street and nearby streets, including significant industrial enterprises, attended a council meeting. At the meeting, they lashed out against the Central's actions. Joseph Leeret, coproprietor of a planing mill and box-making manufactory on Water Street (located one block north of Washington Street, Water paralleled Washington), "and others" protested "against the raising of the railroad track." The petitioners also asked the council "to take measures to protect the property owners from damages and injuries incident to the raising of said track."[80]

Jefferson Street was also contested terrain in 1877. The conflict over Jefferson Street, located two blocks south of Washington Street, involved a railroad bridge over Onondaga Creek. The bridge, located at the western end of Jefferson, blocked the street.[81] In April 1877, "several wealthy firms" petitioned the common council. The petitioners opposed the Syracuse and Binghamton Railroad Company's plan to rebuild the deteriorating bridge. Indeed, their petition to the council was front-page news in the *Morning Standard.* As the petitioners observed, the railroad bridge was built "at such an angle to the street as to absolutely close" the western end of the thoroughfare. The petitioning firms and their supporters also claimed that "the growth and population of the fifth ward of Syracuse renders it necessary" that all of Jefferson Street "be opened." Hence, the petitioners asked that "the present railroad bridge [be] removed" so that it would not "obstruct" the street.[82] At least one of the petitioners asked the council to tear down the railroad bridge and replace it with a "road and foot bridge." The council acted immediately on the petition, passing a resolution giving the railroad twenty days to tear down its bridge "and all obstructions erected or maintained . . . in or upon" Jefferson Street. In its place, the council stated, the city would build a foot-and-road bridge that would not obstruct the street.[83]

The eleven signers of the petition included some of the city's major manufacturing establishments: Sweet's Manufacturing Co., an iron foundry and steel producer; Bradley Manufacturing Co., a maker of agricultural implements and trip hammers; and George Barnes & Co., a manufacturer of knives for mowers and reapers. In addition, the opposition to the railroad's obstruction of Jefferson Street included a nearby hotel and meat market; a manufacturer of soda water; a general ticket office; a canning business; a hardware, seeds, and agricultural implements dealer; and a planing mill. A closer examination of the petitioners and where their businesses were located suggests that it was more than a matter of opening Jefferson Street, as the petitioners themselves maintained. Sweet's Manufacturing Company was located on West Street, about a block from the railroad bridge. Jefferson Street ended at West Street; West was also intersected by a railroad crossing—just a block and a half north of Sweet's and roughly two blocks from the Jefferson Street railroad bridge. The same tracks that crossed the Jefferson Street bridge crossed West Street. Forcing the railroad to remove its Jefferson Street bridge would probably have compelled the railroad to abandon the West Street crossing as well. In fact, six of eleven of the petitioners were located on West Street; two were located on Wyoming Street, one block to the west. Economic factors were probably not the only consideration of the petitioners. Petitioner Oscar F. Soule, for example, was a partner with G. L. Merrell in the canned fruit and vegetable packing business on West Street. Yet Mr. Soule also resided on West Street. Petitioner P. B. Brayton was a general ticket agent located on West Washington Street; the Jefferson Street railroad bridge seemingly did not affect his business interests. His home, however, was on West Street.[84]

For years prior to the "Great Strike," many urban residents faced the frequently injurious and disruptive consequences of the railroads' intersection with streets and neighborhoods. Working men, poor women and children, small business owners and their working and nonworking-class customers, and others faced an array of threats from the steam locomotives that rumbled through their streets. The harmful consequences of the railroads running through dense city streets and residential areas included the "unearthly roar" of the locomotives' whistles, as well as showers of soot, smoke, and occasionally ashes and embers hot enough to ignite fires. Small businesses located on streets intersected by railroads sought to have the tracks removed or the obstruction posed by tracks and trains lessened. Residents of all kinds were impacted by the appalling toll in human lives exacted by railroad use of streets; this consequence in particular generated anger at the railroads among the family and friends of those killed or injured by trains.

A variety of urban residents in all three cities opposed railroad use of the streets. Truckmen and cartmen in Albany joined forces with merchants and other property owners in a struggle with railroads over who would have "the primal right" to use of Quay Street. The residents in the vicinity of Steamboat Square fought to stop the railroad from laying tracks in the square. The square, it was argued, was a public space for "the use and convenience of the residents, tax-payers, merchants and traders." Merchants and traders opposed the obstructions and danger posed by the tracks and trains, and so did many of the area residents. Indeed, in the summer of 1876, as the railroad attempted to lay tracks, neighboring residents gathered at the construction site and angrily protested against the encroachment. The Broadway crossing in Albany—the "terror" that killed on average one person a month—was the focal point of a similarly protracted struggle between railroads and residents who had to use the crossing or who lived in the vicinity of the crossing. In conjunction with the municipal government, these people sought to compel the railroads to run the tracks over the street via a bridge; to the consternation of residents and the common council, the bridge, promised in 1875, had still not been built by the summer of 1877.

The residents of Syracuse faced similar but less severe problems with railroads. The 1874 by-pass carried many freight trains around the city rather than through it. As a result, the city expressed relief that a major source of noise, accidents, and "amputations of limbs" was gone. But railroads still intersected a number of streets. Salina Street, intersected in four places by railroad tracks, was the subject of conflict. Property owners, including an ice dealer and a grocer, petitioned the municipal government in vain to address the railroads' obstruction of the street. Similar grievances were present among property owners and residents on and near Washington and Jefferson Streets.

In Buffalo, a variety of residents and small business owners, among other property owners, opposed the railroads' injurious intersection with streets and neighborhoods. The opposition of residents and property owners on Carroll Street to what they termed the railroads' "encroachment" on that space surfaced in the common council—but to no avail. Grocers, saloon keepers, and other small retail establishments in various other streets and neighborhoods crossed by tracks also petitioned the municipal government for assistance in eliminating or at least lessening the harmful consequences of railroad use of the streets. The residents of Fulton Street sought to have the city government compel the railroads to post a flagman at one of the railroad crossings on their street; the common council passed such a ordinance, but the impact of the ordinance was uncertain. In fact, despite numerous conflicts throughout the central and eastern part of the city over railroad use of the streets, the railroads proposed building an intracity rail route in order to link two depots and provide direct rail access for a number of large manufacturing and commercial establishments. A variety of residents and smaller property owners opposed this project. Nevertheless, the common council approved the project—on the eve of the Great Strike in Buffalo.

The July 1877 railroad workers' strike occurred within the context of these ongoing struggles between railroads and a variety of urban residents. Indeed, the railroad workers' strike unleashed the reservoir of anger the conflicts had generated among urban residents. Much of the strike against the railroad corporations was conducted within the clear and immediate view of hundreds, if not thousands, of the same urban residents who had been unsuccessfully battling the railroads for years. It was the strike of portions of the railroad work force that triggered what became known as the "Great Strike"—crowds of strikers and urban residents with no wage relationship to the railroads, stopping trains, battling police, and, much to the alarm of railroad workers, attacking railroad property. When striking railroad workers acted to stop the movement of trains in order to make their strike successful, many urban residents, workers and nonworkers, could not resist the opportunity to take to the streets and "strike" a blow against the railroads.

3 Striking against the Railroads

The great event of the summer . . . was the railroad strike, and the consequent wide-spread disorder.

Harper's New Monthly Magazine, October 1877

Syracuse

To the Citizens of Syracuse: In view of the feverish state of the public mind throughout the country and in this city . . . People should abstain from congregating in the streets, nor should they be idle spectators of events other than at their own places of business.

Syracuse Morning Standard, July 24, 1877.

Syracuse learned of the start of the Great Strike on Wednesday, July 18, as did the people of Buffalo and Albany. By Sunday, July 22, the Strike was "the principal topic of discussion before church and after church." Large numbers of people spent the day congregated around the bulletin boards of telegraph offices. Indeed, throughout the day, "crowds congregated in the news rooms, the hotels and on the street corners discussing the situation." Nervously, the speculations of "all classes" turned to what might happen in their city and neighboring East Syracuse. Fear not, the press unanimously declared, the Strike would not trouble Syracuse.[1]

Despite the veneer of confidence expressed in the city's newspapers, "anxious inquiries" were directed at the railroad workers in East Syracuse, a village of about 1,000 people.[2] Questions were also directed to the railroad shop workers at the New York Central's facilities in the Fifth Ward of Syracuse. At both locations, everything was quiet on Monday, July 23. Indeed, workers told a newspaper reporter that "no serious trouble would exist on the Central road." But as the *Morning Standard* noted, local railroad workers were "a good deal more quiet than the citizens of Syracuse proper."[3] City and railroad authorities acted in anticipation of a

70

strike. Elements of the militia mobilized, and a contingent of troops were stationed at the city armory on West Jefferson Street. City police were sworn in as county sheriffs; they were part of a "posse of more than one hundred picked men" to be the first to act in the event of a strike or any related violence. By Monday evening, the armory housed a strong force of local militiamen. No railroad workers were yet on strike, and not a single crowd incident of any kind had occurred.[4]

Railroad workers, for their part, held a meeting early Monday afternoon in East Syracuse. "About one hundred trainmen" attended the meeting. No reporters were allowed inside the meeting place, but workers did speak to the press afterward. It had been decided at the meeting to send a telegram to William H. Vanderbilt, owner and president of the New York Central Railroad, demanding a restoration of the July 1 pay cut that many railroad workers throughout the country had suffered. But attendance was poor, and those present decided another meeting should be held later in the day. Notices of the second meeting, to be held at 7 P.M. in a barn behind the National Hotel, were posted at various spots in East Syracuse.[5] A "large and enthusiastic [group] of freight conductors, brakemen and firemen," numbering about 250, attended the 7 o'clock meeting. Again, all "outsiders" were excluded. Messages from railroad workers in Buffalo and Rochester were read (these messages were already rendered moot by the pace of events, as will be seen below). The messages stated that "they had determined to strike if the old prices were not given them," and asked "the Syracuse men what they would do." East Syracuse workers sent a reply stating that, if Vanderbilt did not rescind the wage cut, they would also strike.[6]

A majority of railwaymen passed a number of other resolutions. Evincing a determination to protect railroad property, the East Syracuse men agreed "that in no instance would the property of the company be destroyed or molested." Second, striking railroadmen would not drink during the walk-out; anyone who might become intoxicated "would not be recognized as belonging to their number." Finally, the railroadmen agreed to send a committee to a gathering of the Brotherhood of Locomotive Engineers in Syracuse.[7]

The committee of railroadmen created to meet with the engineers left East Syracuse around 9:30 P.M. on a locomotive and tender. A number of other railroad employees accompanied the committee for the short ride to Syracuse. "At several points" in the city, the locomotive was "vociferously cheered by gatherings of workingmen," who apparently knew beforehand of the men and their mission. The same evening, a number of railroad workers visited the offices of the *Morning Standard*. They announced again their intention to strike if Vanderbilt did not rescind the wage cut. Furthermore, "if they did strike, no freight or passenger trains would be permitted to move, but [that] the United States mail would not be interfered with."[8] Despite the lack of a declared strike, train traffic was at a standstill. The trainmen at East Syracuse had decided not to go out on their scheduled runs.

Everything remained fairly quiet in the city of Syracuse Monday evening. Yet the *Daily Courier* wrote that "a large number of strangers and tramps" were in the city. The paper declared that after dark these strangers and tramps "were seen together in squads on different streets." Most likely, the paper was referring to working-class people, who on warm summer nights congregated in the streets of their neighborhoods. The tramp and stranger designation also showed the considerable uneasiness in the city, particularly among the middle and upper classes. Would the Great Strike afflict Syracuse? Those in the streets, according to the paper, "were watched by the authorities, and their movements known to them."[9]

Efforts to prevent the formation of crowds were the centerpiece of the local government's plans to manage any railroad workers' strike and avoid the violent scenes occurring in other cities and towns across the nation. On Tuesday morning, July 24, city residents were greeted with a frank warning printed on the front page of the *Daily Journal*. The admonition told people how to behave during a strike, even though there was as of yet no strike in the city. Entitled "The Importance of Preserving Good Order—The Duty of Citizens," the notice declared that "the following is published with official approval." The pronouncement acknowledged "the feverish state of the public mind throughout the country and in this city" as a result of "the unusual demonstrations in various parts of the country." Yet, it proposed that "if all people will abstain from that which shall create excitement, there will be a peaceful and happy settlement of the present disturbing elements." City residents, though, must heed one critically important reality: "People should abstain from congregating in the streets." The *Daily Journal* admonition warned that, in other towns and cities, gatherings of people in the streets were "dangerous in their tendencies." Those tendencies, the paper failed to note, were a willingness to participate in stopping trains and attacking railroad property. The front page declaration warned that "should a disturbance occur," people should not go into the streets. If they did, Syracuse would "suffer such consequences as may come."[10]

Freight trains remained idle in East Syracuse Tuesday morning;

brakemen and firemen still refused to leave, apparently in anticipation of a strike. A well-attended morning meeting of conductors, firemen, and brakemen convened in "the school house." This time railroad workers allowed Syracuse newspaper reporters into the proceedings. A railroad official was also present, and he read Vanderbilt's response to the railroadmen's telegram requesting a restoration of the pay cut. As he had all along, Vanderbilt refused to negotiate with employees or strikers until "the excitement is over." In the face of Vanderbilt's rejection, the railroad workers unanimously voted to strike "till our pay is restored as it was prior to July 1, 1877." And they sent a reply to Vanderbilt specifying just that. Then the conductors, brakemen, and firemen sought the support of the engineers, who were also present. But the engineers would only state that "they are bound by rules of their own, and act as a body." In short, the engineers had not yet decided what to do, and they would make that decision themselves.[11]

The strike meeting also reaffirmed the resolutions regarding drinking and the protection of railroad property. In fact, a body of strikers was formed to patrol the yards and protect railroad property. The meeting also decided that "none but employees should take part in the strike." Indeed, the strike committee formally requested the press "to announce that the conductors, firemen and brakemen, do not wish any person or persons not employed by the company to take any part whatever in the strike that has been ordered. No one, other than railroad employees will be allowed on or about the company's grounds." The meeting then took steps to inform other railroad workers of the strike vote, and a committee was sent to Syracuse to notify railroad shop workers of the strike. The prohibition against the participation of nonrailroad people was probably due in part to an awareness that strikes in other towns and cities had triggered widespread antirailroad violence among urban residents who bore no wage relationship to railroad companies.[12]

The strike formally started around noon. The strikers' committee reached the New York Central's machine shops in Syracuse in mid-afternoon, where it urged the shopmen to strike immediately. The shop workers replied that they would make that decision for themselves; a shopmen's committee already "had the subject under consideration." The East Syracuse men also learned that the shopmen were asking Vanderbilt for a 25% wage increase—not just a restoration of the 10% pay cut. As Syracuse's railroad shop workers contemplated their course of action, the railroad strike broadened. At some point on Tuesday, about 150 machinists employed in the railroad shops at East Syracuse went on strike, thereby joining the conductors, firemen, and brakemen. They sought to roll back the July 1 paycut.[13] In the evening, Syracuse shop workers gathered to consider their own grievances and the request of the striking East Syracuse trainmen. The shop workers, consisting of boiler makers, carpenters, and machinists, among others, met around 8 P.M. in central Syracuse. "Between one and two hundred men were present," and a large group of people collected outside of the meeting place. The men discussed whether to strike, but the meeting adjourned without taking decisive action. It was decided, however, that another meeting should be held the following morning. Perhaps the shop workers hoped for a favorable response from Vanderbilt.[14]

Notwithstanding the strike of conductors, brakemen, firemen, and machinists at East Syracuse, and suggestions of an impending strike among shop workers in Syracuse itself, Tuesday passed rather quietly in Syracuse. During the day, crowds gathered at the armory on West Jefferson Street where the local militia was stationed, but no incidents were reported. On some streets, however, there were indications of unrest. People the newspapers viewed as "meddling outsiders," who were "talking rather loud," congregated in a number of unnamed streets. The police, however, continued their crowd prevention tactics. They kept close surveillance of the situation and immediately threatened the arrest of "loud" individuals found on street corners. The *Courier* was so pleased with the general state of affairs in the city's streets that it commended the striking railroad workers. The strikers "behave[d] themselves in a circumspect manner," and, most important, they made "no attempt to excite sympathy or gather crowds."[15] Despite the *Courier*'s identification of those in the streets as outsiders, the paper implicitly recognized the dynamic relationship between the actions of striking railroad workers and the formation of potentially dangerous crowds.

More serious indications of unrest that might pose a danger to railroad property and interests surfaced in East Syracuse. Indeed, moves were made toward attacking railroad property in East Syracuse. A number of unidentified people entered the freight yards with the hope of damaging railroad property. On two separate occasions, individuals labeled as "tramps" were driven from the yard after they openly proposed to the strikers that railroad property be damaged. On one occasion, the interlopers were put to flight by gunfire. On a third occasion Tuesday evening, people again marked as "tramps" entered the yard, claiming to be Erie railroad strikers. The East Syracuse strikers, however, did not believe they were railroad workers. Indeed, these men, whatever their status, were imprisoned in the engine house until sunrise, "when they were released and marched out of town." There could be no clearer demonstration of the strikers' commitment to protect railroad property and prevent people unconnected to the railroad from participating in the conflict. Left alone, strikers "dumped" a number of engines—they extinguished the fires and drained the water out of the locomotives' lines, rendering them temporarily inoperative.[16]

The morning of Wednesday, July 25, commenced with the striking trainmen of East Syracuse approaching a group of trackmen at work in the yard. The strikers asked the trackmen to quit work, and the thirty or so men obliged. The strikers also held another meeting in the schoolhouse, and a committee of trackmen attended. The committee informed the strikers that "as the recent reduction of wages did not affect them, they did not propose to join in the strike." Efforts to gain the voluntary support of the trackmen failed; the trackmen were not going to strike. But they were "compelled to stop work for the present by the trainmen," that is, they would return to work as soon as they were allowed to by striking trainmen.[17] The railroad shop workers of the city of Syracuse remained "divided over the question of striking." There were no reports on their planned Wednesday morning meeting. Apparently some of the shop workers—boilermen and blacksmiths—decided to quit work while waiting for word of the efforts to negotiate with Vanderbilt. But "a large number of the men in the machine shops" were still at work.[18]

Two trains were stopped, as the East Syracuse strikers continued to shut down freight traffic. There were few trains to stop, for the Strike to the west and the east had largely ended train traffic. Railroad management, however, was able to move a livestock train to nearby Manlius, where it was left waiting for another locomotive. It did not have long to wait. A regularly scheduled train carrying cheese, normally destined for East Syracuse, sped through the yards in an attempt to avoid the strikers and reach the livestock train. Caught off guard, the strikers quickly jumped on a switch engine and gave chase. They reached "the cheese train" as it was trying to link up with the livestock cars. The strikers "ordered the firemen to leave the engine," and both trains were idled.[19]

The city remained tense Wednesday, and again there were indications suggestive of unrest. During the day it became public knowledge that a regiment of New York City militiamen was going to stop in Syracuse en route to another destination. That was good news in the view of the *Journal,* for the local "militia had become more like a mob than custodians of the public peace, and nobody felt any confidence in their efficiency."[20]

What led the *Journal* to claim that the local militia was "like a mob"? Crowds had gathered at the armory on more than one day, and some militiamen may have openly sympathized with striking railwaymen. Perhaps some troops went so far as to express a measure of hostility toward the railroads. Others may have indicated an unwillingness to risk their lives in defense of the interests of powerful and wealthy railroad corporations. The newspapers, however, never reported any incidents of any kind at the West Jefferson Street armory. Speculation aside, what the militia did or did not do to earn such reprobation from the newspaper's editors went unreported.

Concomitant with news of the New York City troops, "rumors were current" that Vanderbilt would pass through the city in his personal train. Vanderbilt may or may not have passed through the city; if he did, his passage went unreported. But when a passenger train entered Syracuse in the early evening, a large crowd occupied Washington Street. The street was one of the city's central thoroughfares, and much of it was occupied by the tracks of the New York Central (see fig. 2). Yet the train passed without incident.[21] The *Courier* alleged the crowd had formed in the expectation that the train might be carrying Vanderbilt. One hour later, when another passenger train entered the city via Washington Street, as most passenger trains did, the "large" crowd was still present. This second train, however, bore some 500 troops from New York City. Arriving at the depot at the west end of Washington Street, the troops disembarked. "Headed by their drum corps," they marched to the armory. Even though the New York City militiamen were destined for another community, they were definitely trumpeting their presence in the city. Any prostrike or antirailroad sentiments behind the Washington Street crowd must have cooled considerably with the arrival of out-of-town troops.[22]

The afternoon had brought important news to the East Syracuse strikers. At the behest of railroad management, a committee of railroad engineers from Rochester arrived in East Syracuse. The engineers carried pivotal news: the strike was over in Rochester. In light of this information, a full meeting of all strikers was called, and in the early evening 300 railroad workers gathered in the engine house. Now that the strike had ended in Rochester, they voted to end their strike as well. The workers announced that "Mr. Vanderbilt asks all of us to continue work until the excitement is over, and then have a conference." Given that "the Rochester men have gone to work, we all resume work ourselves immediately." But, the trainmen declared that "we do not yet give up what we ask."

Indeed, "[W]e ask still our ten per cent restored." Nevertheless, the strike at East Syracuse had ended.[23]

The Syracuse shop workers in the Fifth Ward also gathered to consider their course of action. A number of unidentified "outside parties" addressed the meeting, and shop workers were urged not to strike. They agreed, at least for the time being, and ended the meeting without a strike vote. But they would meet again on Thursday. If it was not true, as the *Courier* wrote, that "a very large portion of the men are opposed to striking," it was evident that the shop workers were unsure of what action to take. Yet the very fact they continued to work as other segments of the railroad work force were on strike in neighboring East Syracuse was perhaps statement enough of their position.[24]

To date, there had not been a single serious crowd incident in Syracuse. Yet two final pieces of evidence suggest that crowds may have been gathering in the city. News of the end of the strike at East Syracuse reached the city after midnight Wednesday. At that time, the *Daily Journal* wrote, a "very large number" of people were "in the streets." What these people were doing in the streets was not mentioned. Second, after the strike was clearly over in East Syracuse, the *Daily Courier* asserted that, on two consecutive nights during the preceding week, people "gathered together on obscure streets."[25] Were these gatherings crowds or simply working-class people congregating in their streets? If the former was the case, what had they done?

The railroad workers' strike was over in East Syracuse, and Syracuse's railroad laborers had not struck at all. With the strike over in East Syracuse, train traffic resumed normal operations Thursday morning.[26] The strike of railroad workers in neighboring East Syracuse did not trigger a Great Strike in the city of Syracuse. The city was in a unique position during the Strike in upstate New York. By the time the East Syracuse trainmen were striking, the Strike was well underway in Buffalo, and it was starting in Albany. With most trains stopped to the west and the east, few trains approached Syracuse. The bypass in East Syracuse had also lessened the level of train traffic that Syracuse city residents experienced in the years prior to the Great Strike. The bypass, built in 1874, sent freight trains around the central city, not through its center as had been the case before. Railroad encroachment on city streets had been considerably less than that experienced in Albany and Buffalo. East Syracuse's striking railroad workers focused their activities on the rail center in East Syracuse, and the railroad workers in Syracuse's Fifth Ward did not join the strike. Even if the precipitant of striking railroad workers had been present in Syracuse, residents would have had few trains to confront. Lacking the precipitant of striking railroad workers trying to stop trains in city streets, and with few trains moving, the residents of Syracuse did not rise up to strike blows against the railroads. Nor had workers in other sectors of the city's economy gone on strike.

Albany's railroad strikers conducted their strike activities in the sprawling railroad yard in West Albany, located on the outskirts of the city. In this critically important spacial and social sense, the situation in Albany resembled that of Syracuse. But at times, striking railroad workers in Albany took their strike into the very heart of the city itself. When that happened, a strike of railroad workers prompted a Great Strike.

Albany

> Albany being considerable of a railroad centre, the events of the past few days have aroused intense interest in this city, and the question "will the strike reach here?" has been asked a thousand times.
>
> *Albany Evening Times,* July 23, 1877

On Wednesday, July 18, the residents of New York's capitol city learned of the start of what was to become the Great Strike. By Saturday, news of the Great Strike in various towns and cities dominated the front page of the press.[27] During the first few days of the Strike in other cities, particularly as it became apparent the strike of railroad workers involved huge crowds and frequent violence, residents anxiously followed the news. Naturally, they speculated on the possible behavior of local railwaymen. The question of the hour was whether the railroad workers in the Albany area would strike. Also, if they did, there was concern as to what might follow in the wake of their strike. There were grounds for concern. Central Albany contained relatively few railroad workplaces. There were a few depots and roundhouses and some freight facilities. But of more immediate importance was the fact that the New York Central Railroad operated an immense rail facility at West Albany, employing about 1,000 workers. The facility was located on the northwestern outskirts of the city, two miles from the city center. Across the river in East Albany (see fig. 10), there were railroad workplaces that employed significant numbers of workers. As in Syracuse, people "gathered around the telegraph offices" throughout Sunday to read (or hear about) the dispatches as they were posted on the office's streetside bulletin boards. The news was "anxiously discussed and commented upon."[28] Yet the news prompted different predictions.

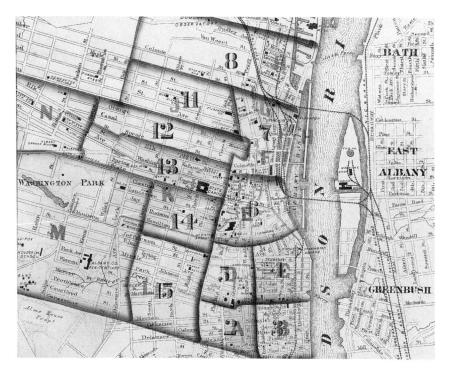

Fig. 10. City of Albany, 1876.

The *Albany Argus* reported in positive terms that the railroadmen at West Albany "do not intend to strike." The *Albany Evening Times* was decidedly ambiguous, even with the benefit of some additional time to appraise the situation. Noting the "innumerable rumors in the air," the paper reported two. First, "a strike would take place" at midnight on Sunday, and, second, "during the week a demand will be made for an advance in wages, and if it is not granted a strike will be inaugurated." For its part, the *Albany Express* wrote that interviews with West Albany railroadmen indicated a strike was imminent.[29]

Railroad authorities, the city government, and Governor Lucius A. Robinson (who resided in Albany) prepared for a strike and the possibility of widespread antirailroad violence. On Sunday evening, July 22, police and units of a militia in the process of being fully mobilized were stationed at various depots. In addition, they occupied the two bridges that spanned the Hudson River and connected Albany to East Albany, an area of about 12,000 people.[30] In doing so, authorities hoped to divide the railroad work force, for significant numbers of railroadmen lived in East Albany. Of equal importance was the fact that controlling the bridges would separate all residents of the two areas.[31] As in Syracuse, Albany deployed the militia before railroad workers went on strike and before any serious crowd disturbances. Nevertheless, railroad management moved engines and rolling stock out of the West Albany yards in anticipation of trouble.[32]

On Monday morning July 23, an informal meeting of railroad workers was held at the West Albany rail center. The railroad workers agreed to "hold a meeting in the Capitol park" at 7 o'clock that evening. That night, 1,000 people assembled in the park in central Albany. Railroad workers dominated the group, but there were a significant number of people present who were not railroad workers—"dry goods clerks," for example.[33] The meeting was formal in nature and was called to order by Matthew J. Tiernan, a railroad worker. Unaware of the strike in Buffalo, which was well underway, Tiernan stated that "information had been received to the effect that the men in Syracuse and Buffalo were ready to strike." In fact, a committee of railroadmen from those two cities would arrive in Albany the following day for the purpose of arranging "harmony of action."[34]

After a committee of Albany men was formed to meet with the Syracuse and Buffalo men, the meeting turned its attention to what Albany railroad workers should do. The meeting agreed that railroad workers would demand a 25% pay increase; a restoration of the 10% paycut of July 1 would not suffice. A motion "to suspend work at once and not to resume" until the pay increase "carried uproariously." Some proposed that a committee be formed to meet with Vanderbilt, prior to striking, in order to negotiate the wage increase; that motion was rejected. Notwithstanding the earlier adoption of a resolution to go out on strike, the meeting also agreed to send a telegram to Vanderbilt informing him of the intentions of his employees; railroadmen would await a response before deciding whether or not to strike.[35]

What a majority at the meeting finally decided is unclear. One of the more detailed newspaper accounts declared that "the meeting adjourned to re-assemble at eight o'clock . . . [Tuesday] morning, in the Capitol park, from which it is proposed to proceed to West Albany and order the men who attempt to work there to desist." In other words, a strike had been agreed upon, at least by a majority of those at the meeting. The other two reports of the meeting differed. One stated only that it had been agreed upon to meet Tuesday morning "to march to West Albany." The final account stated that railroad workers would wait for a reply to their telegram to Vanderbilt; if the wage increase was not forthcoming, they would strike immediately. From the outset, Albany's railroad workers were ambiguous, if not divided, over what course to pursue.[36]

On Tuesday morning, July 24, nearly 500 men, about half of the West Albany work force, showed up for work. Arriving with their "dinner pails, according to their every day custom," they "held a meeting and decided to work until they received a definite answer" from Vanderbilt.[37] These men were following one of the resolutions adopted the previous evening. It is not clear whether the planned morning meeting at the Capitol park was held,[38] but a large crowd "numbering five or six hundred" converged on the West Albany rail facilities. The railroad workers in this crowd were on strike. Most of the crowd consisted of "employees of the shops." But there were "also some men from the city" who were not railroad workers. Their presence was "contrary to the expressed wishes" of many of the railroad workers. Indeed, throughout the Great Strike in Albany, most railroad men felt the conflict with the railroad concerned employees only.[39]

Arriving at the West Albany yard, the crowd divided into three groups. The strikers and city residents who joined this crowd entered various shops, telling those at work to "quit and join them." Shop workers "left work, some quietly going home, and others joining the strikers."[40] Some shops attempted to keep the crowd out—the coach shop slammed its doors shut as the crowd approached. But it would take more than a closed door to keep this crowd out. Indeed, the crowd smashed its way through the entrance "by rolling a car truck against the door."[41] After shutting down the shops, the strikers and other people from the city moved throughout the sprawling yard. They called on the switchmen, trackmen, and lumber hands to join them. Switchmen's shanties were closed and locked. Switches were spiked. Strikers uncoupled a freight train being put together, and the brakemen on board were removed. Climbing aboard the locomotive, a number of the strikers "compelled the engineer to take it to the roundhouse." Several other locomotives met the same fate.[42]

The crowd encountered two more trains. In one case, a freight train attempted to move out of the yard. Charging the locomotive, a number of people jumped on board and stopped the train. The coupling pins were then removed and "thrown down the bank" on one side of the yard.[43] The crowd also intercepted a passenger and freight train as it entered the yard. Once the train was stopped, its fifteen freight cars were switched over to another track. There was no dispute among striking railroad workers over the fate of freight trains; the transportation of freight had to be halted if the strike was to be successful. But there was contention over other trains, for a segment of the crowd sought to keep the passenger portion of the train from continuing. A "majority held that it should not be impeded" and the passenger train was allowed to continue. As was the case in many other cities, although not Syracuse, striking railwaymen in Albany typically allowed passenger trains to pass. A current of the Great Strike, though, would seek to stop the passage of all trains.[44]

After bringing a halt to work in the shops and the movement of freight trains, crowd participants held a meeting. One or two unidentified individuals proposed inflicting serious damage on the trains and equipment. Such a proposition, not uncommon among those in the 1877 crowds who were not railroad workers, was decisively rejected by the striking railwaymen. The meeting then called for another large, public meeting at the Capitol park in the late afternoon, allegedly for the purpose of making "the movement general among the working-men of the city." Indeed, "one speaker declared that this was not a strike of railroad men alone, it was a strike of all kinds of labor against capital." When the strike got "downtown" among the city's major workplaces, he declared, it would find a great deal of support. In addition, a majority at this meeting decided "to visit all the freight houses, roundhouses, etc. in the city and East Albany and invite the men to join." Before leaving the yard, the crowd extinguished "the fires of the locomotives" and left a "patrol to see that no freight trains passed." Nevertheless, after the crowd left, at least one freight train managed to depart. In addition, some shop workers returned to work. And about two hours later, Albany police arrived. Their arrival was apparently not contested by the crowd's patrol.[45]

As the railroad workers' strike developed on Tuesday, military forces continued to arrive in the city, as they had since before the start of the strike. Indeed, on Monday, the press reported the "entire militia" mobilized and "on duty." Nevertheless, a militia corps arrived from nearby Troy, and in the evening a full regiment of troops (about 600 men) arrived from New York City. Unlike the situation in Buffalo, where local police and the militia were not effectively mobilized and positioned within the city until the railroad workers' strike had triggered a Great Strike, armed forces were stationed at key points in the city before any serious crowd disturbances. Their presence lowered, but did not eliminate, the probability of crowds forming and attacking railroad property.[46]

Local officials opposed the use of the state militia. On Tuesday afternoon, Mayor A. Bleecker Banks and the chief of police met with Governor Robinson (who arrived at his Albany residence on Monday evening).

Banks and the police chief argued that deployment of the state militia was not necessary and should be avoided unless absolutely required. The local police force, in their view, was sufficient to maintain order, particularly in light of the fact that no disorders had occurred in East Albany. In short, they suggested that troops would make a tense situation worse. Not surprisingly, Governor Robinson, a stockholder and director of the Erie Railroad, disagreed.[47]

Mayor Banks also addressed himself to "the citizens of Albany" on Tuesday. Via the newspapers, Banks proclaimed his "entire confidence in the good citizenship and intelligence of the workingmen" of Albany. Yet the mayor voiced his fear that the "workingmen of the city, and particularly employees of the railroad companies, are greatly pressed by evil disposed and designing persons against their will and disposition to lawless and riotous conduct." Riots and other unlawful acts, the mayor declared, would harm the property of the railwaymen's "fellow citizens" and would also be injurious to workingmen themselves. As "taxpayers," they would be liable under state law for the costs of any destruction wrought upon persons or property.[48]

Banks's proclamation acknowledged the role played by crowds in other cities. He feared the same was in store for Albany. Just as elite opinion had done in Syracuse, Banks advised all citizens, including workingmen, to "abstain" from "collecting in crowds." Indeed, the mayor went so far as to caution against participating in "exciting and heating discussions." Finally, he asked for abstention from "the use of all intoxicating liquors" and the assistance of everyone "in the prevention of all acts of lawlessness and disorder." The laws would be upheld, the mayor swore. In order to see they were, he called on "all able-bodied male citizens" to sign up as "special policemen." In fact, "special policemen" were part of the armed forces assigned to guard the city's depots on Sunday evening. Now, however, the call was front-page news, and Banks's proclamation was reprinted over the next few days.[49]

The mayor's plea to the community, particularly his attempt to dissuade people from gathering in streets, lest they turn into dangerous "crowds," stemmed from an awareness that there was "a good deal of hearty sympathy with the strikers" in Albany. No doubt the mayor was also cognizant of widespread hostility toward the railroads. The railroads' injurious intersection with streets and neighborhoods killed and injured people with appalling regularity. Passing locomotives had even set homes on fire. The noise of locomotives frightened horses, causing innumerable "runaways," some of which ended in injury to people and property, all of which were part of the hazardous disorder railroads sowed in urban areas. Merchants, joined by truckmen, cartmen, and teamsters, fought the railroads' disruption of Quay Street, and a variety of people fought against the railroads' encroachment on Steamboat Square. "Citizens" in the northern part of the city opposed the deadly grade crossing on Broadway. As a result of such injuries and conflicts, people were prone to join crowds and assault the interests of the railroads. As the *Evening Times* succinctly put it, "[T]he danger lies in crowds. Keep away from them."[50]

As feared by the mayor and the chief of police, the ongoing mobilization of the militia triggered the first crowd incident in Albany itself (outside of the West Albany rail yards). A number of "crowds" formed "in the vicinity of the armories and the arsenal" and "insults were offered to the soldiers passing to and fro."[51] At one armory, an unidentified individual repeatedly harangued people, trying "to induce the crowd to molest" the soldiers. Albany police arrested the "young fellow." But the arrest and the man's cries for assistance prompted the crowd to "close upon the officer, loosening their tongues upon him and threatening a rescue." People reconsidered their intentions, however, when the arresting officer flourished his revolver and made it clear that the prisoner would go to jail, not to the crowd. That was precisely what happened.[52]

Late Tuesday afternoon, between 800 to 1,000 people gathered at the Capitol park. Matthew J. Tiernan again presided. This meeting was planned by the striking railroad workers, but it included many strike sympathizers and urban residents who had their own reasons for "striking" against railroads. The *Evening Times* asserted that the meeting contained "railroad men, of course, but many more were idlers drawn to the spot by curiosity or sympathy with the movement." While foregoing the "idler" pejorative, the *Argus* agreed that the crowd was "very scantily sprinkled with railroad employees."[53] John Van Hoesen, a railroad brakeman, addressed the gathering. Van Hoesen said "he was proud to see that the employees of the New York Central Railroad" and "laboring men generally" were present. He "deprecated violence," but he also felt that "the next move must be the compelling of the trainmen to join in the strike," most especially, the engineers. In fact, Van Hoesen lashed out at the elite of the railroad work force, the engineers, who "had not assisted in resisting the reduction of ten percent, because they knew that they still would have good wages." The engineers in general, he complained to the assembly, "had never made friends with their firemen."[54] For those at the meeting who did not know, Van Hoesen announced that New York City militiamen, "the roughs of New York," were in the city to suppress the strike. Although the strike was by railroadmen over wages, Van Hoesen proposed "to invite every man who has no capital, but his two hands to join us."[55]

Many railroadmen did not agree with Van Hoesen's offer to other workers to join in the strike. Tiernan, the chair of the meeting, "advised the railroad men to reach a conclusion as soon as possible" as to their course, "and get away from the crowd so that they could do their business by themselves." With the same concerns in mind, George McKenna, a West Albany railroad carpenter, sought the creation of a committee "of West Albany men" to oversee the strike. Aware of the danger posed to railroad property from crowds comprised of people with no wage relationship to the railroads, the great majority of city residents, McKenna "denounced any man or men who would touch one dollar's worth of property at West Albany." When a motion was made "to march in a body to the freight house and drive away the men working there," McKenna stalled, asking "the object of that motion." When it was stated "that if freight could not be loaded no trains could be moved," Tiernan "declared that he would not put motions of men who had no interests at West Albany," in other words, of men who were not employed by the railroad. But with railroadmen apparently a minority in this meeting, the motion "to proceed in a body to the freight house" carried, and "the greater portion" of those at the park moved down State Street.[56]

As the crowd moved down State Street from Capitol park, it ran into a corps of Troy militiamen marching up State Street. Remarkably, this unexpected encounter resulted in no violence. The militiamen continued toward their temporary post—the armory. They were, however, subjected to "jeers and hisses."[57] Once the crowd reached the intersection of State Street and Broadway, it followed the railroad tracks of the Delaware and Hudson Canal Company to the company's freight houses. At some freight houses, the crowd found no one at work. At others, the crowd persuaded or forced laborers to cease work. Freight houses with closed doors were forcibly entered. The crowd continued to a railroad roundhouse on Lumber Street, where a number of machinists, blacksmiths, and wipers were at work. Upon the arrival of the crowd, they also quit work. One old employee of the roundhouse, however, objected to having to quit work under the pressure of this particular crowd. He stated "that while he would be willing to leave work if requested by the strikers themselves," he "objected to being dictated to by a lot of boys and others who now had no connection whatever with the road and probably never had." In addition to closing the roundhouse, the crowd spiked some of the switches on tracks running into and out of the roundhouse. As a result, no trains would be leaving or entering the roundhouse, nor crossing through neighboring streets. The crowd's participants then proceeded to cross the upper bridge over the Hudson into East Albany.[58] The significance of the bridges was about to be demonstrated, as the Great Strike in the city hit flood stage.

Once in East Albany, the crowd stopped trains and continued spiking switches. In fact, people removed entire rails. The sloppy and inefficient manner in which many of the switches were spiked was further evidence of the participation of people who were not railroad workers. As the crowd moved through East Albany, it nearly doubled in size to 2,000 people, drawing railroad workers and nonrailroad people from surrounding neighborhoods.[59] The two major currents of the Strike in Albany were coursing together. Pausing on occasion, a number of unidentified individuals exhorted people to continue their efforts to disrupt and stop rail traffic. What they said, and upon what basis they made their appeals, we will never know, but people from the crowd began to carry off entire switching mechanisms, leaving some lines impassable. When the crowd reached the lower bridge across the Hudson, it confronted a train carrying workers from Albany to Troy. Stopped by the assembly of people on the tracks and the engineer's concern that switches or the rails themselves might have been tampered with, the train's conductor entered the crowd. Meeting a well-known traveling peddler and former Albany resident, he asked to see someone in charge. After the conductor spoke with John Van Hoesen, striking railroad workers in the crowd removed selected spikes; the train was allowed to proceed, due to the fact it was a passenger train and one carrying workingmen on their way home. After "interfering with several trains and parts of trains," the crowd crossed back into Albany over the lower bridge and dispersed. The crowd's trek and its attack on railroad property had lasted for about two-and-a-half hours.[60]

As Tuesday came to a close, a large crowd gathered at the Spencer Street railroad crossing in central Albany (see fig. 11). As a train crossed the street, it was subjected to a barrage of stones. The same train was stoned twice afterward as it continued through the city. The Spencer Street crowd was probably formed chiefly of people who bore no wage relation to the railroad, with railroad strikers a small minority. As the addresses of those arrested in Buffalo suggests, most of the people who participated in the 1877 crowds lived within easy walking distance of railroad tracks and crossings. The area of a crossing suggests the core constituency from which many crowds formed. The Spencer Street crossing was

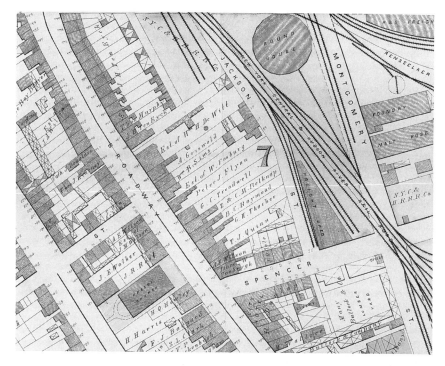

Fig. 11. Railroad crossing on Spencer Street, Albany, 1876.

but one block from Broadway, Albany's major thoroughfare. A Presbyterian church, residences, and various small, retail businesses were located within a block or two of the site.[61] There was at least one other crowd incident on Tuesday. As one of the trains carrying New York City militiamen departed East Albany for West Albany, it encountered a "large crowd" at the bridge. Fearing that the rails or the bridge may have been tampered with, the train stopped. A squad of soldiers, "forming in line," dispersed the crowd and then "preceded the train across the bridge" and into Albany.[62] If residents of Albany sought to stop trains from entering the city from the east, there was no better place to do so than the east end of the bridge.

After the events of Tuesday, in which the two bridges spanning the Hudson River served to dramatically enlarge the scope and intensity of crowd activity (in spite of the presence of guards at both bridges), armed force at both bridges was strengthened. These augmented forces closely "guarded and patrolled" the bridges. In fact, the first crowd incident on Wednesday, July 25, occurred early in the morning when fifty-five local militiamen "marched to the upper railroad bridge." Arriving at the bridge, they ran into a crowd of 200 "men and boys." But after jeering the militiamen, the crowd backed off. Some of the troops crossed the bridge into East Albany, where they encountered yet another crowd of people. This crowd also broke up upon the arrival of rifle-toting soldiers. Evidently, all parties in the conflict realized the tactical and strategic value of controlling the bridges over the Hudson.[63]

Curiously enough, Wednesday's newspapers carried advertisements of future meetings of striking railroad workers. These advertisements point to the continuing efforts of many striking railroad workers to distance themselves from other segments of the community not employed by the railroad, yet participating in crowds. The ads are also suggestive of the multiple currents of the Great Strike. As railwaymen and newspaper editors were aware, it was the element in the crowd with no wage relationship to railroads, yet carrying grievances against railroads generated by the very structure of urban life, that posed a dangerous threat to railroad property. Siphoning off this current of the Strike by separating the railroad strikers from the general population would significantly lower the chances of railroad property being seriously damaged; if successful, it would dramatically reduce the level of disorder in the city. The *Express's* advertisement, "Meeting This Morning," stated that "the railroad men are to hold a meeting at West Albany at nine o'clock." It also announced that "hereafter all meetings will be held at that place instead of Capitol Park" in central Albany. The notice in the *Argus* made the same crucial, spatial, and social point, in addition to stating that it was printing the ad upon request of a "committee" of strikers. Consciously or not, many striking railroad workers recognized the relationship between their strike activities in urban settings and the generally unwanted participation of city residents in crowds. Geographical distance from the center of Albany— returning to the West Albany rail yard—would hopefully lower the number of people unconnected to the railroads participating in meetings and efforts to stop trains.[64] City authorities and railroad management must have been pleased with the apparent change in venue.

Striking railwaymen had other problems to contemplate besides the generally unwanted participation of people who were not connected with the railroad and the threats such people posed for railroad property. So did the hundreds of Albany residents who joined crowds, for the streets, depots, and rail yards of Albany and West Albany "presented rather a warlike appearance." By Wednesday, the city and the yards at West Albany were occupied by hundreds of soldiers—over 600 from New York

City alone. The city had become an armed camp.[65] At 8:30 A.M., 300 New York City militiamen marched down State Street and proceeded through two other main streets to the Union Depot at the foot of Steuben Street. At the depot, they boarded a train for the short ride to West Albany. As the train approached the passenger depot in the West Albany yards, it encountered a mixed crowd of strikers and nonrailroad people. Suddenly, a number of men who were not railroad workers threw a switch to derail the approaching train. But a switchman from the same crowd ran forward to reset the switch. As he did so, "15 or 20 of the mob" threatened him. Nevertheless, he reset the switch. And then he told those who threatened him:

> "[T]here is not a railroad man amongst you; you have no business here. This is a matter between railroad men and their bosses. We want no destruction of property, and as these soldiers have come here to protect property, they must go on."

With the arrival of hundreds of soldiers, as well as a "posse" of local police, the crowd generally broke up. Control of the West Albany rail yard passed into the hands of the military and railroad management.[66]

Pushed out of the West Albany rail yard, the crowd reconstituted itself on an adjacent hillside. Occasional yells and shouts of derision were hurled at the soldiers, but little else. The striking railroad workers in the crowd tried to organize a railroadmen-only meeting, but troops forbid it. The second attempt to hold the meeting succeeded, although the entire meeting took place under the watchful gaze of New York City militiamen. About 150 strikers gathered in conference, and Matthew Tiernan presided once again. He informed his fellow railwaymen that their counterparts in Syracuse had formed a committee to personally call upon Vanderbilt. Furthermore, the Syracuse railroaders were asking the men at West Albany to form their own committee. Together, the Syracuse and Albany strikers would meet Vanderbilt and present their grievances.[67] The meeting appointed Tiernan and another railroad worker for that purpose. Tiernan, the chair of the large public meetings and a key strike leader, asked the meeting to elect a temporary replacement for him. But no one wanted to replace Tiernan, even temporarily.[68]

The military occupation of the West Albany rail yard allowed a number of freight trains to be assembled and sent on their way. In addition, troops escorted a number of workers into the yard. Some of these men were new employees; others were regular employees who took the opportunity to return to work. As both groups went to work, they were taunted by the crowd: "[D]id you kiss your sweetheart?" Indeed, those returning to work should "give us a lock of your hair." Why? Because they would not "reach home again alive." Threats aside, work commenced in the yard.[69]

Military occupation, the start of work, and the resumption of train traffic did not go uncontested. One unidentified individual "threw over a switch which would have thrown [a] train from the track," but the sabotage was discovered and corrected. A more serious challenge was in the making, however, and the source of the challenge is suggestive. As a freight train rumbled through the city on its way to West Albany, a group of "men and boys" jumped aboard. As it entered the outskirts of the rail yard, the train passed between two others sitting on parallel tracks. Momentarily hidden from view, the group jumped off. Immediately, they charged toward the stacked rifles of one regiment. Within but "a short distance" of the weapons, they were intercepted. Surrounded by armed soldiers, they were taken to the edge of the rail yard and ejected from the grounds.[70]

With the massive military occupation of the rail yards at West Albany, the full deployment of armed force throughout Albany, and firm control of the bridges, the Great Strike in the Albany area was nearly over. But not quite yet. The currents of the Strike ebbed and flowed: while the railroad workers' strike was literally under the guns of hundred of troops, Albany residents had a little more space within which to operate—troops could not guard every inch of track in the city. Late Wednesday evening a crowd gathered in Albany at the Van Woert Street railroad crossing (see fig. 12). The Van Woert Street crossing was one block from Broadway, and from that intersection, but one block removed from the infamous Broadway railroad crossing, known locally as *"the terror"* (emphasis added). St. Peter's Hospital at 881 Broadway was only a block away from the Van Woert Street railroad crossing. Public school no. 13, as well as residences, saloons, retail grocers, and other small, nonindustrial businesses were also in the immediate vicinity of the crossings. This crowd, most likely drawn from the surrounding blocks, hurled "stones and missiles" at a train as it crossed Van Woert. Troops were quickly sent to the area. When they arrived, along with the police, they also were "assailed with stones." Then the crowd broke up and ran off.[71] By evening's end, the city was quiet. Calm apparently also reigned on the other side of the river in East Albany. Indeed, as testimony to the critical importance of separating the two areas, conductors on trains passing over the bridges were ordered "to allow no one to cross the river on the trains except regular

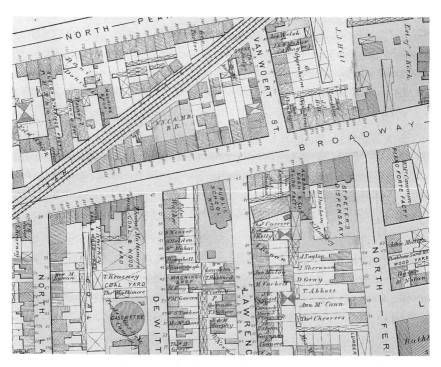

Fig. 12. Van Woert Street and Broadway railroad crossings, Albany, 1876. The crossing on Broadway was known locally as "the terror" given the frequency with which pedestrians and horse-drawn wagons were hit by passing trains. The Van Woert Street crossing, but a block away, was the scene of attacks on railroads in 1877.

passengers." And the troops guarding the bridges were instructed "that no civilian should be allowed to cross, unless a clear statement showed it imperative that he should."[72]

Thursday, July 26, was but two hours old when police arrested one of the most prominent of the West Albany strikers in a Broadway saloon. They detained John Van Hoesen, the man who had a leadership role in the only crowd to traverse the bridges and carry the Strike to both sides of the Hudson.[73] His arrest pointed to the unraveling of the railroad workers' strike. The Great Strike as a whole was almost at an end as well. In fact, no crowds formed anywhere for the better part of Thursday. Train traffic continued at West Albany. The rail center and the city of Albany were bursting with troops, local police, special citizen's patrols, as well as Civil War veterans from the Grand Army of the Republic. The massive employ-

ment of armed force throughout much of the city and the military occupation of the West Albany rail center continued to work strongly against
serious popular crowd actions against the railroads.

The strike of railroad workers, however, continued. About 300 strikers
met in the morning on the outskirts of the West Albany rail yards. Tiernan
reported that the joint negotiations of Syracuse and Albany railroad workers with Vanderbilt failed to resolve their grievances. Vanderbilt received
the committees, listened to their presentations, and flatly rejected any
bargaining until after the strike. Vanderbilt also stated that the shops
would be closed until the strikers agreed to return to work. Notwithstanding Vanderbilt's position, the meeting voted to continue the strike. The
officer in command of the troops occupying the West Albany rail center
sent Vanderbilt the news of the reaffirming strike vote.[74]

In addition to hearing the results of the failed meeting with Vanderbilt
and voting to continue the strike in Albany, the strikers' meeting turned
to the critical and divisive issue of whether striking railroad workers
should seek the active support of workers from other parts of the local
economy. Should striking railroadmen try to bring about a general strike
in Albany? Some strikers clearly felt that such an effort should be made.
But a motion to create committees of railroad men "to invite other workingmen's unions of the city to act with the West Albany railroad strikers"
did not pass.[75] The striking railroad men formally decided to "go it alone."
Nevertheless, some strikers still believed that the strike should be extended dramatically. Ignoring the position of a majority of their fellow
railroaders, by day's end they had met with "the employees of manufacturing firms in the city and invited them to join" in the strike.[76] Finally,
the meeting appointed a committee to meet with the firemen and
brakemen of the Central in an effort to secure their full participation in
the strike. Until now, the strike was spearheaded by railroad workers who
labored in the West Albany shops and yard. The meeting adjourned with
plans to hold a larger meeting of railroad workers. Rather than meet at
West Albany, though, the strikers planned to meet at the Capitol park.

The Capitol park meeting convened in the afternoon. Four hundred
people attended, and most of those present were railroad workers. Perhaps the militarization of the city was working sufficiently to keep non-
railroaders at home. There were, however, some "prominent citizens" in
the gathering. Indeed, prompted by the violent events of the past few
days, members of Albany's elite tried to address the issues facing striking
railroad workers. When the meeting opened, the first order of business
was another announcement of the failure of face-to-face negotiations with

Vanderbilt. Second, a number of leading railroad strikers reiterated and emphasized the desire of railroad men to see no violence enacted on persons and property. These speakers stressed the self-identification of many, if not all railroad workers, as "good citizens." As such, railwaymen were part and parcel of the larger Albany community. Furthermore, railroad workers had a vested interest in protecting property, particularly the property of the New York Central Railroad. "All their little capital invested in the tools now in the shops" was at risk in the face of widespread anti-railroad violence.[77]

In addition to publicly forswearing lawlessness and the destruction of property, other strike leaders reported successful efforts to garner the support of all railroad firemen and brakemen. These segments of the railroad work force were "ready to co-operate" fully in the strike. As the meeting was about to end, Albany's police chief took the podium. He declared that a petition would be circulated throughout the city by the police, with the backing of the mayor and other "influential citizens." The petition would ask Vanderbilt to open the West Albany shops and restore the pay cut enacted July 1. In fact, Mayor Banks pledged to meet with Vanderbilt in an effort to end the conflict on terms favorable to the strikers. In exchange for these efforts, the strikers should return to work and "quietly await the action of Mr. Vanderbilt upon his receipt of their petition."[78] Those at the park greeted the proposal favorably. A majority again rebuffed efforts by some to expand the strike into other sectors of the economy. Indeed, a proposal that the assembly "proceed to the different manufactories and workshops" and persuade or compel other workers to quit work was decisively rejected. The meeting adjourned, but not without a call to meet again in the park Friday afternoon.[79]

As Albany's elite intervened to try and end the railroad workers' strike, and thereby the spark for generalized antirailroad violence, violence directed at trains traveling through streets flared again. At Van Woert Street, where the railroad tracks crossed the thoroughfare, a small crowd of men and boys gathered. This group pelted a passing train with rocks and stones. Local police arrived at the crossing and "dispersed" the crowd. Given the still tense environment in the neighborhood of the Van Woert Street crossing, Mayor Banks telegraphed the military at West Albany. He told the commanding officer that the Albany police had "cleared the street" and would remain at the crossing to prevent another incident. The mayor also requested that no troops be sent to "that locality." The military agreed.[80] In fact, with the stoning of the train at the Van Woert Street crossing on Thurday, July 26, the Great Strike was sputtering to an end. One current of the Strike, the railroad workers' strike, still had a little life left.[81]

The combination of overwhelming military force (employed before any serious crowd incidents), the efforts of most railroad strikers to distance themselves from anyone not employed by the railroad, divisions among the strikers over what course to pursue, and the pledges of the Albany elite to petition Vanderbilt, left the remaining West Albany strikers in an untenable position. In fact, their ranks shrunk as more railwaymen opted to quit the strike. Nevertheless, around four o'clock Friday afternoon, July 27, a meeting of railroad strikers convened in the Capitol park. "Almost entirely composed of railroad workingmen," the gathering again numbered about 400. Thomas O'Neil, reportedly one of the original strike leaders (although the press had not given him much attention), addressed the meeting. The petition circulating on behalf of the strikers was noted. A new executive strike committee was created; some members had quit the strike or were informed by the railroad they would not be allowed to return to work. Apparently, the fired were no longer considered railroad workers and, hence, could not continue to participate in the strike.[82] In addition, the mayor "had advised and requested that future meetings be held at West Albany."[83] Banks knew of the danger present when city residents witnessed the activities of striking railroad workers.

As the petition circulated throughout Albany, particularly "among business men,"[84] and railroad workers mulled their future, the military force that played an important role in sharply limiting the number, scope, and intensity of popular attacks on the railroad displayed itself in central Albany. A grand review of over 2,000 troops, including eight artillery pieces, paraded in front of the governor's platform as the final act in the military's intervention in the Strike.[85] In fact, it is significant that troops were withdrawn from both the West Albany yards and central Albany when a portion of the railroad work force was still on strike. It suggests that the great fear of those who requested the militia derived from a realization that widespread popular anger at the railroads might be released in the course of a strike of railroad workers. That danger had evidently subsided to a point where troops could be sent home.

The various shops in the West Albany yard reopened for work on Saturday, July 28. One last meeting on the outskirts of the yard marked the railroad workers' strike. Only 150 strikers showed up. The meeting produced recriminations, announcements of the firings of strike leaders, and an admission that the strike was over. It was hoped that the petition would gain for workers what the strike had not. The New York Central, for its part, posted notices all around the yard and in every shop that employees had until 8 A.M. Monday to return to work. Those who failed to do so would be "considered as having left the company's service." In fact, with but a few policemen and militia officers on hand, work in the yard commenced in full by Monday morning.[86]

The railroad workers' strike had ended; both currents of the Great Strike in Albany had drained away. But there was lingering concern that the broad grievances generated in the city through the railroads' intersection with streets and neighborhoods might erupt again. Both bridges spanning the Hudson River remained guarded the week following the Great Strike. In fact, the governor's public declaration of the state penalties for people placing obstructions on railroad tracks, tampering with switches or tracks, or throwing stones or other objects at passing trains was on the front page of the *Evening Times* throughout the next week. This concern was not unwarranted. Despite the absence of striking railroad workers or crowds of any kind, sabotage occurred. In East Albany, a freight train on its way to Albany roared through the Second Avenue grade crossing. Instead of continuing on course to Albany, however, the train veered off onto another track and crashed into an old roundhouse. It was "the general belief that some one tampered" with the switches. Whether the act was accomplished by disgruntled, former railroad workers or people from the area who still sought to stop the passage of trains through their communities was never ascertained.[87]

In Albany, railroad shop workers were in the forefront of the strike. In Buffalo, firemen and brakemen would lead the strike. In fact, the Great Strike in Buffalo was underway for three days before a segment of Albany's railroad workers decided to strike. From the start, however, Albany railwaymen were divided over the wisdom of striking, much as their counterparts in Syracuse had been. This division not only weakened their strike, but it was partially mirrored in lower levels of crowd activity in the streets of Albany and East Albany. In addition, many of those railroad workers who did strike defined the strike as a struggle involving only the railroad and its employees. On more than one occasion, a majority of strikers rejected efforts to enlist the support of other workers from the city or the people of Albany in general. This decision on the part of the strikers worked to dampen the development of a Great Strike in the city. And as we shall see, the element of the Strike in Buffalo that fits the traditional view of the event as a rebellion of labor—working-class crowds moving from workplace to workplace trying to create a general strike—was largely absent in Albany.

The urban framework of the Strike undercut the possibilities of a city-wide uprising against the railroads on the scale we shall see in Buffalo. Spatial arrangements and relationships were crucial in prompting or constraining the formation of antirailroad crowds composed of people with no wage relationship with the railroads. The focal point of the railroad workers' strike was the New York Central's sprawling rail center in West Albany. That facility was located on the western edge of Albany—fairly well removed from central Albany. Physical distance from the central city divorced many of the activities of striking railroad workers from the general population. Efforts to stop trains at the West Albany rail center did not take place under the very eyes of hundreds of city residents. In addition, both the railroad work force and the Albany community (Albany and East Albany) were fractured by the Hudson River and its two militia-guarded bridges. Indeed, the most serious crowd incident of the Strike in Albany involved stopping of trains, spiking of switching mechanisms, and even removing entire rails. That attack on the railroads, not coincidentally, occurred when a crowd crossed over the bridge from Albany to East Albany, thereby drawing residents and railroad workers from the ranks of both areas. Finally, the mobilization and use of the militia prior to the railroad workers' strike and any crowd incidents in the city constrained the frequency, scope, and intensity of crowd behavior. Despite these constraints, though, hundreds of people in Albany and East Albany had lashed out against the railroad corporations in the course of the railroad workers' strike. It would be in the city of Buffalo, however, that the Great Strike would reach tidal wave proportions.

Buffalo

On a visit to Superintendent Taylor's office, we learned that no
signs of sympathy with the strikers had been expressed by men
on this division, and it is thought that there will be no trouble at
this point.

                                        Buffalo Express, July 21, 1877

Do the thousands of small property-holders in Buffalo realize that
. . . they are not and cannot be disinterested spectators of the insurrectionary proceedings in our midst?

                                        Buffalo Daily Courier, July 24, 1877

In the early morning hours of Saturday, July 21, 1877, "some 35 or 40 men, mostly firemen," boarded a switch engine in the yard of the Erie Railroad's passenger depot at the intersection of Exchange and Michigan Streets in central Buffalo. They demanded the engineer take them to the

Union Depot and railroad yard in East Buffalo. The engineer refused, and the firemen got off the train. But the firemen informed the recalcitrant engineer and other railroad employees within earshot that "they had better quit work quickly if they knew what was good for them," for a strike would commence at sunrise. As in Syracuse and Albany, their action followed the 10% pay cut enacted three weeks earlier. Aware of the impending strike, local Erie Railroad officials immediately requested aid from the Buffalo police. City authorities obliged, and police were dispatched to many of the city's major railroad facilities. In addition, Erie Railroad officials requested that the militia be mobilized.[88] The firemen had been correct: as the day proceeded, more railroad workers joined the strike.

Throughout Saturday, policemen guarded railroad depots and installations. Although striking railroad firemen attempted to prevent trains from departing, the police managed to keep them running. The 6 P.M. train to Hornellsville, New York, left the Erie Depot without incident, but upon arriving at the Union Depot in East Buffalo at the intersection of William and Curtiss Streets, the fireman on board the train "left his post at the orders of his striking brethren." Railroad management procured another fireman and managed to get the train out of the depot. But striking firemen stopped the train again, a mile down the line. A number of the strikers boarded the train and attempted to persuade or coerce the new fireman to abandon his post. Unexpectedly, a switch engine with railroad officials and Buffalo policemen on board pulled up behind the train; one of the strikers, a fireman, was promptly arrested. The arrest apparently dissuaded the handful of strikers from further delaying the train. With the exception of this episode, most of Saturday passed rather quietly.[89]

Yet, near midnight on Saturday, "an immense crowd" gathered at one of the city's depots as a company of local militiamen prepared to board a train to Attica, New York. The troops were bound for strike duty in that town, where striking railroadmen were stopping trains. Most, if not all, of the people in the crowd were "railroad men." The militia boarded the train, but the engineer balked at having four armed soldiers stationed in his engine cab. Railroad officials, the militia, and city police tried to convince the engineer of the need for soldiers in his cab, as the crowd grew in size and "fears were expressed as to the safety of the train." Indeed, there was "some talk about brick-bats" within the crowd, and one man yelled that "he hoped the train would run off the track before it reached the strikers" in Attica. Nevertheless, the train (with a soldierless engine cab) managed to leave without incident.[90]

Throughout Sunday, July 22, crowds of striking railroad men gathered at or near major rail facilities. Most of these railroad centers were adjacent to major streets, and the railroad tracks leading into the centers crossed the avenues at grade level.[91] Indeed, most of Buffalo's railroad workplaces, depots, roundhouses, freight yards, and tracks were embedded within the structure of the city's streets, residences, and nonrailroad workplaces. As the day wore on, people who were not railroad workers and bore no wage relationship to the railroad companies joined in crowds. They did so for any number of reinforcing or overlapping reasons: to express support for a striker whose wages had been slashed in the continuing depression; to help strike a blow against the interests of the railroad companies and thus express anger over the disruption and hazards the railroads sowed in streets and neighborhoods, frequently at the cost of the lives of family, friends, and neighbors; to strike at the property of the unrivaled symbol of industrial capitalism.

At the roundhouse of the Lake Shore and Michigan Southern Railroad, next to the Perry Street grade crossing, at least "fifteen hundred people" gathered. In addition to striking railwaymen, "boys and young roughs," "women and children," and anonymous "others" were part of the crowd. Another crowd formed at the Erie Depot, one composed of "a large number of railroad employees" but also "a great many non-railroad citizens."[92] Yet the main focus of crowd activity on Sunday was the Lake Shore and Michigan Southern roundhouse and the Perry Street grade crossing (see fig. 13). The area of the crossing suggests the primary constituency of that current of the Strike consisting of people with no wage relationship to railroads. But one block south of Perry was Fulton Street. The same railroad tracks that intersected Perry sliced through Fulton, where five months earlier residents had expressed concern about the dangers the crossings presented to pedestrians and others. In addition, the tracks leading out of the roundhouse first cut across Scott Street, one block north of Perry. In 1875, residents of Scott Street had fought off the encroachment of the Lake Shore and Michigan Southern Railroad when the company tried to lay track along two blocks of the street. As Scott Street residents most likely knew, it was only a matter of time until the railroad tried again. And of course, the crossings in the vicinity of the roundhouse adversely impacted the saloons, retail grocers, and other small businesses in the area dependent upon pedestrian and horse-drawn wagon traffic.[93]

Throughout the day, the people in the roundhouse–Perry Street crowd stopped all freight trains that came their way. The firemen on board were "taken off, whether it was their wish or not." Passenger trains were al-

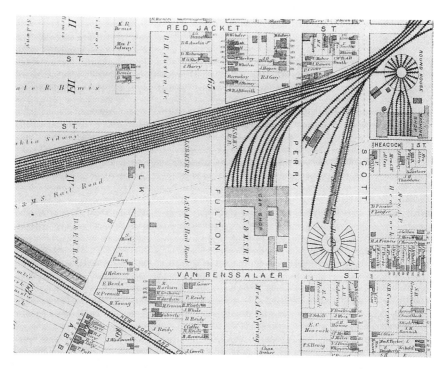

Fig. 13. Buffalo, 1872. The tracks of the Lake Shore and Michigan Southern Railroad cut through many of Buffalo's major thoroughfares. This area was not only the site of railroad workplaces, such as roundhouses and car shops, it was also the scene of conflicts between residents and railroads over the railroads' intersection with streets and neighborhoods. A number of crowd disturbances occurred here in 1877.

lowed to run without interference—a deliberate strategy on the part of striking railroad workers to avoid alienating the traveling public and provoking federal intervention to protect the U.S. mail (sometimes carried by passenger trains). As a striker proposed to a reporter of the *Buffalo Express,* "we know that we have the sympathy of the public so long as we do not interfere with the passenger trains, because we are in the right. But as soon as we stop passengers they begin to grumble and in this way they hurt our cause."[94] A portion of the roundhouse–Perry Street crowd, some of the "strikers," according to the *Express,* left to take possession of the Buffalo Creek railroad bridge in order to stop trains from entering the city at that point. At the bridge, police arrested five people—all railroad workers—and took them to the nearest police station. In spite of the arrests, this crowd stopped a ninety-car freight train loaded with livestock. Some of its coupling pins and links were then removed "and thrown into the creek or ditches along the track."[95] In short, the train was disassembled.

As Sunday progressed, the roundhouse–Perry Street crowd grew larger. Around 2 P.M. "an attempt was made to take a train of loaded freight cars" from the roundhouse to the East Buffalo rail center on William Street. Striking railroad workers from the crowd, however, dashed along the length of the freight train, "pulled the pins and threw them away." The vastly outnumbered city police were deployed along either side of the track to try to prevent the uncoupling of the cars. Their efforts were futile. People in the crowd "would attract the officers attention in some way" so that "some nimble fellow" could dart between the line of police, "pull a pin and make his escape." All done, of course, to the crowd's triumphant cheers.[96] The demeanor of those in the crowd was generally "good natured." "Shouts of laughter" frequently greeted police efforts to prevent decoupling of the cars. Yet, the strikers were determined to stop freight trains (the majority of train traffic). They achieved this with the help of people who were not railroad workers.[97] The two major currents of the Great Strike—striking workers, in this case, railroad strikers, and residents angry at the railroads' deadly and disruptive enroachment on urban life—streamed together in this crowd. The mood of the crowd could change quickly. Having failed to prevent the uncoupling of the freight train, the police arrested one of the strikers. Almost immediately, "the crowd encircled the police," and shouts of "mob the s-ns of b–hs" filled the air. The police, greatly outnumbered and facing people who were threatening violence to prevent the arrest, released the striker. That decision undoubtedly "prevented the police from being roughly dealt with."[98]

Around 4 P.M. the railroad again attempted to put together a freight train and move it out of the roundhouse yard. With two policemen guarding each car coupling—and twenty-five militiamen "drawn up in line" alongside—the train inched forward. The crowd "quickly gathered round and began to hoot and deride" the militiamen. People taunted and threatened the soldiers with such cries as "Fourth of July soldiers," "What are you goin' to do with the shootin irons?" "Big Injuns," "Ain't they pretty," "Does your mother know you're out?" and "Look out or you'll shoot yourself!" When someone in the crowd attempted to snatch a musket from one of the militiamen, "a scuffle ensued." The militia's commanding officer drew his revolver, and the situation hovered on the brink of bloodshed. The officer then commanded his troops to retreat into the roundhouse. Their withdrawal was encouraged by a painful barrage of rocks.[99]

If units of the militia (not fully mobilized) were in retreat, the local police were not. Early Sunday evening, police arrested another person from the roundhouse–Perry Street crowd. Managing to separate him from the main body of the crowd and move him along toward the precinct jail house, the police and their prisoner "were followed by a hooting, yelling mob, who made desperate attempts to rescue" the man. Rocks were hurled at the police, seriously cutting some, and prompting them to draw their revolvers. But they did not fire on their attackers and pursuers, and the crowd failed to free the prisoner. After depositing their prisoner at the jail, the police returned to the Perry Street crossing. As they proceeded through the streets, they were jeered again, this time by neighborhood women. Most of the militia, for its part, was still in the process of being armed. The Erie Railroad had asked for the mobilization on Saturday, and on Sunday the first two units to be fully assembled were sent to the Erie Depot in central Buffalo, where they remained around the clock.[100]

As Sunday came to an end, "about three hundred of the strikers" gathered in the New York Central and Hudson River railroad's yard at East Buffalo. Nonstriking firemen were removed from trains in the yard and switch lights put out. All work ceased in the machine shops and other buildings. Throughout the city, police and militiamen were stationed at all the major rail points, although not in sufficient numbers to control striking railwaymen and the many residents of Buffalo who were beginning to take to the streets.[101]

On Monday, July 23, "a large crowd of strikers" gathered in the Central's East Buffalo yard, and as time passed "they were largely increased . . . by accessions of strikers from the other roads." The strike of Erie Railroad firemen and brakemen now included railroad workers from the three major rail lines in Buffalo: the Erie, the New York Central, and the Lake Shore and Michigan Southern. In addition, engineers of the various roads decided "not to go to work until the trouble was stopped." This was not a sympathy strike but a refusal to work under conditions deemed dangerous.[102] In the East Buffalo yard, a train carrying livestock was put together, but the attempt to move it out of the yard failed. The crowd of strikers, numbering about 150, took possession of the train. They set the brakes and removed the firemen and brakemen as well as the coupling pins. For good measure, they also turned the switches. Perceiving the hopelessness of trying to put the train back together and move it out of the yard, railroad management unloaded the livestock and herded the animals back to the stock yards.[103]

In mid-morning, "a large crowd of strikers" several hundred strong descended on the Lake Shore and Michigan Southern roundhouse "armed with clubs and stones." This crowd of striking railroadmen also contained "men from Uniontown"—an area on the southern outskirts of Buffalo where iron and steel workers lived and worked. With the addition of some iron and steel workers, a portion of the Great Strike was now developing into a broader, working-class strike over grievances generated at the workplace. This crowd forced all roundhouse workers to quit work immediately. Then the crowd continued along the railroad tracks to the machine shops of the Erie Railroad at the corner of Louisiana and Exchange Streets. (After the crowd left the vicinity of the roundhouse, three companies of militia occupied it.) At the machine shops, crowd participants "pushed their way past the soldiers" posted at the entrance. The shop workers "were told to put on their coats and suspend work at once," which they proceeded to do under the additional direction of the master mechanic.[104] Meanwhile, the crowd that had prevented the departure of the stock train at the Central's yard in East Buffalo moved on to the shop of the Buffalo, New York and Philadelphia Railroad. The employees at work there "were all driven out," and a number of trains had their firemen removed. By noon, "all work was suspended about the shops." The strikers then held a meeting where they agreed "there should be no resort to violence." Furthermore, mail trains would continue to be allowed to travel.[105]

Early in the afternoon, "some 400 or 500" of the strikers, some "armed with heavy sticks"—along with "their friends," as a newspaper expressed it—gathered at the major grade crossing on Hamburgh Street. The "friends" of the strikers probably included, for example, the wives and daughters of some of the strikers. Yet, it is likely, too, that the crowd consisted of women who had no familial connection with striking railwaymen but whose reasons for disliking the railroads resulted from the socioeconomic connections between their households and streets, and the railroads' injurious impact on those streets. In brief, their "friends" encompassed people drawn to the grade crossing from the streets and neighborhoods adjacent to it for a variety of reasons, as those arrested during the Strike in Buffalo suggests (grade crossings, of course, were a good spot from which to confront trains). The strikers in the crowd took the lead in intercepting and stopping trains trying to run through Hamburgh Street. The crowd cheered the stopping of every train. Around 1 P.M. a passenger train of the Buffalo and Jamestown Railroad was stopped. A number of strikers "quietly boarded the train and took the fireman and two brakemen off"; the train was then allowed to proceed. This decision on the part of the strikers was apparently accepted by the crowd as a whole. Shortly afterward, the crowd moved over to the Central's tracks to intercept the 2 o'clock express train. The local police, however, were stationed around this grade crossing in large numbers, and they effectively blocked the crowd from interfering with the express. Perhaps the speed of the express discouraged standing on the tracks or attempting to intercept it. Nevertheless, this crowd of railroad strikers and residents from the surrounding blocks spent most of the day at the Hamburgh Street crossing.[106] At 4 P.M. on Monday a militia regiment moved from the Erie Depot to the old abandoned shop of the New York Central next to the grade crossing on Seneca Street, out of fear that "an attempt would be made to burn it." Whether the fear was well-founded, or the militia itself acted as the magnet, "a large crowd" assembled around the building after soldiers arrived. Striking railroadmen were present, but they were probably outnumbered by people who were not railroad employees. Some "boys" in the crowd began to throw rocks at the shop. Striking railroad workers, however, suppressed the stone throwing, and apparently nothing of further consequence transpired.[107]

Around 6 P.M. "a large delegation of strikers" showed up at the Central's East Buffalo machine shop as the shop workers finished their shift. The strike delegation told the shop employees "they must not go to work" the next morning. The shop workers, for their part, informed the delegation they would comply. Around the same time, a Central passenger train started to depart from an unidentified depot in the city. Policemen were stationed on the locomotive and at other spots along the cars. With a crowd occupying the track leading out, "the train came along at quite a good speed, and for some moments, it looked as though she would succeed in passing through." As the train sped through the crowd, however, several men jumped onto the locomotive and forced the engineer to stop. The crowd immediately gathered around the engine, and the firemen on board were "taken off." The passenger cars, apparently empty, were detached from the train "and pushed back to the depot." Only the single car carrying the mail was allowed to continue.[108]

In the early evening, the Hamburgh Street crowd stopped another Buffalo and Jamestown train at the crossing. Strikers who boarded the train, however, were told that the Buffalo and Jamestown Railroad had not reduced the wages of its workers and that "they had no desire to strike." Learning of this fact, the striking railroad workers in the Hamburgh Street crowd "told their friends to allow the train to go on." But now those in the crowd who were not railroad workers proposed a different agenda: all train traffic should come to a halt. Thus, as the train started to move, they pulled a coupling pin and the train split into two. What followed was quite revealing. As the militia and police had done earlier, striking railroad workers "surrounded the engine and baggage car, and threatened to thrash anyone" attempting to prevent the train from moving. The strikers recoupled the train. Yet the sentiment that all trains should be stopped was apparently so strong that they had to maintain their protective positions and "walk[ed] along each side of the train" until it had "passed through the assembly." Once out of the reach of those who sought to prevent it from traveling over the crossing, railroadmen boarded the train. They proudly "told the passengers that they owed their safe passage to the strikers."[109] Not for the last time would striking railwaymen have to act against the sweeping antirailroad sentiments of some of the people who joined crowds. The different currents of the Great Strike frequently flowed together; but this phenomenon did not preclude the existence of different, or opposing, agendas within a single crowd. The question was whether passenger trains would be allowed to continue traveling or whether all trains would be stopped. The merging of the two currents of the Great Strike—urban residents with a multiplicity of reasons to assault railroads and striking workers—would quickly prove a volatile mix.

During Monday afternoon, word reached Buffalo that a militia company from Westfield would arrive by train sometime after dark. A large crowd of perhaps 300 people, striking railroad workers and other people from the city, lay in wait for the train at the Buffalo Creek bridge. As the train carrying the troops approached the bridge, the crowd forced it to stop. Striking railroad workers demanded that the militia "give up their arms" before proceeding into Buffalo; the militia's commander refused. While that officer and some of the strikers continued to speak with one another, strikers—a few armed with revolvers—crept into the rear of one of the cars containing the militiamen and forced some soldiers to turn over their muskets. The commanding officer happened to return to this car as some of his men were being disarmed; when he saw what was taking place, he "gave orders to clear the car." At that point, the confrontation erupted into gunfire and rock throwing. Those in the crowd with guns "fired through the windows and doors" of the car. The militia returned fire, many times over. Indeed, once out of the car and on the ground, the troops fired "another volley" at the fleeing crowd.[110] At least a dozen people from the crowd and the militia were seriously wounded by the gunfire. Ten people from the crowd were wounded by the militia. Of the ten, four were railroad workers, two were clerks, another was a clerk or a bookkeeper, and the fourth nonrailroader was a mason.[111] One person was killed—eighteen-year-old Michael Lyons, the only confirmed fatality of the Great Strike in Buffalo. He was not a striking railroad worker but a clerk. His presence in this crowd was emblematic of the participation of people who were not railroad strikers nor strikers of any kind, but who nonetheless had reasons for disliking railroads. According to the *Express,* he came from a "respectable" family living at 613 Elk Street. The Lyons's residence, it might have been noted, was sandwiched between two major railroad crossings.[112]

News of the shootings provoked anger and fueled further attacks against railroads. The railroads' intersection with streets had killed and injured people with appalling regularity for years; now guns in the service of the railroad corporations were shooting people. One of the cars used to carry the militia was "run down" from the creek bridge to a crossing outside of the Lake Shore roundhouse "and set afire." A crowd of 500 people then "surrounded the burning car and refused to let any one approach it." When a fire company arrived at the scene, the crowd would not allow it to put out the blaze. A second fire company was "received with shouts of derision and taunts." Told to "go home and put out the fires in [their] stoves," both fire companies were blocked from the burning railroad car. The crowd contained striking railroad workers and seemed to be "composed mostly of young fellows." Once again, a portion of a crowd revealed an agenda sharply at odds with that of striking railroad workers. But now that current of the Great Strike consisting of urban residents angered by the railroads' deadly and disruptive presence in their streets threatened to overwhelm the railroad workers' strike. This time people proposed not just the stopping of all trains but the destruction of a major railroad facility located in the heart of the city. Not content merely to burn a single railroad car, the crowd tried "to push the car down to the roundhouse"—in order to set it afire. But striking railroad workers in the crowd would not hear of it, and their strenuous efforts to protect their workplace, the Lake Shore roundhouse, somehow carried the moment.[113]

Earlier on Monday, as the dimensions of the Strike grew, Mayor Philip Becker had issued a proclamation addressed to "all law abiding citizens." The proclamation—printed in the evening papers and distributed throughout the city in the form of handbills and fliers—declared that "the life and property of the inhabitants of this city are greatly endangered" by the strike of railroad workers and the consequent disorders. Becker noted that the state militia had been called out by the governor, and the local police were fully mobilized. But the mayor expressed fear that the militia and police "will not be sufficient." Therefore, he declared, "the citizens themselves should take immediate action." For that reason, the mayor called a public meeting, to be held at the Pearl Street skating rink, "to consider what precautions, if any, should be adopted, and what action should be taken" by Buffalo's residents "for the protection of the city."[114]

The juxtaposition of this invitation with the day's events would prove difficult for the mayor. In fact, the mayor's meeting was probably well attended by people who participated in crowds. Indeed, an "immense assemblage" of city residents gathered at the rink. Becker appointed a member of the common council, L. C. Woodruff, as chair of the meeting. Within minutes after doing so, he slipped away and left the rink. Perhaps the mayor recognized that the "citizens" in attendance were "the strikers and their sympathizers," as they surely were in the view of the *Buffalo Daily Courier*.[115]

Woodruff, the owner of a paper manufacturing business located on Pearl Street, was now the chair of a huge gathering assembled at the behest of the city government. He proceeded to dismiss the wage reduction suffered by railroad workers "as of no consequence at this time." Furthermore, railroadmen had every right to quit work, but "they had not the right to derange the whole business of the country." The alderman decided that "the whole force of the State and Federal government" should be brought to bear on the strikers and anyone who sought to stop trains and prevent laborers from going to work for the railroad. The strikers, the alderman concluded, "should do no violence" if they wished to retain "the respect and sympathy of the whole community." But as the actions of many residents suggested throughout the day, the railroads presented a problem that extended beyond their striking employees. Not surprisingly, then, "numerous expressions of uneasiness" and "exclamations of dissatisfactions" interrupted Woodruff's speech.[116]

Another common council member in attendance, Nathan C. Simons, moved that the meeting form a committee "to confer with the Mayor and report at a subsequent meeting some plan for the protection of life and property." His motion was greeted with "loud shouts of 'no,'" followed by "three rousing cheers . . . [of] . . . 'for the workingmen.'" Nevertheless, the chair appointed a committee, as the meeting chanted "'put workingmen on, put workingmen on.'"[117] A committee of seven people chaired by an alderman was the result. After the creation of the committee, a number of its members addressed the assembly. As striking railroad workers and Buffalo residents prepared to intercept the Westfield militia at the Buffalo Creek bridge, J. V. Hayes, the owner of a steam engine manufactory located in the midst of crowd activity, announced his "great interest in all that pertained to the welfare of this Queen City." He expressed his fear that Buffalo was "on the eve of a great disturbance" if the strike was not "rightly handled." He appealed to "the railroad men" in the meeting "to come forward and tell what they were fighting for." M. Callahan, an Erie Railroad engineer and a member of the newly created committee, came forward and promptly attacked the mayor's appointed chair of the entire proceeding, L. C. Woodruff. Men such as Woodruff, Callahan declared, "had made their fortunes out of the poor men," including railroad workers, who "had to live on salt and potatoes." He stated that the strike of the Erie employees "was not because of the ten per cent reduction" but because members of a workers' committee that tried to negotiate with management had been fired.[118]

As the gathering of city residents grew more restless, alderman Simons "succeeded in making himself heard." The alderman, a prosperous commission merchant, reiterated that "the object of the meeting was to consider the propriety of organizing in the wards for patrolling, that property be protected." But Simons's assertion was shouted down. Apparently unable or unwilling to deal with a gathering at odds with the purposes of those who convened it, L. C. Woodruff declared "in the midst of much confusion" that the meeting was at and end.[119] One wonders how many people at this meeting knew that, earlier in the day, the common council approved construction of the Crosstown railroad—a major rail route that would enable locomotives and freight trains to penetrate further into the very heart of the city.

Crowd activity continued the next day, Tuesday, July 24, and the scope of the Great Strike continued to expand. Indeed, a strike of a segment of the railroad labor force precipitated a major strike among other sections of Buffalo's working classes. In fact, this current of the Strike tended to dominate the streets of Buffalo on Tuesday. Yet, inhabitants of the city who were not strikers of any sort continued to strike blows against the presence of the railroads in their streets and neighborhoods. In midmorning, a group of "men and boys, numbering perhaps one hundred and fifty," appeared at the Niagara Elevator on Buffalo's waterfront and "demanded that the men quit work." The elevator's workers informed the crowd they did not wish to quit work, for they were generally satisfied with their wages. The response of the elevator's workers, and the arrival of the city police, prompted the crowd to move away and march to the City Elevator, the chief elevator of the New York Central railroad. There the crowd attempted to persuade elevator workers to quit work and join them. As was the case at the Niagara Elevator, the crowd's efforts were fruitless. At both workplaces, the "work of unloading vessels and loading canal boats" continued, although no railroad cars were being loaded, as was usually the case.[120]

In other parts of central Buffalo, crowds "visited" various manufacturing establishments to persuade or coerce workers to stop work and join the strike. This current of Buffalo's Great Strike was clearly a working-class event based on conflicts arising from workplaces. Indeed, throughout Tuesday, crowds stopped at many of Buffalo's largest manufacturers, a fact that suggests that this portion of the Great Strike was planned and coordinated. A "large mob" visited Boller and Recktenwalt's planing mill on Chicago Street and Quipp and Durke's manufactory on Seneca Street. At both establishments, the workers were persuaded or "compelled to stop work." The same crowd proceeded to John T. Noye and Sons' factory on Washington Street in the hope of persuading its employees "to quit work." The police arrived and "quickly scattered" the crowd, however, before it could approach Noye's employees. Undaunted, the crowd of "tramps, boys and women," according to the *Express*, re-formed and continued on to other factories and workshops. George W. Tifft & Sons and Farrar & Treft's, manufacturers of steam engines, boilers, and other kinds of machinery; Dempster and Comstock's; and Jewett and Root's, an iron foundry, were targeted as well. The police, however, continued to successfully break up the crowd at each location. Indeed, its participants finally gave up, at least for awhile, and "left to go to different saloons."[121]

Later in the day, however, crowds had greater success in closing manufacturing establishments. Around mid-day, "about 200 men and boys" marched down Exchange Street. Again a crowd stopped at Buffalo's largest and most important manufacturing workplaces: the Buffalo Scale Works, Drullard and Hayes' foundry, and Boller and Recktenwalt's planing mill. At each location (all on the same block), "they effected an unopposed entrance and ordered all the men at work to put on their coats and leave." These workplaces "closed up for the day." Although the police were in the area and made two arrests, they were unable or unwilling to stop the crowd from closing these workplaces. The car works of J. C. & N. Scoville were "also visited by the mob and the employees driven home."[122]

Separate crowds with the same goals roamed other streets in Buffalo on Tuesday. On Clinton Street, a crowd systematically stopped at that avenue's principal workplaces: the tannery of Laub & Zeller, the planing mill of Joseph Churchyard, the bolt-and-nut works of Plumb & Burdict, and the tin manufactory of Sidney Shepherd. At each place, "the employees were forced to quit work." Yet, "no violence" was employed. The workers were simply informed "that they must put on their coats and leave," and they apparently did so without incident.[123] Yet another crowd moved about in parts of the eastern section of Buffalo. This assembly of people, which included many "boys between the ages of 16 and 20," visited Farthing's distillery at the corner of William and Spring Streets and a nearby construction site employing a crew of carpenters. This particular crowd was apparently more "boisterous and turbulent" than others. It successfully persuaded the carpenters to vacate their construction site. But as the crowd moved toward the distillery, a squad of city police rushed out from a nearby station house and arrested at least seven people. In the early afternoon, the city's predominantly Irish coal heavers "struck for higher wages." As coal heavers struck in one yard, they marched to other coal yards and induced their fellow laborers to strike. Their efforts were largely successful, as most of the heavers quit work, notwithstanding the arrests of some of their cohorts.[124]

On Tuesday evening, crowd activity continued. But the railroads' presence and property once again became the primary target. "Shortly after twilight an immense crowd of men and boys" formed on Exchange Street near the Central and Erie Railroad Depots. This crowd occupied the tracks at the point where they entered the streets. Exchange Street not only contained some of the city's larger manufacturing establishments, which crowds had visited earlier in the day, but also residences and various small businesses (at least two grocers and seven saloons) within blocks of the crossing. The militia assigned to the depots tried to control the huge crowd but to no avail. The police, however, decided to clear the tracks and the street. Charging the crowd, they "quickly [drove] them back to Michigan street." The people in this crowd offered little opposition and "shortly afterwards began to disperse."[125] Around the same time, about 500 people converged on the old car shops of the New York Central Railroad. Adjacent to the Seneca Street grade crossing, the shops continued to house a company of militiamen. Impulsively, the crowd stormed through the main doors of the shops; the great majority of the militiamen fled out the back. The few soldiers caught inside were rudely relieved of their weapons.[126]

Another "large crowd" gathered near the depot in East Buffalo, in particular, where the railroad tracks intersected William Street (see fig. 14). According to the *Daily Courier*, the people in this crowd "were not railroad men nor strikers of any kind." With no trains moving, people turned their attention to a streetcar turn table. The crowd took possession of the

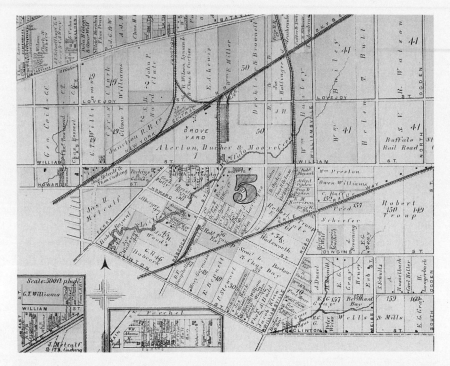

Fig. 14. The railroad crossings on William Street, Buffalo, 1872. The site of crowd disturbances in 1877.

table and promptly drove spikes into it so that it was inoperable. Police drove off the crowd, but only after the turntable was rendered useless. The fact this crowd attacked a turntable belonging to a streetcar company is significant. The crowd's anger at the railroads' presence in city streets was momentarily, yet revealingly, diverted to what was perceived to be a similar threat. Streetcar companies had tested steam-powered cars in Buffalo prior to the Strike. These tests worried residents that more steam-powered vehicles would soon be using their streets, with similar consequences. Particularly in the context of crowd activity, tracks and railways of any kind were worthy targets.[127]

Attacks against railroad property crested, when railroad cars were torched at two locations late Tuesday night. A number of freight cars in the Central's rail yard at East Buffalo were set afire, and a single car near the cattle yards was also burned. Both blazes were extinguished. But the fire bells "caused considerable excitement in the city." Testimony to the fear and anxiety in the city, the alarms triggered brief pandemonium. Indeed, the streets were "alive with people greatly excited and running to and fro." Beset by "rumor" as to "the nature of the fire," many panicked people fled their residences in anticipation of fire—or perhaps they headed for the streets to find out what was happening. Memories of the Great Fire in Chicago and a lesser "great fire" in Boston probably added to the strain created by the Strike and helped trigger the panic. But the panic was short-lived. The bell towers soon signaled that the fires were out, and the evening streets returned to normal.[128] Shortly after these fires, the mayor ordered a curfew. He "admonish[ed] and advise[d] every citizen to keep himself and those under his charge within his own domicile" from 10 P.M. to 5 A.M. In fact, anyone in the streets during those hours would be viewed as an "enemy to the public peace" and subject to immediate arrest. Finally, the mayor's proclamation directed "all places of business" to close during the curfew—a directive aimed primarily at saloons.[129]

Both currents of the Strike continued on Wednesday, July 25, but they were receding. Popular crowd actions against railroads and crowds of striking workers attempting to enforce strikes were rapidly losing strength. At 9 A.M. "a large crowd of men and boys" marched to Haines lumber yard and attempted "to drive away the employees at work." The police interceded and dispersed the crowd, arresting a number of people. Two hours later, with work continuing in the yard, a crowd returned to persuade or coerce the lumber-yard workers to stop work. The police "charged" this group, "laying lustily about them with their batons, and scattering the crowd in all directions." At least a dozen crowd participants were arrested in the melee.[130] At 1 P.M. a large crowd formed at Dakin's coal yard near the intersection of Louisiana and Ohio Streets. The coal yard laborers, numbering about seventy-five, quit work and "joined the crowd." The crowd then commenced "riotous demonstrations." Police arrived and violence immediately flared. People hurled stones at the police and generally "offered strong opposition." But the police charged with their batons and managed to drive the crowd off. After the crowd was driven off, about thirty men returned to work in the yard. A few hours later, a crowd again marched on the yard "vowing vengeance against the men" at work if they did not cease their labors. Again the police arrived, and dividing into three groups "charged on the dense mob from different directions." Some in the crowd threw rocks at the police, but the baton-wielding assault proved too much, and the crowd again scattered. In spite of having driven off the crowd, the police escorted the remaining coal-yard workers to the nearest police station. Remnants of the crowd "hooted and ridiculed" these workers.[131]

Around 4 P.M. a "large crowd" gathered "on Chicago street between Seneca street and the railroad." This crowd seemed unconnected to the crowds of striking workers that descended on the lumber and coal yards earlier in the day. Its object was probably the railroad crossing. Although with train traffic largely at a standstill, there were few if any trains to intercept. Nevertheless, a "disturbance" ensued, either before or after a policeman arrested one of the crowd participants. The policeman "was set upon, and the prisoner released." More police arrived at the railroad crossing, including a dozen officers on horseback. On foot and horse, the police attacked. Yet these people, perhaps putting to use painfully acquired lessons, "quickly divided up into small squads." The police charge was consequently blunted and targets for baton blows more elusive. But these smaller groups could do no more than hurl the "occasional shout of derision" at the police. A few arrests were made, and the disintegrating crowd left the railroad crossing in the possession of the police.[132]

Wednesday evening striking railroad workers tried to symbolically distance themselves from the people who comprised the majority of many crowds and were responsible for much of the violence. A group of strikers traveled on rail handcars to the residence of a West Seneca doctor "where a number of the wounded Westfield soldiers were under treatment." The strikers made it clear their visit would be friendly and sympathetic. Upon receiving word of the intended visit, however, the wounded were moved to another location; the strikers' proffered sympathy was for naught.[133] The burning of railroad cars and the attempted burning of the Lake Shore roundhouse, among other acts of violence directed at railroads, drove the elite of the railroad work force, the engineers, to interject themselves into the Strike. At the offices of the *Express,* two Erie Railroad engineers, authorized to speak for over a dozen of their brethren, pledged "their utmost in maintaining the public peace in the city." The engineers promised to help break up crowds with their own "muscular force," if necessary.[134] Their strength would not be needed, though, for the Great Strike in Buffalo was close to an end.

At all of "the rallying points of the mob on the previous day, scarcely anybody was to be seen" for most of Thursday, July 26. In late afternoon, though, three final crowd incidents occurred. The first involved the ongoing coal heavers' strike. From sixty to 100 striking coal heavers appeared at the coal yard of Frank Williams. The crowd tried to stop work in the yard, but the police arrested fifteen of the strikers; the remainder fled.[135] The final two crowd episodes revolved around people gathering at the intersection of railroad tracks and streets. At the Hamburgh Street railroad crossing, a "mob" stopped a train bound for Niagara Falls. The crowd "uncoupled the cars, pushed the coaches back to the depot, and sent the mailcar on its way." This action strongly suggests that striking railroad workers were present and in control of the crowd, although none of the arrested could clearly be identified in city directories as railroad workers. This crowd also included middle-class people, as did other crowds. Not surprisingly, the four policemen riding on board the train had been unable to prevent the uncoupling of the cars. But upon the arrival of a large contingent of police, the crowd was broken up. The police clubbed many people and made about two dozen arrests.[136]

Last, police moved in upon a crowd of people that "gathered on the L.S. & M.S. Railroad track at the Elk street crossing." The police attacked this crowd as well, arresting nearly a dozen people. Most of the arrested could not be identified in city directories, but a brief look at the immediate vicinity of the crossing suggests what sorts of people were in this crowd and some of the reasons why. The Lake Shore and Michigan Southern Railroad crossing on Elk Street was four to five blocks east of public school no. 4 (with 814 students) and two blocks from St. Mark's Catholic church. In addition, the tracks that crossed Elk at this point were the same tracks that, to the consternation of residents, intersected Fulton Street but one block to the north. Within two blocks of the crossing on Elk, there were also at least three saloons, six retail grocery and provisions stores, as well as other small businesses and residences.[137] Actual and potential recruits abounded in the area of the crossing.

As the day ended, police patrolled the city. They concentrated their efforts on "the railroad tracks and street corners," breaking up incipient crowds and making arrests. In fact, "many arrests" were made by the Buffalo police. Not surprisingly, most of the arrests occurred "in the precincts through which the railroads run." A few people who had participated in crowds were arrested throughout the following week, but with the attack on the crowd at the Elk Street railroad crossing on Thursday, July 26, the "Great Strike" of 1877 in Buffalo was over.[138]

The Strike in Buffalo contained a number of basic elements: the initial strike of railroad workers; the subsequent strike of parts of the Buffalo working classes, such as the coal heavers, and some of the factory workers who left their workplaces upon the arrival of crowds seeking to foment a general strike; and city residents who gathered in streets, particularly at railroad crossings, to stop trains and attack railroad property. At the urging of railroad management, units of the militia were mobilized and dispatched to various railroad facilities. The militia, however, was only partially in place when serious crowd incidents erupted. In other words, notwithstanding the fact that by the end of the Strike Buffalo was occupied by thousands of troops, the Strike developed significant momentum before the militia was in a position to be effectively applied against city residents, both strikers and nonstrikers. Even then, it was the Buffalo police who took the lead in attacking crowds and making scores of arrests. The militia played at best a supporting role when it came to directly confronting the thousands of people who participated in crowds.

Compared to the situations in Albany and Syracuse, Buffalo's railroad workers were relatively united in their course of action: a strike was agreed upon and carried out in a more unified manner. Although dismayed by the violence their strike triggered, Buffalo's striking railroad workers as a whole did not seem to define the struggle against their employer as a fight which precluded the participation of other people (most notably, in the stopping of trains). Railroad workers that may have wished to exclude city residents were in all likelihood simply unable to do so. In any event, the goals and behavior of striking railroad workers were at times overwhelmed by the sheer numbers of residents who demonstrated their willingness to confront the railroad in the streets of Buffalo. Geography played a role in intertwining the actions of railroad workers and city residents with no wage relation to the railroad. In fact, as evident in Albany, spatial arrangements and relationships were crucial. Most of Buffalo's rail facilities were embedded in the central city, surrounded by a multitude of residences, churches, schools, offices, and small businesses. The railroad workers' strike was physically conducted within the view of hundreds of city residents, many of whom had concrete grievances against the railroads. Many had only to step out of their residence to be in the streets—and among strikers trying to stop trains.

In Buffalo and Albany, the actions of striking railroad workers triggered what became known as the "Great Strike." In Buffalo, the railway strike soon led to strikes among workers unconnected to the railroad. This current of the Strike clearly revolved around workplace-centered grievances. Another powerful current of the Strike, however, involved a wide array of urban residents—women, boys, "citizens," striking and nonstriking workers, and people not of the industrial working classes—forming or joining in crowds. Many of these crowds gathered at railroad grade crossings to contest the movement of trains through the streets.

Others attacked railroad property. The two currents combined to produce the "Great Strike" of 1877. The Strike in Albany, although different in some important respects and less intense than that in Buffalo, was composed of essentially the same two currents. As will become clearer in the next chapter, the crowds in both cities contained striking railroad workers, striking and nonstriking workers who bore no wage relation to the railroad, and nonworking-class individuals. In Buffalo and Albany, a variety of people who were residents of streets and neighborhoods intersected by railroads participated in crowds.

4 Who Was in the Crowd?

What kinds of people were in the July 1877 crowds that stopped trains from running down city streets, battled police, and attacked railroad property? The strike of segments of the railroad work force clearly precipitated the Great Strike, and striking railroad workers were parts of many crowds. Indeed, their effort to make the strike successful by stopping train traffic (freight trains, for the most part) sparked others to enter the streets and join in crowds. But who were those people who were not railroad workers? Specifically, what concrete evidence do we have concerning the social composition of the 1877 crowds? Those in the crowd who were not railroad workers came from the surrounding streets, residences, and neighborhoods. Indeed, most of those arrested for participating in crowds lived on streets intersected by railroad tracks or lived in the immediate vicinity of a grade crossing.[1] As outlined in previous chapters, they had compelling reasons to hate railroads in the 1870s and to join striking railroad workers in their attempts to stop freight trains, even though their actions, at times, went well beyond stopping freight trains, threatened railroad property, and clashed with the self-defined interests of most striking railroadmen.

Determining the social composition of the 1877 crowds is problematic, as are most historical inquiries. Ideally, we would like to have comprehensive data on all the people who formed crowds in 1877. Such data, however, does not exist. The people for whom we can generate some information were not randomly selected; they are only those people whom the police wanted to arrest and were able to arrest—and whose names appeared in the press. For all practical purposes, the local police forces chose which crowd members we can study. In other words, we cannot generate a valid sample of the crowd from which we could legitimately draw inferences regarding all crowd participants. In short, our sample is skewed from the start. Nevertheless, we must and can use what evidence exists.[2] The existing evidence, despite its limited nature, paints a picture of the 1877 crowds as a broadly drawn collection of urban residents. A majority was working class, although a significant number were not of the industrial working classes. Indeed, some crowd participants are best defined as middle class.

Previous studies of the Great Strike have examined the identities of those who were arrested (and killed or wounded). The results of these analyses of the social composition of 1877 crowds make one fact very clear: many crowds were composed of people who were not railroad workers. In addition, crowds also contained numbers of people who were not of the industrial working classes. Robert V. Bruce's seminal study of the Strike nationwide makes it clear that the crowds of 1877 were not, for the most part, composed of striking railroad workers. Indeed, Bruce's description of crowds in many cities and towns evidences the prominent roles played by "citizens," women, "boys," and the forever anonymous "others." Of the fifteen people killed or wounded in the bloodiest clash of the Great Strike in Baltimore, for example, Bruce discovered that "none of the known dead or wounded were railroad strikers." Two out of the ten casualties about which occupational status could be ascertained were white-collar employees—a salesman in a clothing store and a grocery clerk. The remainder were a tinner, a poultry peddler, a newsboy, a fresco painter, an unemployed fisherman, a cobbler, a carpenter, and a messenger boy. In Martinsburg, West Virginia, the crowds were composed of "hundreds of strikers and citizens, including 'a number of half-grown boys.'" In Pittsburgh, where the most violent attack against the railroads occurred, the crowd at the Twenty-eighth Street railroad crossing—the location of the fateful clash with Philadelphia militiamen—was one in which "railroad men were outnumbered by others." "Men, women and children," and especially "boys" filled this crowd, according to Bruce. In Harrisburg, Pennsylvania, "all witnesses agreed that throughout the upheaval it was the 'boys and halfgrown men' who were so prominent."[3]

James Francis Caye provides the most in-depth analysis of an 1877 crowd, specifically, the crowd involved in the Roundhouse "riot" in Pittsburgh—the single most violent and destructive event in the Great Strike nationwide. Based on an examination of the 139 people arrested or indicted in connection with the Roundhouse "riot," Caye writes that the crowd "represented all ranks of working class men . . . the mob included substantial numbers from all occupational levels save the professional and managerial classes." Hence, Caye characterizes the crowd as of "the laboring classes of Pittsburgh." Yet, the professional and managerial occupations, which in Caye's view were not present in "substantial" numbers, accounted for 8.6% of the people arrested or indicted for the Roundhouse riot, while "skilled" workers comprised 11.6%. "Semi-skilled" workers accounted for 32%, "operatives" 20.4%, and "unskilled" workers 23.4%. The Pittsburgh crowd was multi-ethnic, in numbers roughly proportional to the city's population. In terms of age, Caye found that nearly 70% of the "rioters" were from twenty to thirty-nine years of age. Nearly half of the rioters were unemployed, and the vast majority (82.7%) were married.[4]

Based on newspaper descriptions of crowd participants in the Great Strike in Chicago, and an analysis of those killed and wounded, Richard Schneirov illustrates that the social composition of crowds could change from day to day, and could also be a function of what type of ward or neighborhood the crowd gathered in. Railroad workers sparked the Strike in Chicago, but "their participation thereafter steadily receded." Depending upon the nature of the area surrounding crowd activity—whether it was, for example, an Irish neighborhood, a commercial district populated by lumber and coal yards employing large numbers of casual day laborers, or an area characterized by heavy industry—crowds were at various times and places composed of specific ethnic and occupational groups, and women and teenagers, according to Schneirov. "When the crowd actions shifted to the neighborhoods," as opposed to lumber yards or industrial areas, "women became more actively involved." Additionally, "at least half of most crowds were young men between the ages of twelve and twenty." In general, "outdoor laborers, followed by teenagers and factory hands . . . played a precipitating and continuing dynamic role in the events of the week" of the Great Strike in Chicago. Most of those reported as killed or wounded in the press had Irish surnames, and 45% of the reported victims were nineteen or younger.[5]

David R. Roediger's account of the Great Strike in St. Louis also presents an extensive analysis of the participants in crowds, along with the composition of the strike's leadership. In terms of rank-and-file crowd members—those arrested or otherwise identified as crowd participants in the press—62% were "unskilled" workers, and 32% were "skilled" workers. The remaining 6% were left unidentified as "other." The mean age of rank-and-file crowd members was thirty-seven. Of the rank-and-file, 95% were male and 6% female; 12% were black. In terms of place of origin, 35% were native-born, 29% were German, 18% were Irish, and 12% were English. In terms of the composition of the "strike leaders," Roediger found that "skilled" and "unskilled" workers accounted for 68% of the leadership. "Small proprietors" accounted for 13%, "white collar employees" 9%, "professionals" 6%, and "others" 4%. Of the strike leaders, 32% were German in origin, 21% were Irish, and another 21% were native-born; 11% had been born in England and Wales.[6]

Most analyses of the social composition of the 1877 crowds conclude with a general characterization of the crowd as multi-ethnic and working class in nature, which most crowds were. Yet this general characterization is also shaped by the available data we can generate from city directories and censuses, and the fact that occupational status and ethnicity are arguably the most salient pieces of data in those two sources. Although some of the authors of these analyses would disagree, there were substantial numbers of Strike participants who were not of the industrial working classes. Caye found that professional and managerial occupations accounted for 8.6% of those arrested or indicted for participating in the Roundhouse riot in Pittsburgh. (In other words, in a crowd of 1,000 people, eighty-six would be from professional and managerial occupations.) Roediger's analysis of the Strike in St. Louis found that among rank-and-file crowd participants, 6% were not of the working classes, while small proprietors, white-collar employees, professionals, and similar "others" accounted for nearly one-third of the leadership of the Strike. Likewise, Bruce's study of the Strike nationwide gives evidence of the participation of people not of the working classes: among the dead in Baltimore, 20% were white-collar employees. In general, Bruce's account suggested the importance of viewing the crowd in terms other than (in addition to) that of occupation. "Citizens" were present in many crowds, along with women, children, and boys. Last, Schneirov's analysis of the Chicago crowds noted that when crowd activity occurred in residential neighborhoods, women and children—in a sense, the primary residents—became much more involved. Indeed, both Schneirov and Roediger observed a relationship between place and crowd composition.

Similar characteristics are found among the 1877 crowds in Buffalo and Albany. Over 150 people were arrested during the Strike in Buffalo. Those who were arrested and whose names appeared in the press provide the "crowd" we can analyze. No such data are available, however, for Albany and Syracuse, for few arrests were made. In Albany, three individuals were arrested: one of the railroad strike's leaders, a railroad man; an anonymous "young fellow" who tried to incite a crowd to attack militiamen; and an itinerant peddler who resided in New York City but participated in a crowd's attack on railroad property in Albany.[7] In Syracuse, only one arrest was reported in the press—that of a striking railroad man, and he was arrested after the Great Strike ended. For an analysis of the crowd in Albany and Syracuse, then, we will have to rely almost exclusively on general newspaper descriptions.

In Buffalo, over 150 people were arrested for a variety of offenses: "leading" crowds, "obstructing sidewalks," and "riot." Some of those who were listed in the newspapers as arrested did not have their alleged offense included in the account of their arrest, or were not mentioned as arrested in connection with any crowd. For this analysis, only those individuals arrested as part of a crowd were examined. In addition, the arrests must have occurred during Strike week; the handful of arrests occurring the week after the Strike (usually of railroad workers) was also excluded. In short, we are examining only those who were crowd participants and were arrested as such during the Strike. Information on these individuals was obtained from the city directory for 1877 and newspaper accounts of the week of the Strike; most were identified in the city directory.

Ninety-nine people were arrested for identifiable crowd incidents during the week of the Strike in Buffalo. Of these, forty-six could be identified in some respect in the 1877 city directory or the newspapers. Table 1 presents the entire list of occupations and the number of cases for the forty-two individuals who could be identified with respect to occupation. There were 17% who were not of the industrial working class; these seven individuals ranged from the proprietor of a soap and candle business to foremen and white-collar employees, specifically, clerks. An occupational breakdown of the remainder reveals that 31% were skilled or semi-skilled workers, and 29% were unskilled workers. The railroad workers comprised 24%, mostly firemen and brakemen, the two segments of the railroad work force that started the railroad workers' strike in Buffalo.[8] Such aggregate data, however, obscure the differing composition of some crowds. Overall, for example, 24% of those identified with respect to occupation were railroad employees, yet one cannot generalize, therefore, that one-fourth of all or even most crowds were made up of railroad workers. A better way of analyzing the occupational status of crowd participants (those arrested or wounded) is to break down the arrested and wounded into the specific crowds of which they were a part and then examine their occupational status. As previous research demonstrates, the social composition of crowds could change from day to day and from location to location. Such was the case in Buffalo.

On Sunday, July 22, as the strike was unfolding in the city of Buffalo, a part of the crowd that had gathered at the Lake Shore roundhouse and the adjacent Perry Street crossing moved off to take control of the Buffalo Creek railroad bridge. At that bridge, a crowd stopped trains from enter-

Table 1. Occupational Data on Buffalo Crowd Participants
(Those Arrested: $N = 42$)

Skilled and semi-skilled occupations (31%)	Machinist (3); blacksmith (2); mason (2); molder (2); roller (1); turner (1); marble polisher (1); painter (1)
Unskilled occupations (29%)	"Laborer" (12)
Railroad employees (24%)	Brakeman (4); fireman (3); engineer (1); switchman (1); unspecified (1)
Nonworking class occupations (17%)	Foreman (2); clerk (2); soap and candle proprietor (1); stove mfr. (1); unspecified, white-collar (1)

ing the city. The *Buffalo Express* described this crowd as composed of "strikers," and railroad workers did indeed dominate the earliest stages of the strike. The occupational status of those arrested supports the *Express's* contention that this was a crowd in which "strikers" predominated. Buffalo police arrested five people from this crowd. All five were railroad workers: three brakemen and two firemen.[9]

The second crowd we can examine is that composed of those who were recorded in the press as crowd participants wounded in the clash between the Westfield militia and the crowd occupying the Buffalo Creek railroad bridge on Monday evening, July 23. To reiterate, a large crowd stopped a train carrying out-of-town militia at the bridge. Some people from the crowd entered the cars carrying militiamen, a scuffle over arms ensued, and the confrontation exploded into gunfire, with the militia firing volleys at the crowd, and at least a few in the crowd firing at the militia. Although the only newspaper description of this crowd described it as also being composed simply of "strikers," an analysis of those wounded confirms that the "strike" in Buffalo was expanding into something more than a strike of railroad brakemen and firemen. Ten people were listed in the newspapers as being wounded participants in this crowd. Of those ten people, four were identified as railroad workers. Of equal or greater importance, four were not railroad employees. Two of the wounded (one of whom died) who were not railroad strikers were listed as "clerks" in the city directory. The other two individuals who were not railroad workers were a mason and a "young" man whose occupation cannot be determined but who was clearly not a railroad worker. According to the directory, the young man was the stepson of John Avery, one of two proprietors of the Continental Hotel. Avery's stepson was either a clerk or a bookprinter.[10] The two other people who were wounded could not be identified with respect to occupation. One was a "young man," while the other remained unidentified except for his address.[11] A powerful current of the Great Strike, existing at times side by side with striking railroad workers (and other strikers), consisted of urban residents with no wage relationship to the railroad joining in attacks against the railroad corporations.

A segment of the Strike in Buffalo does fit a key part of the traditional labor interpretation—crowds of striking workers "visiting" work places in an attempt to foster a general strike. On Tuesday, July 24, a crowd containing many "boys between the ages of 16 and 20," according to the *Buffalo Express,* moved about in the area of William and Spring Streets, visiting various work sites and attempting to persuade or coerce laborers to quit work and join the crowd. The police arrested seven individuals from this crowd. Of the six legible names printed in the press, only two could be identified in the city directories. One of the individuals was a foreman of a planing mill; the other person was a machinist.[12] On Wednesday, July 25, a "large crowd of men and boys" attempted on two occasions in the morning to force the employees at Haines lumber yard to quit work. Both times the police interceded, and a total of fifteen people were arrested. Of these fifteen people, only three could be identified in the city directory. None of the three had any direct work connection with the lumber yard: a turner, a molder, and a foreman of a floating grain elevator.[13] Clearly, an important element or current of the Great Strike in Buffalo consisted of working-class crowds visiting various work places in an attempt to foment a general strike. This segment of the Strike continued on Thursday, July 26. At Frank William's coal yard, a crowd composed for the most part of striking coal heavers converged on the yard in order to shut it down. Thirteen people in the crowd were arrested. Of these thirteen people, one was a roller, and ten were identified in either the directory or the press as simply "laborers," probably the striking coal heavers. The remaining two individuals could not be identified.[14]

The final two crowd incidents involved people gathering at railroad crossings—these were not crowds attempting to close manufactories or other work sites but, rather, were crowds of people, railroad workers and people who were not railroad workers, attempting to prevent some or all trains from moving through street level crossings. The first of these two crowds gathered at the Hamburgh Street crossing and managed to stop and uncouple a train bound for Niagara Falls; the mail car was allowed to proceed, a fact suggesting that striking railroad workers were present and in control of the crowd. Thirty-two people were arrested from this crowd. Of these thirty-two individuals, ten could be identified in the city directories or newspapers. The occupations of these ten people illustrate the diverse nature of the people in the crowds that gathered at grade level railroad crossings. Three of the ten were not of the working classes, indeed, one was the proprietor of a soap and candle business on East Seneca Street. Another was a white-collar employee of a large Main Street retail clothing store, and the third person was listed as a stove manufacturer. The occupations of the other seven people arrested at the Hamburgh Street railroad crossing were laborers (two), a blacksmith, a painter, an engineer, a molder, and a machinist. None of the arrested was clearly identified as a railroad employee.[15]

Last, a crowd gathered at the Elk Street crossing of the Lake Shore and Michigan Southern Railroad. If the people in this crowd encountered any trains attempting to pass across Elk Street, it went unrecorded in the press. Nevertheless, the Buffalo police attacked the crowd, making numerous arrests in the process. Of the fourteen people arrested at the crossing, only three could be identified. They were a blacksmith, a mason, and a marble polisher.[16]

In both the accounts of crowd activities and general editorial responses to the Strike, the Buffalo newspapers contained a number of references to the social composition of the crowds. In addition to the descriptions of the composition of crowds already noted, Buffalo's newspapers noted some other features of the crowd. These descriptions seem to be accurate because they were frequently repeated throughout the Strike, and because research on the Strike in other cities has ascertained much the same. First, although not a single woman was reported as arrested in Buffalo during the Strike, "women were also among the crowd[s]." The fact that no women were arrested is revealing, for it indicates again the skewed nature of arrests and therefore the data; nearly every newspaper in Buffalo noted the presence of women in crowds. The *Buffalo Express* observed of one crowd that "many of them [were] women and young girls." The *Daily Courier* wrote of another crowd that "there were also a good many women." The *Buffalo Christian Advocate* simply stated in its review of the Strike in Buffalo that "women and children were noticeable in the crowds." In fact, the *Buffalo Express* asserted that "women carried clubs and uttered threats as loudly as men."[17] Whether or not crowd participants carried "clubs," women were clearly present in significant numbers. Particularly in poor working-class neighborhoods, women and their children were frequent users of the streets. The railroads' deadly intersection with those streets alone made women logical participants in the crowds of 1877. When situating the Great Strike in its urban environment, the participation of women is no longer solely a function of their relationship to men—the wives and daughters of strikers, to cite the most common explanation. As residents, and as poor and working-class women with close attachments to what transpired in the streets, female crowd members had good reasons for attacking the interests of the railroads, quite apart from any relationship to male strikers.

The presence of "boys" in crowds was also repeatedly noted. "Mischievous boys" frequently took the lead in hurling stones and verbal taunts at the militia, much to the consternation of not only the press but also striking railroad workers. In one particular crowd, the *Express* observed that "a great many of the crowd were boys between the ages of 16 and 20." Indeed, "men and boys" was perhaps the most common description of "the crowd" in Buffalo.[18] Yet, it is not quite clear just what the term "boy" referred to in the 1870s, absent an age range like the one cited above. While "boy" usually referred to a male child from birth to the age of puberty, it was also used as a derogatory term for "a young man, indicating immaturity, want of vigor *or judgment*" (emphasis added).[19] Perhaps some of these boys were actually young men derided as "boys" by the newspapers for their presence in crowds.

There was also recognition of the fact that railroad workers were a minority in many if not most crowds. The *Buffalo Express,* the paper containing the most detailed and extensive descriptions of crowds and their behavior, noted from the onset of the Strike that "it is clear that wherever riot has ensued, the railroad employees have been but a small part of those engaged." In a particularly suggestive editorial passage, the paper wrote that the railroad workers' attempts to protect railroad property and avoid violence had helped to control "the striker in the citizen." This offhand remark acknowledged the fact that residents from many walks of life in Buffalo joined in crowds and participated in "striking" against the railroads.[20] The *Daily Courier* also recognized that in many cases "these were not railroad men nor strikers of any kind" but rather "non-railroad citizens"—in short, a wide array of urban residents. The *Commercial Advertiser,* which virtually ignored the Strike in Buffalo, stated flatly that "most of the rioters" were not railroad strikers "but men out of employment." In the most detached observation, written after the Strike ended in Buffalo, the *Sunday Morning News* concluded that few "strikers" were found in most of the crowds. For the most part, the paper asserted, crowds had been composed of "other citizens," "women," and "children," in addition, of course, to some "roughs and vagabonds."[21]

In Albany and Syracuse, crowds were not nearly as numerous as in Buffalo. Hence, we find fewer descriptions of crowds in the Albany and Syracuse newspapers. When we add the fact that we have no arrest/casualty lists of people to examine, our portrait of the crowd in these two locations is quite sketchy. Nevertheless, there were similarities in the newspapers' descriptions of the crowds. In Albany, it was immediately stated that most crowds were not composed of striking railroad workers. The *Argus* wrote that the crowds which gathered for the mass meetings held in Albany (as opposed to the meetings of railroad workers held in West Albany) were "made up largely of men not in the employ" of the railroads. The paper observed at the meetings that "there was little in the appearance of the men to indicate that they were railroad employees, and many of them evidently were not." The paper added in the same passage that many of the men were also not "skilled mechanics of any kind."[22] Other Albany papers made the same observation: many, if not most of the people who gathered for the mass meetings in Albany were not railroad workers. Furthermore, it was pointed out that in these gatherings (a point also made by railroad workers who were present) there were people who were not of the working class; the unwanted presence of people such as "dry goods clerks" was highlighted at more than one meeting.[23] The constant efforts of striking railroad workers in Albany to distance and separate themselves from the many people in these gatherings who were not railroad workers also supports the newspapers' observations. Once again, these accounts are evidence that a powerful current of the Strike consisted of people with no railroad wage connection, workers and nonworkers, participating in attacks against railroads.

As was the case with crowds in Buffalo, "boys" were present in large numbers in many crowds in Albany. "Men and boys" was again the most frequently employed descriptive term. In particular, these "boys" were, it was asserted, between the ages of fifteen and twenty. One paper simply labeled them the "boys of sixteen."[24] While the presence of women in the Buffalo crowds was commented upon by the press in that city, no mention was made of the participation of women by any of the Albany newspapers. It is difficult to believe, though, that women were absent from Albany's crowds.

In Syracuse, a city which witnessed no violent crowd incidents (nor the stopping of trains in the city proper), the skimpy press accounts of those who did gather in the streets were significantly different from the descriptions of crowd activity found in Buffalo and Albany newspapers. The *Daily Courier,* which was the only paper to really notice and mention gatherings of people in the streets of Syracuse, asserted that these people were from outside the Syracuse community. The paper asserted on July 24 that "tramps and strangers" were congregating on some of the streets of the city. The following day it stated again that the people who were milling around in various streets (unnamed) were "meddling outsiders," and on July 27, when even the probability of violent crowd incidents had passed, the *Courier* reasserted that these people had been "outsiders."[25] There were only two other references to gatherings or crowds of people in Syracuse in the city's press. On July 23, when a committee of striking railroadmen from East Syracuse entered Syracuse on its way to meet with other railroad workers, the train was greeted along the way by "gatherings of workingmen," the *Morning Standard* wrote. And when two trains—one purported to be carrying Vanderbilt, the other carrying militiamen—entered Syracuse via the tracks running the length of Washington Street, a "large crowd" of "people" was on hand, although for what purpose remains unknown. When describing the events in East Syracuse, the Syracuse papers observed what was true: the crowds in the yards at East Syracuse had been composed exclusively of striking railroadmen.[26]

Conclusion

Railroad workers were a minority in many if not most crowds. In Buffalo, Albany, and Syracuse, the limited evidence indicates that a variety of people joined crowds. As evidenced in newspaper accounts (Buffalo, Albany, and Syracuse) and information taken from city directories on those arrested and killed or wounded in clashes with the police and militia (Buffalo), crowds contained: "non-railroad citizens," "men out of employment," "a good many women and children," "boys," and "other citizens," in short, many people who were "not railroad men nor strikers of any kind." To be sure, crowds did contain "strikers"—workers on strike from the railroad and other economic sectors. The roving crowds in Buffalo that moved from work place to work place attempting to shut down businesses were clearly taking part in a working-class event stemming from grievances generated at the point of production. It is this current of the Strike that clearly fits the widely accepted view of the Strike as a "rebellion of labor." Another kind of crowd, however, manifested itself: the crowd that gathered on city streets at grade level railroad crossings in the hope of stopping or at least hindering the movement of trains. Some of these crowds contained railroad workers, and at times railroadmen controlled these gatherings. At other times, however, the behavior of these crowds was at odds with the wishes of striking railwaymen. Some of these crowds were composed primarily of people who were not strikers of any kind. In the city, and as a result of particular features of the city, a wide range of reasons moved a variety of working-class people, and a small minority of middle-class people, to strike a blow against the interests of the railroads.

5 The Aftermath

After the Great Strike of 1877, residents continued to struggle against the encroachments of the railroads on their streets and neighborhoods. In Albany, Steamboat Square continued to be a source of conflict. In March of 1878, the New Jersey Steamboat Company asked the common council for permission "to lay a switch track on the Steamboat Square." The company apparently did not see fit to wait for the approval of the city, for in May, the aldermen created a special committee "to inquire by what authority the switch tracks were laid upon" the square.[1] The infamous railroad crossing on Broadway continued to plague area residents and users of that major thoroughfare. The city continued to fight to force the New York Central to remove the tracks from the street by way of a viaduct. But the aldermen apparently realized the futility of passing resolutions "directing" the railroad corporation to build the viaduct. And earlier commitments from the Central to build a bridge over Broadway had resulted in no action on the part of the railroad. So aldermen turned to the state legislature. By March 1879, an assemblyman had introduced legislation to prohibit "the New York Central and Hudson River Railroad Company from maintaining its track across Broadway," and the council was exerting whatever influence it had to secure passage of that bill.[2] If the Central's actions are any indication, it did not seem to be concerned with its public image in the state's capital city. In May, the Central saw fit to summarily close a street in Albany, prompting the common council to protest, "[B]y what authority [has] the New York Central Railroad Company . . . closed Quackenbush street east of Montgomery street?"[3]

In November 1879, unidentified property owners protested in a petition to the council "against the blockading of Church Street . . . by the railroad cars." A week after the petition was presented to the council, one aldermen who supported the petition offered a resolution threatening to rescind the grant to the Albany and Susquehanna Railroad Company to run trains in certain streets, specifically, Church, Madison, and Broadway Streets, because the tracks and trains presented a "danger to life and the use of the streets and sidewalks." In addition, they prevented the "owners of property in said neighborhood from the enjoyment of their property."[4]

The Broadway crossing was finally bridged in the early 1880s, eliminating the worst railroad menace in the city. In the mayor's annual message to the common council in May 1882, it was noted that the Central had finally begun constructing a bridge over Broadway (at the same time, the grade of Broadway at the site of the bridge was being lowered). Indeed, construction would be complete within a few months. The crossing had been, as the mayor noted, and as residents and users of that major avenue knew from personal experience over the years, "a source of danger." Indeed, the crossing of late had become "almost insufferable." The completion of the crossing, the mayor observed, "will be of great advantage to the northern section of Albany and to adjacent farm lands, the owners of which have hither to been deprived of a safe and available means of entry into the city."[5] The elimination of the Broadway crossing did not remove the encroachments of the railroads in other streets. Two months after the mayor's annual message, aldermen proposed a resolution threatening the New York Central with legal action if the corporation continued to blockade Water and Montgomery Streets with its cars and freight.[6]

In Syracuse, conflict continued to be focused on the railroad crossings on North Salina Street. In October 1877, S. D. Evans, the superintendent of the horse-powered Central City Railway—"and others"—petitioned the common council asking the city to force the New York Central and other railroad corporations "to raise the roadway and approaches at the crossings on North Salina Street so that it may be passable for teams to and from the lake." Evans was probably not the only petitioner who lived on North Salina Street. Six weeks later, the aldermen approved Evans's petition. But at the same meeting, an alderman proposed a resolution that noted part of the problem with the railroads' use of Salina Street. The alderman's petition noted that Salina Street had been extended in 1871 to Onondaga Lake and that the street was "the only street running to the lake." Ice merchants in particular, with the support of "one hundred of our citizens, have petitioned this Council" to compel the railroads to improve the grade crossing "so that teams and vehicles may pass." The proposed resolution specifically asked that the mayor be directed to personally take up the matter with the railroads. The resolution, however, did not pass; rather, one passed noting the same problems but directing the street commissioner to approach the railroad corporations.[7] Resolutions continued to have little impact, however, for in early 1878, the common council unanimously adopted another resolution—it noted that the railroads had failed to rectify the problems with their crossings on Salina Street. The city attorney was ordered to sue the railroads for "obstructing the streets."[8]

The Jefferson Street railroad bridge conflict appeared to be settled, if not to the satisfaction of everyone. The city engineer devised a plan for constructing a combined road and railway bridge that would open up Jefferson Street, and presented it to the council in late September of 1877. Neither the railroad companies nor the residents in the area of the bridge complained about the plan. The new bridge would be constructed by the railroad according to the city's plan and under the supervision of the city engineer. The council unanimously adopted the plan and work commenced quickly.[9] The conflict over the obstructionist bridge on Jefferson Street was resolved, but conflicts developed in other streets as railroad expansion continued: in late 1878, a petition for permission to lay track through Scott and Lock Streets generated opposition. Adam Theobald, an upholsterer who lived on Lock Street, "and others," remonstrated against track laying on those streets by presenting a petition to the common council.[10] And so the struggle for city streets continued.

The battle against the railroads' injurious intersection with streets and neighborhoods was a losing one in Buffalo as the 1870s expired. The Crosstown railroad struggle disappeared from the pages of the *Proceedings of the Common Council* for three months after July 1877, although the issue did not disappear from the minds of property owners and other residents along the proposed route. Sometime during July or August, the council's committee on streets launched an investigation to determine the degree of support for the project among property owners on the streets through which the railroad was to run. In September, a majority of the committee on streets reported to the whole council "that the rights of citizens owning property" along the proposed route were "sufficiently guarded and protected." So were "the interests of the city at large." The committee's assertion that the proposed railroad would not infringe on the "rights" of property owners or the "interests" of others in the city was not fully shared by the committee's minority. The minority approved of the overall project, but sought to eliminate the railroad from some of the streets through which it was to be built. This minority of aldermen wanted to prevent tracks from being laid in Court and Fourth Streets and the

"Terrace." The two contending reports were tabled, to be taken up at a later meeting.[11]

In September, opposition to the Crosstown railroad venture intensified with the first formal remonstrance to the council. John Gorman—"and others"—protested against "the proposed route of the Buffalo City Railway."[12] Their protest resulted in the two conflicting reports of the committee on streets remaining tabled. On October 15 the council voted yet again to approve the Crosstown railroad project; it was not to be the last vote on the Crosstown. But the unanimity of July, something of a paradox given that the city was in the throes of the Great Strike, wilted into a 17–6 vote in favor of the original route.[13]

The conflict over the Crosstown railroad continued into 1878. In fact, the conflict intensified as opposition to having a major rail line run through the city, including streets west of Main Street, grew. In addition, the New York Central Railroad Company sought to take over the proposed route from the Buffalo City Railway. The Central's takeover attempt fueled the opposition of those who sought to keep railroads out of city streets. The New York Central's renewed entrance into the conflict occurred in April 1878. In April, the New York Central Railroad presented a petition to the council asking for permission to build and operate the same railroad route the Buffalo City Railway had undertaken. Indeed, the Central's application to the council was signed and supported by James D. Warren and J. N. Matthews, who until just recently had been the joint owners/editors of the traditional organ of Buffalo business, the *Commercial Advertiser*. The council immediately voted to give the Central the same grant it had given to the Buffalo City Railway Company. The vote, however, was 18–8 in favor. It had come after "bitter debate."[14]

As the *Express* observed, "[T]he interest felt by the public in the construction of the Cross-town Railway has, within a few days past, been greatly increased" by the council's grant to the New York Central "to connect its lines on the east and west sides by a direct route through the city."[15] Although the Buffalo City Railway Company had received a grant to do precisely that in June of 1877, the same grant to the Central seemed to magnify the issues surrounding the intracity route. The Crosstown railroad was now doubly ominous, for an ideological component had been added to what was essentially a material threat stemming from the development of capitalist industrialization. Lives and businesses were now at risk from the locomotives of a monopolistic corporation controlled by interests outside of the city and not accountable to its residents. On May 4 a letter to the editor was printed in the *Express*. Its anonymous writer decried that the council's grant to the Central would permit "that corporation to run its freight as well as passenger trains along the Terraces and across Main street." This "outrage" would result in the area being "gridironed with railway tracks and freight trains passing to an fro at all hours of the day and night."[16]

As the conflict escalated, the mayor of Buffalo, Solomon Scheu (Becker's successor), moved to try to mediate the dispute. He called for a meeting in his office "of all parties interested in the matter of the Crosstown Railroad." Many of Buffalo's most prominent citizens heeded the call. In addition, nonelite residents were at the meeting. Indeed, one anonymous "working-man" stated at the meeting that the Buffalo City Railway had obtained the consent signatures of many residents on Court Street by telling them that the proposed project would be "a grand central depot" constructed on the Terrace. However, Court Street residents "now knew" that no such depot was planned, and that it was a case of whether or not to have locomotives and trains running on their street. "All the people residing on Court street," the worker declared, "were now opposed to the road."[17]

Two major businesses also presented their grievances at the meeting. Pratt and Company's retail hardware business on the Terrace was adamantly opposed to the construction of any railroad that would run through the Terrace. Hoping to play on sentiment at least, the company argued that it was one of Buffalo's oldest firms, having been located on the park since 1838, and therefore "its history was coincident with that of the city." Pratt and Company argued that the railroad "would necessarily be a difficult road to cross" in the area of the Terrace. Pratt expressed the predicament faced over the years by grocers, saloon keepers, retailers, and many other small and medium-sized businesses; given the firm's physical location relative to the proposed tracks, and the routes most of the store's customers and suppliers took, the company "would be virtually cut off if the railway took the course laid out." The Citizen's Gas Company also opposed the route of the Crosstown railroad at the meeting in the mayor's office. The company was not in principle opposed to the building of an intracity connection, but it was "opposed to having the tracks laid in Court street." The company was the "largest property in the block on that part of the street through which the road was to be constructed, and paid most of the taxes." The tracks, if laid on Court Street, "would injure their property seriously." If they were laid, the company promised to pursue the matter in the courts.[18]

With construction underway on the Terrace and elsewhere, formal protests to the council peaked with the presentation of a lengthy petition objecting to the Crosstown railroad project. The petition, dated May 11 and presented to the aldermen two days later, had thirty-seven signatories. The petition outlined some of the reasons property owners in particular were opposed to the railroads' intersection with city streets. Their objections were some of the same objections made by property owners and others on streets in Albany and Syracuse in the 1870s. The petitioners identified themselves as "owners of land and buildings adjoining the Terrace and along the proposed routes" of the Buffalo City Railway and New York Central Railroad. The construction and operation of a crosstown railroad by "either of them," the petitioners pointedly declared, would "irremediably damage" and "depreciate" their "interests" and "property." Observing that the bulk of the freight transported by rail was presently carried around the city limits, the owners of land and property along the proposed intracity route decried the fact that if the railroad went through the result would be "the obstruction of the ordinary uses of these streets and of free passage across them." As to the issue of consent, the property owners asserted that a majority of those along the proposed route had not consented to the line being built. The alleged consents obtained by the Buffalo City Railway during the course of 1877 had been obtained through "false and fraudulent representations." The petitioners concluded with a plea to the aldermen to stop the "defacing [of] the Terrace" and rescind the grants to build a crosstown rail route. Only when the plans for a crosstown railroad were denied would these citizens be allowed "the full enjoyment of their property."[19]

Of the nineteen petitioners identified with respect to occupation, six were saloon proprietors, the single largest occupational group among those identified. One of the saloon keepers was also a retail grocer. In addition to area saloons that would have to face locomotives and trains running down the streets on which they were located, a variety of other businesses were found in opposition to the Crosstown railroad. W. Somerville & Sons were veterinary surgeons who owned and operated a large horse infirmary on the Terrace. George Dakin, proprietor of a coal yard, also opposed the proposed railroad, which would have created serious obstacles and dangers for the many wagon teams which transported coal into and out of his yard. Similarly, H. Brinkman of Brinkman & Joice opposed the Crosstown for the impact it would have on his teamster firm located on the Terrace. Edward Myers, also on the Terrace, was a contractor; his occupation also placed a high premium on relatively unobstructed streets for the movement of laborers and building materials. Yet the May 1878 petition against the Crosstown railroad project also included people who were not identified in the directories as property owners or business operators, but who are identifiable as users of the street—as pedestrians and drivers, for example—and who lived on or near streets to be used by the railroad and did not want the danger, noise, and pollution the tracks would bring. These individuals were a brakeman, two firemen, a blacksmith, a book printer, a teamster, a schoolteacher, a jobber, and a ship's captain. One-quarter of all the petitioners were women.[20] In terms of place of business and residence, eleven of the twenty-two petitioners identifiable with respect to address lived or worked on streets to be occupied by the Crosstown railroad; ten did not, but lived in the immediate vicinity of streets to be used by the railroad.[21]

Opposition to the intracity railroad continued in the weeks after the presentation of the May petition to the council. John Reynolds "and others" remonstrated "against laying of railroad track along the Terrace." J. B. Roffo, an Erie Street saloonkeeper, "and others," protested again "against laying railroad track on Erie street," another of the city streets to be used by the Crosstown railroad.[22] Opposition to the use of city streets by railroads also developed a different form after the May petition. A "public meeting" was called by those who had signed the May petition, to treat "matters pertaining to the Cross-town Railroad." John Pfeil, the ex-alderman who was the proprietor of a large grocery and bakery concern on Court Street, was elected chair of this meeting of "citizens." Pfeil announced that the meeting had been called "in opposition to the Crosstown Railway." Those who spoke at the meeting were largely unanimous in their opposition to the road. Indeed, when F. F. Fargo, an official of the Buffalo City Railway, spoke in favor of the railroad his company sought to construct, the meeting turned angry. After "some desultory discussion" and an anonymous cry from someone at the meeting that "if they build the road we'll throw it in the canal over night," the meeting disintegrated.[23] Such threats were in the spirit of the Great Strike.

In June, another petition against the Crosstown was presented to the council by the "residents and property holders upon Erie street," some of whom had signed the May petition. The petitioners stated that the Buffalo City Railway's ongoing construction of the Crosstown railroad had caused the street "to be torn up and placed in an almost impassable condition." Noting that "in places the pavement is torn up and is in piles in the street," the signers requested that the council "compel" the railroad to put Erie Street "in a passable condition." Of the seven signers, six could be identified: an attorney whose office was located on a street near Erie Street—one that was to be used by the Crosstown; James Jameson & Co., a retail provisions' store and stable located on Erie Street; Delahunt & Marion, another retail grocer located on Erie; J. B. Roffo's saloon on Erie; the proprietors of the St. James Hotel, located on the corner of Erie and Seneca Streets; and Wm. Somerville & Sons, the veterinary surgeons from the Terrace, who also operated thirty horse stalls at a location on Erie Street.[24] The council granted their petition, but only as a preliminary to revoking the Buffalo City Railway's grant to build the Crosstown railroad. On June 24, the council revoked the railway's grant, but the Crosstown railroad project remained; it was now the exclusive venture of the New York Central Railroad.[25]

The Crosstown railroad was built, notwithstanding continued opposition from property owners and residents. Litigation by Pratt and Co., among other property owners on the streets to be used by the road, continued remonstrances to the common council, litigation by the ousted Buffalo City Railway Company which sought to regain the intracity route from the New York Central, and the efforts of individual aldermen to change the route delayed the project for years, but failed to prevent the eventual construction of the route in central Buffalo. In 1882, the Crosstown was completed; the "hated railroad tracks" crossed the Terrace and other streets where residents and property owners had fought to keep them out.[26] The failed opposition to the Crosstown railroad in central Buffalo was generally the story of opposition to the railroads' injurious intersection with streets and neighborhoods in Albany and Syracuse in the immediate aftermath of the Great Strike as well. After 1877 property owners and residents in all three cities continued to petition common councils for various types of relief from the railroads' frequently deadly and injurious intersection with streets, but successes were rare and sometimes temporary. Yet, there would never again be a "Great Strike" against the railroads.

In the late nineteenth century and early twentieth century, opposition to the railroad's injurious intersection with streets and neighborhoods grew more organized. Progressive elites spearheaded this opposition, which took the form of a peaceful but determined campaign to eliminate dangerous grade crossings. Even so, the elimination of dangerous grade crossings in urban areas took decades to achieve. Before the grade crossing itself came under attack, continued efforts were made to accommodate grade crossings by posting flagmen to warn pedestrians and vehicles of oncoming trains. And the use of movable gates on each side of crossings was an idea that took some time to develop. Once developed, of course, railroad corporations had to be persuaded or compelled, if possible, to install them. It was not until 1883, for example, that an Albany alderman proposed to the common council that the city require the New York Central to "place lift gates on either side" of a dangerous crossing in the city, and his resolution apparently died in committee.[27] When the railroad's centrality to the dynamics of capitalist industrialization was superseded, when grade crossings were represented and viewed by elites (including, perhaps, railroad owners and managers) as an impediment to progress, efficiency, and the aesthetic improvement of cities, and when the railroads collided with another more popular form of transportation—the automobile, most intracity grade crossings and grade level use of the streets were abolished. With their abolition, the worst consequences of the railroads' intersection with streets and neighborhoods disappeared.[28] The elimination of grade crossings was a cause for celebration; the successful grade crossing elimination campaign in Syracuse was commemorated with a bronze plaque that remains embedded in the sidewalk in front of City Hall. While the plaque notes the year tracks were first laid in Washington Street, it notes the year, month, and day they were finally removed—April 21, 1937.

Conclusion:
The Great Strike
as Urban History

In the years preceding the Great Strike of 1877, urban residents fought against railroad "encroachment" on their streets. They had a variety of compelling reasons. Streets were intrinsically linked to the households and neighborhoods surrounding them. As Perry Duis, Clay McShane, Christine Stansell, and others have detailed, streets served a variety of family, social, and recreational uses for most urban Americans, and these traditional uses of the street persisted for decades after the Civil War.[1] The city street also served a variety of economic functions. For some working people, the street was a place where they earned their living. Truckmen, draymen, teamsters, and hackmen, for example, carried out a large portion of their daily labors in streets. Many property owners, particularly nonindustrial businesses, were dependent on the relatively unobstructed flow of people and goods through the streets adjacent to their enterprises. Given the importance of the street in many facets of urban life, railroad use of the streets necessarily brought an array of urban residents face-to-face with the Iron Horse and its accompanying disorder, disruption, noise, and hazards to life. Railroads running through crowded streets killed and injured scores of people with horrible regularity. Commerce and travel were routinely obstructed, delayed, and disrupted. Retail stores, saloons, small manufactories, and others could see their business patrons and suppliers literally cut off with the advent of a railroad in or near the street on which they were located. Many parts of urban life connected to streets were at risk from the railroads.

Formal opposition to the expanding and intensifying use of city streets by railroads in post–Civil War Buffalo was located firmly among nonindustrial property owners, particularly retail store owners, grocers, and saloon keepers. The opposition was quite diverse, however, and included the owners of small manufactories, lumber and coal yards, contracting and teamster firms, as well as the forever anonymous *others* referred to in common council records. Indeed, there was opposition to the railroad's disruptive and destructive impact on the city among people who may not have been property or business owners, but were residents of a street or a neighborhood through which a railroad was to run or already ran. The latter are most likely the "others" noted in municipal government records. Nonindustrial business and property owners, and the blacksmith, teamster, school teacher, ship's captain, and firemen, for example, who signed the May 1878 petition against the Crosstown railroad in Buffalo, shared one important characteristic: they were all residents of an area that would be adversely impacted by the railroad. Regardless of their class differences, as residents they were troubled and affected by the noise, disorder, economic disruption, and death/injury the railroads dealt out in the streets. There was also a social and political connection between residents and small businesses. Many local retail shops, from grocery stores to saloons, functioned as community centers. Local business people were frequently neighborhood leaders or spokesmen who "articulated and championed the interests of the neighborhood." As Alexander Von Hoffman argues, local stores did far more than just sell goods— "[T]hey linked customers to the urban place in which they lived."[2] These social and physical ties to place were operative when local business people and an array of neighborhood residents opposed the injurious consequences of the railroads' intersection with streets.

In Albany, the absence of the names of those who opposed the railroad does not allow for as specific an identification of their social status. But the *Proceedings* and the newspapers make it clear that "merchants, property owners, boatmen, truckmen and cartmen," in addition to the even more widely shared status of "citizens" and "persons residing in the vicinity" of streets used by railroads, worked to stop or limit railroad encroachment and its consequences. In Quay Street, merchants and property owners joined with the street-based occupations, such as cartmen and truckmen, to fight against the railroad's disruptive and injurious use of that street. In other areas of the city, such as the area around the infamous Broadway crossing, it was simply the people residing in the vicinity of the crossing, and those who had to pass over the crossing during the course of the day, who worked to eliminate the "terror." In Syracuse, the smallest city of the three, and the city with the lowest level of industrial development, a number of the "wealthy firms" among the city's manufacturing elite took the lead in seeking the removal of the railroad from Jefferson Street. They were joined by some nonindustrial business concerns, such as a hardware store and a hotel and meat market. In another part of the city, nonindustrial property owners—a lumber dealer, grocer, and ice dealer, among "other property owners"—petitioned the common council to address the disruptive and harmful impact of the railroad's intersection with the streets surrounding their businesses.

Through petitions and litigation, a variety of urban residents worked during the years preceding the Strike to eliminate or mitigate the devastating presence of the railroad in urban space. Their efforts, while sometimes successful in individual cases, could hardly have been expected to stem or roll back the most powerful sector of industrial capitalism in the 1870s. The mid-to-late nineteenth century was the period of the railroad industry's most spectacular growth in terms of track laying, and the railroad's growth and development was the lathe on which much of the economy turned. Population growth and the increasing density of urban life made the space of the street even scarcer. Consequently, the impact of the railroad's intersection with that space was sharply aggravated. However manifested, widespread opposition to the railroad's use of crowded urban space failed to stop the devastating encroachment of the railroad and the increasing volume of traffic the rails were carrying. The high human toll exacted by railroad use of the streets, and the obstruction, disruption, and injury to commerce and travel, gave a multiplicity of residents good reasons to hate and fear the railroads. Nor can it be forgotten that the presence of the railroads in urban areas was a fact that occurred for many Americans in the course of their lifetime. Many Americans could remember a time when the railroad had been absent from urban life, or when the level of encroachment had been much less than what was experienced after the Civil War. As Robert Bruce pointed out in his study of the Great Strike, the "railroads drew the map of the new urban age"—and they did so "within the memory of living men" and women.[3]

In July 1877, a strike of portions of the railroad work force over wages and the right to bargain collectively triggered the "Great Strike." The frequently injurious impact of the railroad on facets of urban life and the consequent conflicts between railroads and city residents provided "the charge" for the resulting explosions which shook America as never before.[4] In Buffalo and Albany, and in other cities and towns across the country, crowds of varying composition confronted the railroad in railroad yards and neighborhood streets. In Buffalo, much crowd activity revolved around groups of striking workers, both from the railroad and from other economic sectors. These workers confronted their employers—railroad corporations and other companies. Such crowds attempted to close down businesses and employers throughout their cities. At the same time, crowd activity developed in Buffalo and Albany focused exclusively on the streets, particularly the point at which the railroad crossed or entered streets. Many of these crowds confronted the railroad primarily as a deadly intruder in the urban community—not as an employer nor as a "symbol" of the emerging industrial order. Many crowds were composed overwhelmingly of people unconnected to the railroad, including a significant number of people not of the industrial working classes. Their goal, judging by their behavior, was not the closing of a manufactory but the closing of streets to railroads and the destruction of railroad property. There was more than one occasion when striking railroad workers labored strenuously to prevent the destruction of railroad property or allow the passage of selected trains through the streets.

The Great Strike consisted of two powerful *currents:* a variety of people assaulting the railroads as a dangerous intruder in their streets and neighborhoods, and workers striking over grievances generated at their work places. These two currents took the form of separate crowds. They also flowed together in individual crowds. In fact, the two currents could be found in the actions of a single person, for it is easy to conceive of a striking worker who was part of a crowd moving from work place to work place trying to foment a general strike, and also part of a crowd attacking the railroad as an unwanted intruder in crowded urban space— stoning a passing train, for example, or setting fire to railroad cars.

For various reasons, the Strike was more intense in Buffalo than in Albany and Syracuse. In fact, the Strike barely touched Syracuse and was almost entirely an affair of railroad workers who worked in East Syracuse. The current of the Strike which stemmed from grievances against the railroad and other economic enterprises as employers, consequent upon capitalist industrialization, was more pronounced in Buffalo given that city's significantly higher level of industrialization at the time of the Strike. Albany and Syracuse were significantly less industrialized, as measured by the levels of capitalization and the average number of workers employed in the most highly capitalized businesses. The precipitant for the Strike, in all of its forms or currents, was the strike of railroad workers. In Buffalo, the railroad workers who went out on strike seemed to have been relatively unified in their decision to do so. This relative unity of action also helps to account for the more pronounced course of the Strike in the city. Swift and fairly decisive action by the striking railroad workers quickly led to the spontaneous unleashing of grievances against the railroad among a wide array of urban residents. By contrast, Albany's railroad workers were less sure of themselves. The strike was not as widely an agreed-upon course of action among Albany's railroad workers. Their uncertainty was partially reflected in lower levels of crowd behavior stemming from earlier and ongoing conflicts over railroad use of urban space. Albany's railroad workers also made more strenuous and repeated efforts to distance themselves from residents of the city who were not railroad workers. These efforts served to dampen crowd activity. Unlike Albany's railroad workers, many railroad workers in Buffalo did not seem to view the strike as being strictly an issue between the railroad and its employees. Buffalo's railroad workers were clearly dismayed, though, by the violent behavior their strike activities evoked from the general urban population.

The timing and extent of the force applied by local, state, and federal authorities constrained the scope and intensity of crowd behavior. Serious crowd disturbances occurred in Buffalo before armed force was effectively mobilized, stationed within the city, and used against crowds. The Strike, in terms of crowd activity, developed momentum in Buffalo before armed force was effectively applied against such behavior. Chronology in another sense affected the differing intensity of the Strike in the three cities. The Strike started at different times in the three cities, and the differential timing was important. Albany, the capitol of the state of New York and the home of the governor, had knowledge about the Strike in other cities, especially Buffalo, before its railroad workers went out on strike. This knowledge led to armed force being more fully and effectively in place prior to serious and sustained outbreaks of crowd violence.

Different urban environments shaped the nature and course of the Strike. Relative to Albany and Syracuse, the sum of Buffalo's railroad yards and depots—and the many tracks that laced the surrounding streets and neighborhoods—were closer to and more a part of the city's hub in a geographical sense. The very fact that the complement of the city's railroad facilities was within the parameters of the heart of the city meant that any conflict originating with the railroads would almost by definition involve the thousands of people who lived and worked in the immediate vicinity of those facilities. The activities of the city's striking railroad workers were carried out quite literally in the view of thousands of nonrailroad residents. In Albany, the socioeconomic geography of relevance to the Strike was fractured in two ways. First, the Albany Strike suggested that, in important respects, Albany and East Albany constituted one community or at least a single urban area. Yet, the urban locale

was physically divided by the Hudson River, a division only partially mitigated by two bridges. Although their efforts were not totally effective, for
the biggest crowd event of the Strike stemmed from the two areas linking
together, city and state authorities realized the importance of controlling
the bridges and thereby erecting a barrier. Significant numbers of railroad
workers lived in East Albany, and they were from the start separated from
their cohorts in West Albany. Second, the New York Central's major rail
yard on the western edge of Albany was the focal point of the strike of
railroad workers. Relative to Buffalo, these facilities were not as spatially
integrated within the hub of the city of Albany. Indeed, they were on the
periphery. Efforts to stop trains in West Albany were not an activity witnessed by the residents of the central city. Hence, the probability that
residents would spontaneously pour into the streets to stop trains and
attack railroads was significantly lowered. The urban environment was an
important factor constraining or facilitating the formation and movement
of crowds during the Strike. Indeed, spatial arrangements and relationships were crucial.

Syracuse was unique with respect to Buffalo and Albany on a number
of levels related to the Strike. The city had a much lower level of industrialization relative to Buffalo and even to Albany, and it was by far the smallest in terms of population. The strike among railroad workers developed
at about the same time as the strike commenced in Albany. But the railroad workers who went out on strike worked in East Syracuse—some
five miles from the city of Syracuse. And like most of their counterparts
in Albany, the striking railroad workers of East Syracuse defined their
struggle as a contest between the railroad and its employees. People who
were not railroad workers were unwelcome intruders into the conflict.
Syracuse's railroad shop workers in the Fifth Ward never went out on
strike. Hence, the residents of Syracuse lacked what both the people of
Buffalo and Albany had—the precipitant of a railroad workers' strike *and*
the sight of strikers stopping trains. Equally significant was the fact that
the residents of Syracuse had few trains passing through their city during the formative period of the Strike. Stopping trains in Buffalo and Albany when the Strike started meant that few trains would be approaching
Syracuse from either the west or the east. Those that did could be routed
around the city rather than through it. The bypass—a two-track freight
line built in 1874 by the Central—meant the city in general had not experienced the intensifying levels of train traffic—and the consequent noise,
disorder, and hazards to life and commerce—that characterized Buffalo
and Albany in the years preceding the Strike. Syracuse had not been free

of railroad encroachment. Indeed, its main avenue was occupied by railroad tracks, and other areas of the city had witnessed conflict over railroad use of the streets. But the level of encroachment was lower, and the necessary precipitants for a Strike in the city were lacking in July 1877.

A powerful current of the Great Strike consisted of a rebellion of urban residents, mostly working class, against the injurious impact of the railroad on facets of urban life. This view of the Great Strike of 1877 is not incompatible with the traditional labor interpretation of the uprisings as a "labor rebellion," that is, a conflict between employers and employees. Much of the uprising was a labor rebellion and a harbinger of the great struggles between labor and capital which marked the subsequent years of the Industrial Revolution in the United States. Concomitantly, however, a powerful current of the Great Strike of 1877 in Buffalo and Albany consisted of a spontaneous rebellion against the railroad's injurious intersection with streets and neighborhoods. This current in the Great Strike consisted, then, of an uprising against one of the most direct and damaging ways in which urban residents experienced capitalist industrialization *outside* of the work place.

Defenders of the traditional labor interpretation of 1877 will be quick to point out that the evidence presented here is far from conclusive: that there is no evidence per se that people joined in crowd attacks against railroads because of the railroads' injurious impact upon the life of the streets. In fact, there is no direct evidence documenting why people joined in assaults against railroads—either in this work or in any other work on the Great Strike. It bears repeating that the overwhelming majority of the participants in the crowds of 1877 remain unknown, not just in Buffalo and Albany but in every city where the Strike occurred. We have neither the names of the vast majority of crowd participants nor direct evidence concerning their intentions and motivations. All interpretations of the Great Strike of 1877 rest heavily on inference; setting and context therefore are crucial. However, the null hypothesis, if you will, that there is no causal relationship between the Great Strike of 1877, and the urban environment within which the Strike occurred, is not plausible. An interpretive "scaffolding"[5] for the Great Strike of 1877 must contain urban braces and supports if it is to stand. The urban environments of the Great Strike are critically important independent variables.

Perhaps the best way to fully comprehend the Strike—and to synthesize the "Great Strike" in terms of both labor and urban history—is to return to the level of the streets and their crowds. In Buffalo and Albany, there were different crowds, both in terms of composition and behavior.

There were also different agendas within crowds. The traditional labor interpretation of 1877 and the interpretation offered in this study are not antagonistic on this most elemental level. Although petitions to common councils sometimes employed the term "encroachment," the word does not adequately convey what was at stake in the struggle for city streets. A person who was not a railroad striker might have participated in crowd attacks against railroads for any number of mutually reinforcing reasons: anger over the railroad's killing or maiming of a friend, neighbor, or family member; smoldering opposition to the railroad's disruption of the social and economic fabric of streets and neighborhoods; support for a striking railroad worker; fear of the concentrated economic and political power of the railroads; animosity over a house set on fire from a passing locomotive. All of these motivating factors, and others, such as hostility toward the railroad's cutting of wages in the midst of a depression and the railroad's unrivaled status as the symbol of the harsh terms of capitalist industrialization, dovetailed in the 1877 crowds. In the process, a multitude of people entered the streets to confront the railroads in July of 1877, and the Great Strike became as much an urban phenomenon as a labor phenomenon.

Railroads encroached on urban space prior to the Great Strike, of course, dating from their entrance into American cities in the 1830s and 1840s. From the start, their use of a vital urban space fulfilling a number of social and economic functions sparked resistance and resulted at times in "riots."[6] The conflicts which ensued as a result of the introduction of the railroad into urban areas did not disappear after the Civil War. Indeed, the period after the war witnessed a dramatic acceleration in the growth of railroads, as visibly manifested by the laying of new tracks and more and more trains traveling over those tracks. The additional tracks and trains were part of the larger process of capitalist industrialization and urbanization occurring in cities throughout the nation. The intensification of industrialization and the growing density of urban life increased the rate and intensity at which the railroad disrupted and even destroyed life. The wholesale killing and maiming of hundreds of people each year, the disruption and obstruction of travel, the hazards to many local businesses, and the general disorder the railroad sowed in the streets generated opposition within multiple levels of the social structure. The strike of railroad workers in July 1877 provided many urban residents with a brief opportunity to lash out against the railroads.

The powerful currents of resistance to and anger at railroad encroachment on urban space present in the 1877 crowds argue for a view of the

Strike which recognizes and acknowledges its similarity with earlier episodes of popular opposition to the railroads. In this sense, the Strike does
not represent as sharp a break with the past as historians assert. While
the Strike was undoubtedly the "clarion call" of the industrial and urban
working class for many participants and observers,[7] it was also a vehicle
for the direct and physical opposition of workers and nonworkers to the
railroad's use of a critical urban space. The Strike contained strong elements of continuity with the past, as some contemporary framing of the
event suggests.[8] The explosive power of the Great Strike flowed from the
hostility and resistance the railroads created in urban areas via their use
of the streets *and* the grievances they generated and symbolized as employers of an increasingly hard-pressed proletariat. Paradoxically, the
very strength of the Great Strike obscured an underlying characteristic
of urban, working-class life in late nineteenth-century America. The
might of the Great Strike was due to the coursing together of two basic
currents: workers striking over grievances generated at work places, and
urban residents, mostly working class, "striking" against railroads as a
result of the death and disorder railroads sowed in streets and neighborhoods. However, the Strike's bridging of the divide between grievances
generated at the point of production and conflicts rooted in the communities of industrializing America was brief and fleeting.[9]

Notes

Introduction

1. Eric Foner, *Reconstruction: America's Unfinished Revolution, 1863–1877* (New York, 1988), 583; C. Vann Woodward, *Reunion and Reaction: The Compromise of 1877 and the End of Reconstruction* (Boston, 1951); Robert V. Bruce, *1877: Year of Violence* (Chicago, 1989 [1959]); Lawrence Goodwyn, *The Populist Moment: A Short History of the Agrarian Revolt in America* (New York, 1978); Nell Irvin Painter, *Standing at Armageddon: The United States, 1877–1919* (New York, 1987).

2. Foner, *Reconstruction: America's Unfinished Revolution,* 583–86.

3. I use "strike" to refer to the railroad workers' strike or other individual strikes of workers, and I use "Strike" to denote the Great Strike as a whole.

On the Great Strike of 1877, see Philip A. Slaner, "The Railroad Strikes of 1877," *Marxist Quarterly* 1, no. 2 (April–June, 1937): 214–36; Clifton K. Yearley, Jr., "The Baltimore and Ohio Railroad Strike of 1877," *Maryland Historical Magazine* 51, no. 3 (September 1956): 188–211; Bruce, *1877: Year of Violence;* David T. Burbank, *Reign of the Rabble: The St. Louis General Strike of 1877* (New York, 1966); Philip English Mackey, "Law and Order, 1877: Philadelphia's Response to the Railroad Riots," *Pennsylvania Magazine of History and Biography* 96, no. 2 (April 1972): 183–202; Bill L. Weaver, "Louisville's Labor Disturbance, July, 1877," *Filson Club Historical Quarterly* 48, no. 2 (April 1974): 177–86; Philip S. Foner, *The Great Labor Uprising of 1877* (New York, 1977); Nick Salvatore, "Railroad Workers and the Great Strike of 1877: The View from a Small Midwest City," *Labor History* 21, no. 4 (Fall 1980): 522–45; Richard Schneirov, "Chicago's Great Upheaval of 1877," *Chicago History* (1980), 3–17; Marianne Debouzy, "Workers' Self-Organization and Resistance in the 1877 Strikes," in Dirk Hoerder, ed. *American Labor and Immigration History, 1877–1920s: Recent European Research* (Chicago, 1983), 61–77; the film, "1877: The Grand Army of Starvation" (New York: American Social History Project, 1985); David R. Roediger, "'Not Only the Ruling Classes to Overcome, But Also the So-Called Mob'; Class, Skill and Community in the St. Louis General Strike of 1877," *Journal of Social History* (Winter 1985): 213–39; David O. Stowell, "Albany's Great Strike of 1877," *New York History* 76, no. 1 (January 1995): 31–55; and Stowell, "'Small Property Holders' and the Great Strike of 1877: Railroads, City Streets, and the Middle Classes," *Journal of Urban History* 21, no. 6 (September 1995): 741–63. See also: Jeremy Brecher, *Strike* (San Francisco, 1972); Herbert G. Gutman, "Trouble on the Railroads in 1873–1874: Prelude to the 1877 Crisis?" in Gutman, *Work, Culture and Society in Industrializing America: Essays in American Working-Class and Social History* (New York, 1976), 295–320; James Francis Caye, Jr., "Crime and Violence in the Heterogeneous Urban Community: Pittsburgh, 1870–1889," Ph.D. dissertation, University of Pittsburgh, 1977; David Montgomery, "Strikes in Nineteenth-Century America," *Social Science History* 4, no. 1 (February 1980): 81–103; Alan Trachtenberg, *The*

Incorporation of America: Culture and Society in the Gilded Age (New York, 1982); Walter Licht, *Working for the Railroad: The Organization of Work in the Nineteenth Century* (Princeton, 1983); Richard Slotkin, *The Fatal Environment: The Myth of the Frontier in the Age of Industrialization, 1800–1890* (New York, 1985), 477–98; Martin Shefter, "Trade Unions and Political Machines: The Organization and Disorganization of the American Working Class in the Late Nineteenth Century," in Ira Katznelson and Aristide R. Zolberg, eds., *Working Class Formation: Nineteenth-Century Patterns in Western Europe and the United States* (Princeton, 1986); Shelton Stromquist, *A Generation of Boomers: The Pattern of Railroad Labor Conflict in Nineteenth-Century America* (Chicago, 1987); and Foner, *Reconstruction: America's Unfinished Revolution, 1863–1877* (New York, 1988); Bruce Laurie, *Artisans into Workers: Labor in Nineteenth-Century America* (Chicago, 1997).

4. "From letter to Frederick Engels (in Ramsgate), London, July 25, 1877," in Saul K. Padover, editor and translator, *The Letters of Karl Marx* (Englewood Cliffs, 1979), 317.

5. Trachtenberg, *The Incorporation of America,* 39; Stromquist, *A Generation of Boomers,* 24; Bruce, *1877: Year of Violence,* 27. The Great Strike is dismissed by some historians. For Robert Wiebe, the Strike is little more than "the first national holiday of the slums"; see Wiebe's *The Search for Order, 1877–1920* (New York, 1967), 10.

6. "Crowd" is a term that obscures more than it illuminates, yet it is employed throughout this work as a linguistic convenience and because the term itself was used in contemporary accounts of the Strike. There is, of course, a rich historiographical tradition relating to the role of crowds in history. The seminal account, published in 1964, remains George Rude's *The Crowd in History: A Study of Popular Disturbances in France and England, 1730–1848* (London, 1981). Studies of crowds in nineteenth- century America include Theodore Hammet, "Two Mobs of Jacksonian Boston: Ideology and Interest," *Journal of American History* 62 (March 1976): 845–68; David Grimstead, "Rioting in Its Jacksonian Setting," *American Historical Review* 77 (April 1972): 361–97; Michael Feldberg, "The Crowd in Philadelphia History: A Comparative Perspective," *Labor History* 15, no. 3 (1974): 323–36; Leonard L. Richards, *Gentlemen of Property and Standing: Anti-Abolition Mobs in Jacksonian America* (New York, 1970); Iver Bernstein, *The New York City Draft Riots: Their Significance for American Society and Politics in the Age of the Civil War* (New York, 1990).

7. Salvatore, "Railroad Workers and the Great Strike of 1877"; Roediger, "Not Only the Ruling Classes to Overcome, But Also the So-Called Mob"; Schneirov, "Chicago's Great Upheaval of 1877."

8. Francis Couvares, *The Remaking of Pittsburgh: Class and Culture in an Industrializing City, 1877–1919* (Albany, 1984), 6; Debouzy, "Workers' Self-Organization and Resistance in the 1877 Strikes," 74.

9. Licht, *Working for the Railroad,* 253. This assertion is repeated in Licht's *Industrializing America: The Nineteenth Century* (Baltimore, 1995), 168.

10. Trachtenberg, *The Incorporation of America,* 39–40. Bruce Laurie's seminal study of labor in nineteenth-century America depicts the Great Strike as an expression of "antimonopoly outrage"; see *Artisans into Workers,* 145. Antimonopoly sentiments are also discussed in Couvares's *The Remaking of Pittsburgh;* and Gutman, "Trouble on the Railroads in 1873–1874."

11. William Deverell's excellent *Railroad Crossing: Californians and the Railroad, 1850–1910* (Berkeley, 1994) treats the multiplicity of reasons people had for disliking the railroads; see especially the introduction, "The Varieties of Railroad Antagonism."

12. Foner, *The Great Labor Uprising,* 9–11.

13. Bruce, *1877: Year of Violence;* David T. Burbank, *Reign of the Rabble: The St. Louis General Strike of 1877;* Philip English MacKey, "Law and Order, 1877: Philadelphia's Response to the Railroad Riots"; Bill L. Weaver, "Louisville's Labor Disturbance, July, 1877." This perspective is strongly and unequivocally voiced by Gabriel Kolko, who writes that

"anyone who examines this strike closely will immediately perceive it was unorganized and wholly a response to the frustrations and wage cuts that accompanied the first serious industrial depression of 1873–1878." See Kolko's *Main Currents in Modern American History* (New York, 1984), 174.

14. Salvatore, "Railroad Workers and the Great Strike of 1877," 523.

15. For antirailroad riots in Philadelphia in the 1840s, see Feldberg, "The Crowd in Philadelphia History," 326, 329–30; and Feldberg, *The Turbulent Era: Riot and Disorder in Jacksonian America* (New York, 1980), 64–72.

16. Alexander Saxton, *The Indispensable Enemy: Labor and the Anti-Chinese Movement in California* (Berkeley, 1971), 112.

17. Chapter 4 studies the crowd in depth. Bruce's 1959 study established that striking railroad workers were a minority in most crowds. Men, women, boys, and "citizens" were the central actors in most crowds that Bruce examined. More recent analyses have confirmed the same. James Francis Caye found a wide variety of occupations among the Roundhouse crowd in Pittsburgh: 9% were from professional and managerial occupations; 12% were skilled workers; 76% were semi or unskilled workers. Schneirov's analysis of the Chicago crowds documented the steadily declining role of railroad workers once the Strike began, and it illustrated the importance of women, outdoor laborers, teenagers and factory workers. Roediger's analysis of the St. Louis crowd found much the same: railroad workers were a minority in crowds that drew heavily from all sections of the working classes. In St. Louis, 6% of the rank and file crowd participants were not of the working classes. See Bruce, *1877: Year of Violence,* 77, 105–8, 119, 123, 186; James Francis Caye, Jr., "Crime and Violence in the Heterogenous Urban Community: Pittsburgh, 1870–1889," 39, 82–83, 86, 97, 99, 112; Schneirov, "Chicago's Great Upheaval of 1877," 4, 6, 10, 14–15; Roediger, "'Not Only the Ruling Classes to Overcome, But Also the So-Called Mob,'" 228–32.

18. Bruce, *1877: Year of Violence,* 15, 27, 29–31.

19. Sam Bass Warner, Jr., "If All the World Were Philadelphia: A Scaffolding for Urban History, 1774–1930," *American Historical Review* 74 (October 1968): 26–43. I am indebted to Theodore Hershberg's, "The New Urban History: Toward an Interdisciplinary History of the City," *Journal of Urban History* 5, no. 1 (November 1978): 3–40, for sharpening my conceptual understanding of the relationship between the Great Strike and cities, as well as defining the structure and content of something rightly called "urban" history.

20. See, for example, Amy Bridges, *A City in a Republic: Antebellum New York and the Origins of Machine Politics* (New York, 1984); Thomas Dublin, *Women at Work: The Transformation of Work and Community in Lowell, Massachusetts, 1826–1860* (New York, 1979); David A. Gerber, *The Making of an American Pluralism: Buffalo, New York, 1825–1860* (Chicago, 1989); Howard Rock, *Artisans of the New Republic: The Tradesmen of New York City in the Age of Jefferson* (New York, 1979); Roy Rosenzweig, *Eight Hours for What We Will: Workers and Leisure in an Industrial City, 1870–1920* (Cambridge, 1985); Ira Katznelson, *City Trenches: Urban Politics and the Patterning of Class in the United States* (New York, 1981).

21. John Kellett *The Impact of Railways on Victorian Cities* (London, 1969), 421; Licht, *Working for the Railroad;* Alfred D. Chandler, Jr., ed. *The Railroads: The Nation's First Big Business* (New York, 1965). Kellett's inquiry into the impact of railroads on nineteenth-century English cities has no counterpart in the literature on railroads and American cities.

22. Kolko, *Main Currents in Modern American History,* 11; Gerber, *The Making of an American Pluralism,* 46.

23. Katznelson, *City Trenches,* 66.

24. In a similar sense, Iver Bernstein has argued that the potency of the 1863 New York City draft riots stemmed from "a multiplicity of grievances" revolving around both the work place and the neighborhood; see Bernstein's *The New York City Draft Riots,* 5–6, 17. For

perceptive observations of the varied reasons why workers might garner "support" in an urban strike, see Sarah M. Henry's "The Strikers and Their Sympathizers: Brooklyn in the Trolley Strike of 1895," *Labor History* 32, no. 3 (Summer 1991): 329–53.

25. Montgomery, "Strikes in Nineteenth-Century America," 86–88, 95–96.

26. Montgomery's most recent work posits a causal link between the Great Strike and conflicts generated outside of work places; see Montgomery, *Citizen Worker: The Experience of Workers in the United States with Democracy and the Free Market during the Nineteenth Century* (Cambridge, 1993), 104–5.

27. Gutman, "Trouble on the Railroads in 1873–1874," 295–96.

28. *Buffalo Express,* July 24, 1877.

29. *Albany Express,* July 26, 1877; *Albany Argus,* July 26, 27, 1877; *Albany Evening Times,* July 26, 1877.

30. Licht, *Working for the Railroad,* 253.

Chapter One

1. Dickens's observation is contained in a March 6, 1842, letter he wrote to John Forster while visiting Philadelphia. See Dickens's *American Notes for General Circulation,* edited and with an introduction by John S. Whitley and Arnold Goldman (New York, 1985), 310.

2. The phrase is cited by Leo Marx, *The Machine in the Garden: Technology and the Pastoral Ideal in America* (New York, 1964), 191, and is attributed to J. H. Chapham's *An Economic History of Modern Britain* (Cambridge, 1926–38).

3. 4-4-0 refers to the placement of wheels on the locomotive.

4. John H. White, Jr., *American Locomotives: An Engineering History, 1830–1880* (Baltimore, 1968), 22, 46, 57, 72, 211; E. P. Alexander, *Iron Horses: American Locomotives, 1829–1900* (New York, 1941), 168–69. The use of the American type or 4-4-0 locomotive declined as the 1870s progressed and rapidly declined in the 1880s. Yet, as late as 1884, they accounted for 60% of new engine purchases.

5. *Statistics of the Population of the United States at the Tenth Census* (Washington, 1883), 453, 538; *Report of the Manufactures of the United States at the Tenth Census* (Washington, 1883), 381, 389, 439–40.

6. David M. Ellis, James A. Frost, Harold C. Syrett, and Harry J. Carman, *A History of New York State* (Ithaca, 1967), 250; James Sullivan, ed., *History of New York State, 1523–1927* (New York, 1927), 564; Franklin H. Chase, *Syracuse and Its Environs: A History* (New York, 1924), 117; Henry Wayland Hill, *Municipality of Buffalo, New York: A History* (New York, 1922), 481–83.

7. Ellis et al., *A History of New York State,* 251–53, 553.

8. Chase, *Syracuse and Its Environs,* 117.

9. Ellis et al., *A History of New York State,* 250; Hill, *Municipality of Buffalo, New York,* 481. On local support and competition for railroad lines, see also Carter Goodrich, *Government Promotion of American Canals and Railroads, 1800–1890* (New York, 1960); and Charles N. Glaab, *Kansas City and the Railroads: Community Policy in the Growth of a Regional Metropolis* (Madison, WI, 1962).

10. Ellis et al., *A History of New York State,* 553, 558. Ellis et al. are not clear in delineating the years during which this money was given to railroads, although they seem to indicate it was from 1865 to 1900; Goodrich more clearly writes that some $33 million was contributed by municipalities between 1861 and 1875. (Syracuse) *Common Council Proceedings,* 1875, 1–2; *Buffalo Express,* May 3, 6, 1876; the Common Council Proceedings reported that 75% of Syracuse's total municipal debt was accounted for by investments in railroads. See also Gabriel Kolko, *Railroads and Regulation, 1877–1916* (Princeton, 1965).

According to William Deverell's *Railroad Crossing: Californians and the Railroad,* the 1870s in California were also marked by intense popular dislike of railroad corporations.

11. Chase, *Syracuse and Its Environs,* 117, 120, 125, 128–29, 131, 179; W. W. Clayton,

History of Onondaga County, New York (Syracuse, 1878), 151; Dwight H. Bruce, ed., *Onondaga's Centennial: Gleanings of a Century* (Boston, 1896), 447–53. See Feldberg, *The Turbulent Era,* for an account of conflicts between neighborhoods and railroads over the use of the streets in Philadelphia in the 1840s.

12. John Ashworth, *Slavery, Capitalism, and Politics in the Antebellum Republic: Commerce and Compromise, 1820–1850* (Cambridge, 1995), 498. Such a characterization of the Civil War is not without controversy, of course. In addition to the recent work of John Ashworth, my interpretation of the Civil War is based primarily on what I have culled from Charles A. and Mary R. Beard, *The Rise of American Civilization* (New York, 1927); William W. Freehling, *Prelude to Civil War: The Nullification Controversy in South Carolina, 1816–1836* (Oxford, 1966); Eugene D. Genovese, *The Political Economy of Slavery: Studies in the Economy and Society of the Slave South* (New York, 1967); James M. McPherson, *Battle Cry of Freedom: The Civil War Era* (New York, 1988); and Bruce Levine, *Half Slave and Half Free: The Roots of the Civil War* (New York, 1992). William Freehling disagrees vigorously with characterizing the planter class as "precapitalist" or fundamentally at odds with the capitalist system; in *Prelude to Civil War,* Freehling writes that "a southern plantation was as much a capitalistic enterprise as a northern factory."

13. George Rogers Taylor and Irene D. Neu, *The American Railroad Network, 1861–1890* (Cambridge, MA, 1956), 28, 54.

14. Taylor and Neu, 30, 45–47, 53. Taylor and Neu apparently did not consider other reasons for this opposition.

15. The use of coal rather than wood as the fuel for steam locomotives produced a sooty and heavier smoke and by 1880 coal accounted for more than 90% of the fuel used by steam locomotives. Railroad managers were aware of the dirt and smoke "nuisance" for both passengers and people residing adjacent to tracks. In 1868, the Illinois Central Railroad, for example, posted instructions in the cabs of its passenger locomotives for various steps that would prevent the engine from "throwing out large quantities of smoke"; see White, Jr., *American Locomotives,* 89–90.

16. Christine Meisner Rosen, "Infrastructural Improvement in Nineteenth-Century Cities: A Conceptual Framework and Cases," *Journal of Urban History* 12, no. 3 (May 1986): 211–12; and Rosen, *The Limits of Power: Great Fires and the Process of City Growth in America* (New York, 1986), 135; Cronon, *Nature's Metropolis: Chicago and the Great West* (New York, 1991), 373.

17. Chandler, ed., *The Railroads;* Douglass C. North, *Growth and Welfare in the American Past: A New Economic History* (Englewood Cliffs, 1974), 117; Licht, *Working for the Railroad,* 3–4; Kolko, *Main Currents in Modern American History.*

18. Taylor and Neu, *The American Railroad Network,* 2, 82; John F. Stover, *American Railroads* (Chicago, 1961), 102, 144; Ellis et al., *A History of New York State,* 552–53.

19. Gerber, *The Making of an American Pluralism,* 46.

20. Katznelson, *City Trenches,* 66.

21. *Syracuse Daily Courier,* January 21, April 3, 1874; *Syracuse Daily Journal,* November 11, 16, 1874.

22. See chapter 2.

23. François Bedarida and Anthony Sutcliffe, "The Street in the Structure and Life of the City: Reflections on Nineteenth-Century London and Paris," *Journal of Urban History* 6, no. 4 (August 1980); Christine Stansell, *City of Women: Sex and Class in New York, 1789–1860* (Chicago, 1987); Perry R. Duis, *The Saloon: Public Drinking in Chicago and Boston, 1880–1920* (Chicago, 1983); Clay McShane, "Transforming the Use of Urban Space: A Look at the Revolution in Street Pavements, 1880–1924," *Journal of Urban History* 5, no. 3 (May 1979): 279–307; Stanford Anderson, ed., *On Streets* (Cambridge, MA: MIT Press, 1978); especially Anthony Vidler, "The Scenes of the Street: Transformations in Ideal and Reality, 1750–1871," 28–111; Susan G. Davis, *Parades and Power: Street Theater in*

Nineteenth-Century Philadelphia (Philadelphia, 1986); Daniel M. Bluestone, "'The Pushcart Evil': Peddlers, Merchants, and New York City's Streets, 1890–1940," *Journal of Urban History* 18, no. 1 (November 1991), 68–92; Stowell, "'Small Property Holders' and the Great Strike of 1877," 741–63.

24. McShane, "Transforming the Use of Urban Space," 283–84, 289–90.

25. *Every Saturday,* July 27, 1878; Joel A. Tarr and Josef W. Konritz, "Patterns in the Development of the Urban Infrastructure," in Howard Gillette, Jr., and Zane L. Miller, eds., *American Urbanism: A Historiographical Review* (New York, 1987), 197.

26. Stansell, "Women, Children and the Uses of the Streets," 310; and Stansell, *City of Women,* 203. Stansell's work treats the antebellum decades, of course, but as Clay McShane and others have pointed out, the traditional uses of the streets persisted for decades after the Civil War.

27. Stansell, *City of Women,* 49, 55–56.

28. Stansell, *City of Women,* 55–61; *Albany Express,* April 23, 1877. For a description of an assault on a temperance advocate which drew a large and supportive crowd as he was being beaten in the street, see *Albany Evening Times,* November 1, 1875.

29. *Buffalo Daily Courier,* August 24, 1877.

30. Stansell, *City of Women,* 49–52, 56; Duis, *The Saloon,* 94–110.

31. *Albany Express,* November 1, 1876; April 9, May 7, June 25, 1877. Mrs. Charles S. Hamlin, "Elk Street and Its Neighborhood," October 1926, manuscript in the Pruyn Library of the Albany Public Library; H. P. Phelps, ed. *The Albany Hand-Book for 1881* (Albany, 1880), 36; McShane, "Transforming the Use of Urban Space," 283; Rosenzweig, *Eight Hours For What We Will,* 131.

32. General S. V. Talcott, "Docks, Wharves, and Basin of Albany, with Many Historic Events and Reminiscences of Olden Times," in *Old Albany* 3 (n.d.): 70–76; *Albany Directory,* 1869, 1880; *Albany Evening Journal,* September 15, 16, 1874.

33. On the importance of streets and location for middle-class enterprises, see also Stowell, "'Small Property Holders' and the Great Strike of 1877"; and Melanie Archer, "Small Capitalism and Middle-Class Formation in Industrializing Detroit, 1880–1900," *Journal of Urban History* 21, no. 2 (January 1995): 247.

34. *Syracuse Daily Courier,* February 4, 1874.

35. Duis, *The Saloon,* 172–76, 202; *Albany Express,* April 30, 1877.

36. *Buffalo Daily Courier,* June 20, 1876.

37. See table 2 in McShane, "Transforming the Use of Urban Space," 292; *Albany Express,* September 17, 1874.

38. See the "Guide for Travelers" column in the *Albany Evening Times,* November 30, 1875.

39. Throughout the 1870s, it was the responsibility of the state engineer and surveyor to collect and organize statistics on railroad accidents. For the most part, this information was provided to the state by railroad corporations operating lines inside the State of New York and was organized into three groups: death and injuries to railroad employees, railroad passengers, and "others." For the purposes of trying to ascertain the level of carnage resulting from the railroads intersection with streets and neighborhoods, we are primarily interested in examining the number of deaths and injuries to "others"—people who were neither railroad employees nor passengers. The three tables covering the years 1870–79 are in the Annual Reports of the State Engineer and Surveyor on the Railroads, *Documents of the Assembly of the State of New York,* 1873, vol. 8, Document 160, 312–13; 1877, vol. 7, Document 69, 375–76; 1881, vol. 7, Document 92, 220–21. Data collected by the state engineers and surveyors included a significant, yet indeterminate, number of deaths and injuries that occurred outside the State of New York, largely Pennsylvania and New Jersey. For example, 22% of the deaths and injuries listed in the Erie Railroad's accident report submitted in 1877 occurred outside of the state.

The year 1868 was used as the starting point, as data for that year (and 1869) were included in the three data sets which together cover the decade of the Great Strike. Once I decided to use 1868 as the starting point, I wanted to examine data for an equal period of time after 1877. Hence, I sought to include data for nine years after the strike. Given the absence of data for three years—1881, 1882, and 1887—I included data for the years 1888 and 1889 in order to end up with figures for nine years following the Strike.

Data for the 1880s were collected and managed by the Board of Railroad Commissioners, created in 1882 by the New York State Legislature. The first annual report of the board is in *Documents of the Assembly,* 1884, vol. 3, Document 25. In the 1880s, the board counted only those victims of railroad accidents occurring within the state. Strictly speaking, then, the data for the 1870s and the data for the 1880s are two disparate data sets.

40. *Documents of the Assembly,* 1886, vol. 3, Document 26, xviii; 1887, vol. 2, Document 12, xi; 1890, vol. 5, Document 28, xiii.

41. *Documents of the Assembly,* 1877, vol. 7, Document 69, 580.

42. *Documents of the Assembly,* 1877, vol. 7, Document 69, 727.

43. *Documents of the Assembly,* 1886, vol. 3, Document 26, xix.

44. *Documents of the Assembly,* 1877, vol. 7, Document 69, 580–600. The year ending in September 1876 was randomly chosen from among the years 1870–79. I chose to look at either the figures for the Erie Railroad or the New York Central, given the fact that they were the two largest railroads in the state. The Erie also was chosen randomly. The standard deviation for the fifty cases is 19.9.

45. Licht, *Working for the Railroad,* 164.

46. The figures for 1877 are from *Documents of the Assembly,* 1881, vol. 7, Document 92, 220–21; the figures for 1889 are cited in Licht, *Working for the Railroad,* 190. Of course, the probability of being killed or injured by railroads was much greater for a railroad worker than an individual who was not an employee, notwithstanding the larger numbers of "others" killed or injured.

47. Georges J. Joyaux, "The New York Peregrination of Armand Parrot-La Riviere," *New York History* (January 1988): 85.

48. Georges J. Joyaux, "A Franc-Tireur in New York: The Observations of Auguste Foubert," *New York History* (October 1988): 466.

49. Max Berger, *The British Traveler in America, 1836–1860* (New York, 1943), 41.

50. *Syracuse Daily Courier,* March 12, 1873.

51. Cited in White, *American Locomotives,* 214.

52. *Albany Express,* September 17, 1874.

53. *Common Council Proceedings* (Syracuse), 1877, 208.

54. *The Buffalo Express,* March 30, April 18, 1877.

55. *Buffalo Express,* August 25, 1875; *Albany Express,* May 19, 1877.

56. *Syracuse Morning Standard,* December 25, 1876.

57. *The Buffalo Express,* October 9, 1876.

58. *Albany Express,* July 3, 1877; *Albany Argus,* July 3, 1877.

59. *The Buffalo Express,* October 9, 1876.

60. *Albany Express,* November 18, 22, 29, 1876; *Albany Argus,* November 18, 1876.

61. *Albany Evening Times,* November 6, 13, 1875.

62. Henry P. Phelps, ed., *The New Albany* 1, no. 1 (May 1891): 4; Cuyler Reynolds, *Albany Chronicles: A History of the City Arranged Chronologically* (Albany, 1906), 681.

63. Frank H. Severance, *Publications of the Buffalo Historical Society,* vol. 8 (Buffalo, 1905), xi.

64. *Albany Express,* June 4, 22, 1877.

65. *Syracuse Daily Courier,* September 27, 1875; *Syracuse Daily Journal,* January [?], 1877 (clipping in the file folder labeled "Tr. R.R.–New York Central 1877" at the Onondaga Historical Association); *Syracuse City Directory,* 1874–75.

66. *Syracuse Morning Standard,* July 9, 11, 1877.

67. Roger Lane, *Violent Death in the City: Suicide, Accident, and Murder in Nineteenth-Century Philadelphia* (Cambridge, MA, 1979), 39. Lane states there are only two periods for which there exist complete records of coroner's juries in Philadelphia—1854–57 and 1878–80. For the period 1878 to 1880, twenty-one out of twenty-seven censures were directed at railroad corporations.

68. *Common Council Proceedings* (Syracuse), 1876, 82.

69. *Syracuse Daily Courier,* August 14, 1873.

70. *Albany Express,* October 30, 1876.

71. *The Buffalo Express,* March 14, 16, 1877. The problem was an ongoing one—the *Express* captioned an account of a boy losing his leg with "Boy's, Keep Away from the Cars," *Buffalo Express,* September 1, 1875.

72. *Proceedings of the Common Council of the City of Albany,* 1874, 918–19.

73. *Buffalo Daily Courier,* July 30, 31, 1873.

74. *Buffalo Daily Courier,* August 1, 4, 13, 14, 1873. In December of 1875, a coroner's jury looking into the deaths of two railroad employees censured the railroad corporation for, among other things, "violating the city ordinance in running their cars faster than six miles an hour inside the city limits," *Buffalo Express,* December 15, 1875.

75. *Buffalo Daily Courier,* August 18–19, 1873; for a similar but less serious accident in Syracuse, see *Syracuse Daily Journal,* January 9, 1877.

Chapter Two

1. Alexander Von Hoffman, *Local Attachments: The Making of an American Urban Neighborhood, 1850–1920* (Baltimore, 1994), 91–92, 101–2.

2. Cited in Bruce, *1877: Year of Violence,* 49; Ellis et al., *A History of New York State,* 552.

3. *Proceedings of the Common Council,* 1875, 260; *Atlas of the City of Buffalo,* 1872; *Buffalo City Directory,* 1875, 1876; *Courier Company's Map of Buffalo,* June 1876, in the directory of the same year; *Buffalo Express,* May 13, 1875.

4. *Proceedings of the Common Council of Buffalo,* 1875, 260, 277; *Atlas of the City of Buffalo,* 1872.

5. *Proceedings of the Common Council,* 1875, 323.

6. *Proceedings of the Common Council,* 1875, 420; *Buffalo Express,* June 4, 1875.

7. *Proceedings of the Common Council,* 1875, 714, 716.

8. *Atlas of the City of Buffalo,* 1872.

9. *Atlas of the City of Buffalo,* 1872; *Proceedings of the Common Council,* 1875, 89, 187, 243.

10. *Proceedings of the Common Council,* 1875, 301, 305, 410. As was typically the case, no breakdown of the vote by alderman was given. In fact, the great majority of council decisions about railroad disputes did not give a numerical breakdown of the vote; the proceedings simply noted whether the resolution passed or failed. Elizabeth Bale remains anonymous: she was not listed in any of the city directories for the period 1870–81.

11. *Proceedings of the Common Council,* 1875, 547, 565, 607; *Courier Company's Map of Buffalo,* 1876.

12. *Proceedings of the Common Council,* 1875, 618, 634, 766, 837; *Buffalo City Directory,* 1876.

13. *Proceedings of the Common Council,* 1875, 725; *Buffalo City Directory,* 1876, 1877; *Courier Company Map of Buffalo,* 1876; Dentinger could not be identified.

14. *Proceedings of the Common Council,* 1875, 766, 770, 837.

15. *Proceedings of the Common Council,* 1875, 618, 629, 714; *Buffalo City Directory,* 1876, 1877; *Courier Company Map of Buffalo,* 1876.

16. *Proceedings of the Common Council,* 1876, 136, 145, 241, 297, 333.

17. *Proceedings of the Common Council,* 1876, 218; *Courier Company Map of Buffalo,* 1876; *Buffalo City Directory,* 1876. The specific crossing at issue was not identified.

18. *Proceedings of the Common Council,* 1876, 682, 904; *Buffalo City Directory,* 1876; *Courier Company Map of Buffalo,* 1876.

19. *Proceedings of the Common Council,* 1877, 572.

20. *Proceedings of the Common Council,* 1877, 50; Wilson could not be positively identified in the directories. There was, however, one James Wilson, a carpenter, who resided on Walden Avenue near the crossing; *Courier Company Map of Buffalo,* 1876.

21. *Proceedings of the Common Council,* 1877, 98, 255; Colligon could not be identified in the directories; *Atlas of the City of Buffalo,* 1872; *Buffalo City Directory,* 1876.

22. *Proceedings of the Common Council,* 1877, 513, 1293.

23. *Proceedings of the Common Council,* 1877, 538, 766.

24. *Buffalo Express,* May 19, June 28, 1875; H. Perry Smith, ed. *History of the City of Buffalo and Erie County* (Syracuse, 1884), 4. The reorganization of the Crosstown so that the Central controlled its board of directors involved the wholesale resignation of the original board and the formation of a new board dominated by the Central. Included on the new board were D. S. Bennett, who was to become the Crosstown's president by 1877; J. N. Larned, editor of the *Commercial Advertiser;* and A. P. Laning, the Democratic candidate for mayor in the fall elections. The streets to be used by the Crosstown railroad were Ohio, Main, Prime, Water, Norton, Erie, Church, Fourth, Court, and Joy; in addition, the tracks were to cross the Terrace and Coit slip.

25. *Buffalo Express,* May 19, June 28, October 23, 25, 29, 30, 1875. Up until the day before the election, the *Express* attacked Laning's candidacy for a number of reasons, none of which had anything to do with railroad use of the streets. The *Express* had not criticized the Crosstown project for the impact it would have on the residents of the streets through which it was to operate when it was a locally controlled project, nor when it was first announced that it was to be an enterprise of the New York Central Railroad. Nevertheless, the paper's editors realized the issue would resonate among Buffalo residents and would perhaps be able to determine the outcome of the election. The issue, if it was a genuine one for the *Express*'s editors, was dropped after the election.

26. *Buffalo Express,* November 1, 1875.

27. The results by ward of city elections can be found in the Common Council proceedings. The two wards which would be most affected by the Crosstown railroad voted for Laning, the Democratic candidate, as they voted for the Democratic candidate in the 1872, 1873, 1877, and 1879 mayoral contests.

28. *Buffalo Express,* July 31, August 18, 31, 1875. No mention of the proposed intracity route was found in the Common Council Proceedings until 1877; *Buffalo Daily Courier,* June 26, 1877; Smith, ed., *History of the City of Buffalo and Erie County,* 4.

29. *Proceedings of the Common Council,* 1877, 725–26.

30. *Proceedings of the Common Council,* 1877, 725–26; *Buffalo Daily Courier,* June 26, 1877.

31. *Proceedings of the Common Council,* 1877, 771–73, 844. At the council meeting two weeks earlier on July 9, the aldermen voted to reconsider the grant to the Buffalo City Railway Company (in effect rescinding the grant), although nothing in the council's published proceedings indicated why the aldermen were having second thoughts about sanctioning an intracity railroad.

32. *Proceedings of the Common Council,* 1877, 726, 844.

33. The events of the Great Strike are examined in the next chapter.

34. *Map of the City of Albany* (Albany, 1857); *City Atlas of Albany, New York* (Philadelphia, 1876).

35. *City Atlas of Albany, New York,* 1876; *Albany City Directory,* 1876; General S. V. Talcott, "Docks, Wharves, and Basin of Albany, with Many Historic Events and Reminiscences of Olden Times," in *Old Albany* 3 (n.d.): 70–76.

36. David A. Gerber, *The Making of an American Pluralism,* 46; Talcott, "Docks, Wharves, and Basin of Albany"; *Albany City Directory,* 1869, 1880; "Minutes of Wharf Association, 1856 et.cet," vol. 2.

37. H. P. Phelps, *The Albany Hand-Book for 1881* (Albany, 1880); *Albany City Directory,* 1876; *City Atlas of Albany, New York,* 1876; Francis P. Kimball, *The Capital Region of New York State: Crossroads of Empire,* vol. 2 (New York, 1942), 125; *Proceedings of the Common Council,* 1875, 175–76.

38. *Proceedings of the Common Council,* 1874, 631.

39. *Albany Evening Journal,* September 15–16, 18, 1874; *Albany Express,* September 17, 1874.

40. *Albany Express,* September 21, 1874; *The Argus,* September 21, 1874. Although in this case, the interests of property owners, such as commission merchants, coincided with the interests of working-class groups like teamsters and cartmen, it is not difficult to envision a situation where their interests over what transpired in streets would diverge. The framing of the conflict as one that pitted abutting property owners vs. railroad corporations implicitly excluded working-class groups like the cartmen.

41. *Proceedings of the Common Council,* 1874, 731–32.

42. *Proceedings of the Common Council,* 1874, 917, 933.

43. *Proceedings of the Common Council,* 1875, 88–89; *Albany Express,* April 16, May 3, 8, 1877; *Buffalo Express,* September 28, 1875.

44. Cited in White, *American Locomotives,* 114.

45. *Proceedings of the Common Council,* 1875, 175–76, 267, 275.

46. *Proceedings of the Common Council,* 1875, 330, 364–65, 407–8; *Albany Evening Journal,* June 22, 1875.

47. *Proceedings of the Common Council,* 1875, 539.

48. See, for example, the Syracuse *Common Council Proceedings,* 1875, 1–2; *Albany Express,* March 30, 1877; *Buffalo Express,* April 13, 1877. For railroads and issues of taxation that helped create widespread anger and episodes of violence in Missouri, see David Thelen, *Paths of Resistance: Tradition and Dignity in Industrializing Missouri* (New York, 1986).

49. *Albany Express,* June 30, 1876; *Albany Argus,* June 30, 1876. The case disappeared from the press and cannot be found at all in the pages of the council's proceedings. The case of the arrested foreman was postponed, then sent to a grand jury, but its outcome went unreported. The fate of the proposed tracks also went unreported; no mention of the tracks was found in the local press from the time of the altercation in June 1876 up to the Great Strike a little over a year later.

50. *Proceedings of the Common Council,* 1877, 384.

51. *City Atlas of Albany, New York,* 1876; "City of Albany, New York" map, *Albany City Directory,* 1877.

52. See the discussion of the Broadway crossing in chapter 1.

53. *Proceedings of the Common Council,* 1874, 729, 770.

54. *Proceedings of the Common Council,* 1875, 584–87, 706.

55. *Proceedings of the Common Council,* 1875, 734–35.

56. *Albany Evening Times,* November 6, 1875.

57. *Albany City Directory,* 1876, 1877; *City Atlas of Albany,* 1876. For saloons and small retail shops such as grocers, it was not uncommon for work place and residence to be within the same structure or adjacent to each other.

58. *Proceedings of the Common Council,* 1875, 809–10.

59. *Proceedings of the Common Council,* 1876, 497, 532, 620.

60. *Proceedings of the Common Council*, 1877, 270, 340.

61. *Albany Evening Times*, October 27, 1875.

62. *Albany Express* January 17, 1876.

63. *Albany Express*, January 17, 22, 1876.

64. *Albany Express*, March 14, 16, 1877.

65. East Syracuse, or DeWitt, was literally created by the New York Central's decision in 1872–73 to add two new tracks to its existing two-track line. The new tracks were to handle freight trains, and it was decided that the additional tracks would bypass the city of Syracuse rather than run through the city as the existing tracks did. East Syracuse was originally nothing more than the point at which the four-track line separated in order to run around Syracuse. In 1880, East Syracuse had a population of 1,099; it was incorporated as a village the following year. Population figures taken from Shupe, Steins, and Pandit, eds., *New York State Population, 1790–1980;* see also *Syracuse Daily Courier,* January 21, 1874.

66. I was unable to determine why the by-pass was built by the Central. Although the Syracuse newspapers expressed relief over the by-pass, there was no indication that it was a result of public pressure. The by-pass was part of the new, four-track freight line the Central constructed from Albany to Buffalo; avoiding the center of the city no doubt shortened the time it took to ship freight.

67. *Syracuse Daily Courier,* January 16, 21, April 3, August 7, November 11, 1874; *Syracuse Daily Journal,* August 7, 1873; January 22, 1874.

68. *Common Council Proceedings,* 1875, 30, 47; *Syracuse City Directory,* 1875–76.

69. Chase, *Syracuse and Its Environs,* 135; *City of Syracuse and Village of Geddes,* 1874 map.

70. *Syracuse Daily Courier,* November 11, 17, 1874.

71. *Common Council Proceedings,* 1875, 69, 79. Hiscock could not be identified with any certainty in the city directories.

72. *Syracuse City Directory,* 1875–76.

73. *Common Council Proceedings,* 1875, 305; 1876, 332, 338; *Syracuse Daily Journal,* January 4, 1876, April 30, 1877; *Syracuse Daily Courier,* January 4, 1876; *Syracuse City Directory,* 1875–76, 1876–77; *City of Syracuse and Village of Geddes* map (Syracuse: H. Wadsworth Clarke, 1874).

74. *Syracuse City Directory,* 1875–76.

75. *City of Syracuse and Village of Geddes,* 1874 map; Washington Street was sometimes referred to as "Railroad Street" in the city's newspapers.

76. Chase, *Syracuse and Its Environs,* 126–27.

77. *Common Council Proceedings,* 1875, 130–31.

78. *Common Council Proceedings,* 1875, 301, 338.

79. *Common Council Proceedings,* 1876, 190.

80. *Common Council Proceedings,* 1877, 175, 183; *Syracuse Morning Standard,* June 26, 1877; *City of Syracuse and Village of Geddes,* 1874 map.

81. *City of Syracuse and Village of Geddes,* 1874 map.

82. *Common Council Proceedings,* 1877, 59, 62–64; *Syracuse Morning Standard,* April 17, 20, 1877; *Syracuse Daily Journal,* April 17, 1877; *Syracuse Daily Courier,* April 17, 1877.

83. *Common Council Proceedings,* 1877, 64; *Syracuse Morning Standard,* April 20, 1877. Whether the railroad bridge was ever removed is doubtful, as an 1884 map of the city published by Andrew Boyd for the 1885–86 *Syracuse City Directory* appears to show the railroad bridge still in place.

84. *Syracuse City Directory,* 1876–77, 1877–78; Clayton, *History of Onondaga County, New York,* 216–18; *City of Syracuse and Village of Geddes,* 1874 map.

Chapter Three

1. *Syracuse Morning Standard,* July 18, 23, 1877; *Syracuse Daily Journal,* July 23, 1877; *Syracuse Daily Courier,* July 23, 1877.

2. In 1880 East Syracuse had a population of 1,099; it was incorporated as a village the following year. Population figures taken from Shupe, Steins, and Pandit, eds. *New York State Population, 1790–1980;* see also *Syracuse Daily Courier,* January 21, 1874.

3. *Syracuse Morning Standard,* July 24, 1877.

4. *Syracuse Daily Courier,* July 24, 1877; *Syracuse Daily Journal,* July 24, 1877; *Syracuse Morning Standard,* July 24, 1877.

5. *Syracuse Daily Journal,* July 24, 1877; *Syracuse Daily Courier,* July 24, 1877.

6. *Syracuse Daily Journal,* July 24, 1877; *Syracuse Morning Standard,* July 24, 1877. The repeated efforts of railroad workers in Buffalo, Syracuse, and Albany (in addition to Rochester) to coordinate their action, however ineffective or effective, undermine the view of the Great Strike as a series of "spontaneous" railroad strikes. Rochester, a city with a population of 89,366 people in 1880, was located on the Erie Canal 70 miles west of Syracuse and 60 miles east of Buffalo. *Statistics of the Population of the United States at the Tenth Census* (Washington, D.C., 1883).

7. *Syracuse Morning Standard,* July 24, 1877; *Syracuse Daily Journal,* July 24, 1877. Just what constituted the destruction or molestation of railroad property was open to interpretation, of course.

8. *Syracuse Morning Standard,* July 24, 1877.

9. *Syracuse Daily Courier,* July 24, 1877.

10. *Syracuse Daily Journal,* July 24, 1877; *Syracuse Morning Standard,* July 24, 1877. The proclamation, with its warning not to participate in crowds, was reprinted again the following day in the *Daily Courier.*

11. *Syracuse Daily Journal,* July 24, 1877.

12. *Syracuse Daily Courier,* July 25, 1877; *Syracuse Morning Standard,* July 25, 1877.

13. *Syracuse Daily Courier,* July 25, 1877; *Syracuse Morning Standard,* July 25, 1877.

14. *Syracuse Daily Courier,* July 25, 1877; *Syracuse Morning Standard,* July 25, 1877.

15. *Syracuse Daily Courier,* July 25, 1877. See Feldberg's *The Turbulent Era* for a discussion of the origins of uniformed police forces and the transition to an emphasis on the prevention of crime. In this case, of course, Syracuse policemen sought to prevent the formation of crowds by threatening to arrest selected individuals. See also Eric H. Monkkonen, *Police in Urban America, 1860–1920* (Cambridge, 1981), especially chapter 1.

16. *Syracuse Morning Standard,* July 25, 27, 1877; *Syracuse Daily Journal,* July 25, 1877.

17. *Syracuse Daily Journal,* July 25, 1877.

18. *Syracuse Daily Courier,* July 26, 1877.

19. *Syracuse Daily Courier,* July 26, 1877; *Syracuse Daily Journal,* July 25, 1877.

20. *Syracuse Daily Journal,* July 26, 1877.

21. *City of Syracuse and Village of Geddes,* 1874 map; Franklin H. Chase, *Syracuse and Its Environs: A History* (New York, 1924), 125, 179.

22. *Syracuse Daily Courier* July 26, 1877; *Syracuse Daily Journal,* July 26, 1877. As demonstrated in other cities during the Great Strike, out-of-town troops were more willing to open fire on people, if necessary, than militiamen drawn from the local community. One can only speculate what this crowd would have done had there been striking railroad workers in its ranks trying to stop trains from moving, or if such an example and spark had been provided for Syracuse residents on other days.

23. *Syracuse Morning Standard,* July 26, 1877; *Syracuse Daily Journal,* July 26, 1877; *Syracuse Daily Courier,* July 26, 1877.

24. *Syracuse Daily Courier,* July 26, 1877.

25. *Syracuse Daily Courier,* July 27, 1877.

26. *Syracuse Daily Journal,* July 26, 1877.

27. *Albany Express,* July 18, 21, 1877; *Albany Argus,* July 21, 1877. The Great Strike in Albany is also examined in Stowell, "Albany's Great Strike of 1877," *New York History* 76, no. 1 (January 1995), 31–55.

28. *City Atlas of Albany, New York* (Philadelphia: G. M. Hopkins, 1876); *Albany Argus,* July 23, 1877.

29. *Albany Express,* July 23, 1877; *Albany Evening Times,* July 23, 1877; *Albany Argus,* July 23, 1877.

30. The East Albany area was composed of three legal entities: the town of East Greenbush, the town of Greenbush, and the village of Greenbush. In 1880, these three entities had a combined population of 12,165. See Shupe, Steins, and Pandit, eds., *New York State Population, 1790–1980.* I am treating the Albany/East Albany area as comprising a single urban community.

31. *Albany Evening Times,* July 23, 1877; *Albany Express,* July 23, 1877. The second bridge was not constructed until the 1870s; "City of Albany" map, *Albany City Directory,* 1877.

32. *Albany Express,* July 24, 1877.

33. *Albany Express,* July 24, 1877; *Albany Evening Times,* July 24, 1877; *Albany Argus,* July 24, 1877; *Albany Evening Journal,* July 24, 1877.

34. *Albany Evening Times,* July 24, 1877. The strike of railroad workers was taking place on two levels—one formal and formally organized—the other spontaneous and informally organized. The pace of events frequently outpaced railroad workers' efforts to coordinate action.

35. *Albany Express,* July 24, 1877; *Albany Argus,* July 24, 1877; *Albany Evening Times,* July 24, 1877.

36. *Albany Express,* July 24, 1877; *Albany Argus,* July 24, 1877; *Albany Evening Times,* July 24, 1877. One other issue was apparently the subject of much discussion at the meeting besides the strike issue—the treatment of the strike in other cities by the Albany newspapers. Indeed, "the subject of the newspapers" was brought up "repeatedly" at the meeting by "several speakers." The newspapers' allegedly unsympathetic coverage of the strike was denounced "in bitter terms." No specifics, perhaps not surprisingly, were reported. After a discussion of which newspapers were the worst offenders, "it was finally agreed to condemn all the papers." A committee was appointed to deal with the issue. Some at the meeting observed that "the press was supported by the laboring men," and they condemned "those who purchased and read" the papers—a not too subtle suggestion for a working-class boycott of the press.

37. *Albany Argus,* July 25, 1877; *Albany Evening Times,* July 24, 1877.

38. The *Albany Argus* and the *Albany Express* of the twenty-fifth state there was a meeting; the *Albany Evening Times* declared there was no meeting.

39. *Albany Evening Times,* July 24, 1877; *Albany Argus,* July 25, 1877.

40. *Albany Express,* July 25, 1877; *Albany Evening Times,* July 24, 1877; *Albany Argus,* July 25, 1877.

41. *Albany Express,* July 25, 1877; *Albany Evening Times,* July 24, 1877.

42. *Albany Express,* July 25, 1877; *Albany Evening Times,* July 24, 1877.

43. *Albany Argus,* July 25, 1877. Coupling pins connect each car of a train to the car in front and behind.

44. *Albany Argus,* July 25, 1877; *Albany Evening Times,* July 24, 1877; *Albany Express,* July 25, 1877. This dispute in the West Albany railyard could have reflected differences among striking railroad workers. On the other hand, the desire to stop all trains may have originated among the people in the crowd who were not railroad employees. If this train was eastbound, allowing it to proceed would mean that it would have traveled through the city

of Albany; allowing a westbound train to proceed meant allowing it to travel away from the city.

45. *Albany Argus,* July 25, 1877; *Albany Evening Times,* July 24, 1877; *Albany Express,* July 25, 1877.

46. *Albany Evening Times,* July 23, 24, 1877; *Albany Express,* July 24, 1877; *Albany Argus,* July 25, 26, 1877.

47. *Albany Express,* July 24, 25, 1877; *Albany Evening Times,* July 24, 1877; Bruce, *1877: Year of Violence,* 54.

48. *Albany Evening Times,* July 24, 1877. The mayor's vague yet ominous reference to "evil disposed and designing persons" was probably his way of referring to anonymous "outside agitators" or "communists," both of whom were frequently blamed across the country for the violence in 1877. Blaming outsiders, communist or noncommunist, was a way of denying that the cause of the disorders was intrinsic to the community.

49. *Albany Evening Times,* July 24, 1877.

50. *Albany Express,* July 23, 24, 1877; *Albany Evening Times,* July 24, 25, 1877.

51. *Albany Argus,* July 25, 1877.

52. *Albany Argus,* July 25, 1877.

53. *Albany Argus,* July 25, 1877; *Albany Evening Times,* July 25, 1877.

54. For the relationships between various segments of the railroad work force, and the relatively privileged position of the engineers, see Licht, *Working for the Railroad.*

55. *Albany Argus,* July 25, 1877.

56. *Albany Argus,* July 25, 1877; *Albany Express,* July 25, 1877.

57. *Albany Argus,* July 25, 1877; *Albany Evening Times,* July 25, 1877; *Albany Express,* July 25, 1877.

58. *Albany Argus,* July 25, 1877; *Albany Evening Times,* July 25, 1877; *Albany Express,* July 25, 1877. No mention was made of the police and/or militia units assigned to guard the bridge.

59. *Albany Express,* July 25, 1877.

60. *Troy Daily Times,* August 6, 1877; *Albany Argus,* July 25, August 10, 1877; *Albany Express,* July 25, 1877; *Albany Evening Times,* July 25, 1877.

61. *Albany Evening Times,* July 25, 1877; *Albany Express,* July 25, 1877; *Albany Argus,* July 26, 1877; *City Atlas of Albany,* New York, 1876. See chapter 4 on crowd composition.

62. *Albany Evening Times,* July 25, 1877; *Albany Express,* July 25, 1877; *Albany Argus,* July 26, 1877; *City Atlas of Albany,* New York, 1876. See chapter 4 on crowd composition.

63. *Albany Express,* July 26, 1877.

64. *Albany Argus,* July 25, 1877; *Albany Express,* July 25, 1877.

65. *Albany Evening Times,* July 25, 1877.

66. *Albany Evening Times,* July 25, 1877; *Albany Argus,* July 26, 1877; *Albany Express,* July 26, 1877.

67. *Albany Evening Times,* July 25, 1877; *Albany Argus,* July 26, 1877; *Albany Express,* July 26, 1877.

68. *Albany Argus,* July 26, 1877.

69. *Albany Express,* July 26, 1877.

70. *Albany Argus,* July 26, 1877; *Albany Express,* July 26, 1877; *Albany Evening Times,* July 25, 1877.

71. *Albany Express,* July 26, 1877; *Albany Argus,* July 26, 1877; *Albany Evening Times,* July 26, 1877; *City Atlas of Albany, New York,* 1876; *Albany City Directory,* 1876, 1877.

72. *Albany Express,* July 26, 1877.

73. *Albany Evening Times,* July 26, 1877; *Albany Argus,* July 27, 1877.

74. *Albany Express,* July 27, 1877; *Albany Evening Times,* July 26, 1877; *Albany Argus,* July 27, 1877.

75. *Albany Express,* July 27, 1877; *Albany Evening Times,* July 26, 1877.

76. *Albany Evening Times,* July 26, 1877.

77. *Albany Evening Times,* July 27, 1877; *Albany Express,* July 27, 1877; *Albany Argus,* July 27, 1877.

78. *Albany Evening Times,* July 27, 1877; *Albany Express,* July 27, 1877.

79. *Albany Express,* July 27, 1877.

80. *Albany Argus,* July 27, 1877; *Documents of the Assembly of the State of New York,* 1878, vol. 1, Document 6, 463. The official reports of the state militia on its mobilization, orders, and actions during the "riots" are contained in this volume. While quite extensive, they are of no real value in ascertaining the social make-up and behavior of crowds during the Great Strike.

81. *Albany Express,* July 26, 27, 1877.

82. *Albany Express,* July 28, 30, 1877.

83. *Albany Argus,* July 28, 1877.

84. The petition, as reprinted in the press, asked Vanderbilt only to make "some ar-rangement" so that "the mechanics and other employees of the company at West Albany [could] resume work"—"as soon as possible." It contained no call for the railroad to rescind the pay cut, as railroad workers had apparently been told it would; *Albany Evening Times,* July 28, 1877.

85. *Albany Evening Times,* July 28, 1877.

86. *Albany Express,* July 30, 31, 1877; *Albany Evening Times,* July 28, 1877.

87. *Albany Evening Times,* July 30, August 2, 3, 1877; *Albany Express,* August 4, 1877.

88. *Buffalo Express,* July 21, 1877; *Buffalo Sunday Morning News,* July 22, 1877.

89. *Buffalo Express,* July 23, 1877.

90. *Buffalo Sunday Morning News,* July 22, 1877; *Buffalo Express,* July 23, 1877. There were five depots in the city of Buffalo; unfortunately, it is not always clear from newspaper accounts which depot is being discussed.

91. *Atlas of the City of Buffalo, Erie County,* New York (Philadelphia: G. M. Hopkins, 1872).

92. *Buffalo Daily Courier,* July 23, 1877.

93. *Atlas of the City of Buffalo, Erie County,* New York (Philadelphia: G. M. Hopkins, 1872); *Buffalo City Directory,* 1876.

94. *Buffalo Express,* July 23, 1877.

95. *Buffalo Express,* July 23, 1877.

96. *Buffalo Express,* July 23, 1877.

97. *Buffalo Express,* July 23, 1877.

98. *Buffalo Express,* July 23, 1877.

99. *Buffalo Express,* July 23, 1877.

100. *Buffalo Express,* July 23, 1877.

101. *Buffalo Express,* July 23, 1877.

102. *Buffalo Express,* July 24, 1877.

103. *Buffalo Express,* July 24, 1877; *Buffalo Daily Courier,* July 24, 1877.

104. *Buffalo Express,* July 24, 1877; *Buffalo Commercial Advertiser,* July 23, 1877; *Courier Company's Map of Buffalo,* 1876.

105. *Buffalo Express,* July 24, 1877.

106. *Buffalo Express,* July 24, 1877; *Atlas of the City of Buffalo, Erie County, New York* (Philadelphia: G. M. Hopkins, 1872).

107. *Buffalo Express,* July 24, 1877; *Atlas of the City of Buffalo, Erie County, New York* (Philadelphia: G. M. Hopkins, 1872).

108. *Buffalo Express,* July 24, 1877; *Atlas of the City of Buffalo, Erie County, New York* (Philadelphia: G. M. Hopkins, 1872).

109. *Buffalo Express,* July 24, 1877.

110. *Buffalo Express,* July 24, 25, 1877; *Buffalo Christian Advocate,* July 26, 1877; *Buffalo Sunday Morning News,* July 29, 1877; *Buffalo Daily Courier,* July 24, 1877.

111. The remaining two could not be identified with respect to occupation.

112. *Buffalo Express,* July 24, 25, 1877; *Buffalo City Directory,* 1877; *Atlas of the City of Buffalo,* 1872. The militia was left fragmented by the confrontation. One militiaman who became separated from the main body decided to head for the city—when he encountered some striking railroad workers from the Buffalo Creek bridge crowd. Threatening to throw him into the creek, the strikers chased after the private; he managed to elude his pursuers and make his way to safety in the city. Another militiaman wounded in the clash found his way to Perry Street and was taken in at someone's home. The main body of the militia proceeded on foot, for the train was apparently unable to start again. Carrying two seriously wounded soldiers, the company made for the nearest houses, one of which happened to be the home of a physician willing to render medical assistance.

113. *Buffalo Express,* July 24, 25, 1877.

114. *Buffalo Express,* July 24, 25, 1877.

115. *Buffalo Daily Courier,* July 24, 1877.

116. *Buffalo Daily Courier,* July 24, 1877; *Buffalo City Directory,* 1877.

117. *Buffalo Daily Courier,* July 24, 1877; *Buffalo City Directory,* 1877.

118. *Buffalo Daily Courier,* July 24, 1877; *Buffalo City Directory,* 1877

119. *Buffalo Daily Courier,* July 24, 1877; *Buffalo Express,* July 24, 1877; *Buffalo City Directory,* 1877. After the meeting, special citizens' patrols were formed from some of the people who had attended the meeting.

120. *Buffalo Express,* July 25, 1877; *Buffalo Commercial Advertiser,* July 24, 1877.

121. *Buffalo Express,* July 25, 1877; *Atlas of the City of Buffalo,* 1872; *Buffalo City Directory,* 1877. The "tramp" label typically referred to the homeless unemployed, although in the context of the Great Strike, it may have been a pejorative used to denigrate individuals in a threatening, working-class crowd. See Paul T. Ringenbach, *Tramps and Reformers, 1873–1916: The Discovery of Unemployment in New York* (Westport, 1973). For the role of the saloon in working-class life, see Licht, *Working for the Railroad;* Duis, *The Saloon;* Rosenzweig, *Eight Hours for What We Will.*

122. *Buffalo Express,* July 24, 1877; *Atlas of the City of Buffalo,* 1872.

123. *Buffalo Express,* July 25, 1877; *Buffalo Commercial Advertiser,* July 24, 1877; *Atlas of the City of Buffalo,* 1872. As the words "driven" and "forced" indicate, the newspapers sought to persuade their readers that the city's manufactories were being closed due to coercion by the crowds. The workers in these establishments, however, may very well have willingly left work as a way of supporting or joining the strike.

124. *Buffalo Express,* July 25, 1877; *Buffalo Commercial Advertiser,* July 24, 1877.

125. *Buffalo Express,* July 25, 1877; *Buffalo City Directory,* 1877; *Atlas of the City of Buffalo,* 1872.

126. *Buffalo Express,* July 25, 1877; *Buffalo City Directory,* 1877; *Atlas of the City of Buffalo,* 1872. The press did not comment on the retreat of the militiamen, but it is worth asking why they fled. Were they simply cowed by the prospect of facing down 500 city residents? Did the militiamen have little interest in risking their well-being in defense of railroad property? Were they refusing to confront people who were in many ways just like themselves?

127. *Buffalo Daily Courier,* July 25, 1877; *Buffalo Express,* July 25, 1877. See McShane, "Transforming the Use of Urban Space" for opposition to the use of steam-powered vehicles by street railway companies in other cities.

128. *Buffalo Express,* July 25, 1877. On the Great Fire in Chicago in 1871, see Karen Sawislak, *Smoldering City: Chicagoans and the Great Fire, 1871–1874* (Chicago, 1995); and Carl S. Smith, *Urban Disorder and the Shape of Belief: The Great Chicago Fire, the Haymarket Bomb, and the Model Town of Pullman* (Chicago, 1995). On the Boston confla-

gration in 1872, see the contemporary account by Charles Carleton Coffin, *The Story of the Great Fire, Boston, November 9–10, 1872* (Boston, 1872).

129. *Buffalo Express,* July 25, 1877.

130. *Buffalo Express,* July 26, 1877; *Buffalo Commercial Advertiser,* July 25, 1877. See chapter 4 on crowd composition.

131. *Buffalo Express,* July 26, 1877.

132. *Buffalo Express,* July 26, 1877.

133. *Buffalo Express,* July 26, 1877.

134. *Buffalo Express,* July 26, 1877.

135. *Buffalo Express,* July 27, 1877; *Buffalo Daily Courier,* July 27, 1877.

136. *Buffalo Express,* July 27, 1877.

137. *Buffalo Express,* July 27, 1877; *Buffalo Daily Courier,* July 27, 1877; *Atlas of the City of Buffalo,* 1872; *Buffalo City Directory,* 1877.

138. *Buffalo Express,* July 27, 1877; *Buffalo Daily Courier,* July 27, 1877.

Chapter Four

1. *Buffalo City Directory,* 1877. The addresses of the arrested were plotted on Hopkins's 1872 map of the city of Buffalo (Atlas of the City of Buffalo).

2. There is an extensive literature dealing with crowd theory and definition. For a recent and excellent discussion of the conceptual and methodological problems inherent in analyzing "crowd" composition, behavior, and motivation, see Mark Harrison, *Crowds and History: Mass Phenomena in English Towns, 1790–1835* (Cambridge, 1988). George Rude's masterful *The Crowd in History, 1730–1848* lays out the essential problems in studying crowds, especially in the introduction, "The Subject and Its Problems."

In some locales, like Buffalo and Pittsburgh, for example, there are other individuals we can inquire about: those killed or wounded by local militias and federal troops. One can continue this discussion of the existing "sample" and its defects, but it would not alter the fact that the names of those arrested and wounded/killed appearing in the press are the only group of crowd participants we can examine. For example, one could assert that police might have been consciously or unconsciously more likely to arrest lower-class individuals rather than the middle-class people also in crowds. Similarly, newspaper editors could have chosen for a number of reasons not to print the names of certain individuals who had been arrested, and so on. It should also be pointed out that once we have the names of people from the 1877 crowds, the information we can gather on them is usually limited to data in city directories: occupation and place of residence. These categories, in and of themselves, are of limited use when trying to determine what motivated people to join or form crowds. We could also attempt to identify those arrested in the census, but such a task would be daunting, and the resulting data on birthplace, marital status, age, etc., are in and of themselves of limited use in trying to ascertain what motivated people to join crowds.

3. Bruce, *1877: Year of Violence,* 77, 105–8, 119, 123, 186.

4. James Francis Caye, Jr., "Crime and Violence in the Heterogeneous Urban Community: Pittsburgh, 1870–1889," 39, 82–83, 86, 97, 99, 112. The occupational status of 3.9% of the Roundhouse crowd remained unknown.

5. Schneirov, "Chicago's Great Upheaval of 1877," 4, 6, 10, 14–15.

6. Roediger, "'Not Only the Ruling Classes to Overcome, But Also the So-Called Mob,'" 228–32.

7. *Albany Argus,* July 25,1877; *Albany Evening Times,* July 26,1877; *Albany Argus,* July 27,1877. On the arrest of the peddler, a former resident of Albany, and the subsequent trial which attracted a great deal of attention, see *Albany Express,* August 6, 1877; and the *Albany Argus,* August 10, 14–16, September 14, 15, 1877.

8. The percentages total 101 due to rounding to the nearest whole number.

9. *Buffalo City Directory,* 1877; *Buffalo Express,* July 23, 1877.

10. *Buffalo City Directory,* 1877; *Buffalo Express,* July 24–26, 1877; *Buffalo Daily Courier,* July 28, 1877.

11. *Buffalo Daily Courier,* July 28, 1877; *Buffalo Express,* July 25, 1877.

12. *Buffalo Express,* July 25, 1877; *Buffalo Commercial Advertiser,* July 24, 1877; *Buffalo City Directory,* 1877.

13. *Buffalo Express,* July 26, 1877; *Buffalo Commercial Advertiser,* July 25, 1877; *Buffalo City Directory,* 1877.

14. *Buffalo Express,* July 27, 1877; *Buffalo Daily Courier,* July 26, 1877; *Buffalo City Directory,* 1877.

15. *Buffalo Express,* July 27, 1877; *Buffalo Daily Courier,* July 26, 1877; *Buffalo City Directory,* 1877.

16. *Buffalo Express,* July 27, 1877; *Buffalo Daily Courier,* July 27, 1877; *Buffalo City Directory,* 1877.

17. *Buffalo Express,* July 24, 30, 1877; *Buffalo Daily Courier,* July 23, 1877; *Buffalo Commercial Advertiser,* July 24, 1877; *Buffalo Christian Advocate,* July 26, 1877; *Buffalo Sunday Morning News,* July 29, 1877.

18. *Buffalo Express,* July 23–26, 1877; *Buffalo Daily Courier,* July 23, 1877; *Buffalo Commercial Advertiser,* July 23, 1877; *Buffalo Christian Advocate,* July 26, 1877; *Buffalo Sunday Morning News,* July 29, 1877. It should be noted that accounts of specific incidents could and frequently did employ fairly objective terms to describe crowds. Editorial commentary, on the other hand, was much more likely to employ derogatory terms such as "tramp" or "rioter."

19. Noah Webster, ed. *An American Dictionary of the English Language.* (Springfield, MA, 1859), 142.

20. *Buffalo Express,* July 23, 26, 1877.

21. *Buffalo Daily Courier,* July 23, 25, 1877; *Buffalo Commercial Advertiser,* July 23, 1877; *Buffalo Sunday Morning News,* July 29, 1877. "Roughs" is perhaps best interpreted as an indication of working-class status; "vagabonds" is probably a linguistic variance of tramps—the transient unemployed.

22. *Albany Argus,* July 24, 25, 1877.

23. *Albany Evening Journal,* July 24, 1877; *Albany Evening Times,* July 25, 1877.

24. *Albany Evening Times,* July 25, 1877; *Albany Argus,* July 25–27, 1877; *Albany Express,* July 25, 1877; *Albany Evening Journal,* July 25, 1877.

25. *Syracuse Daily Courier,* July 24, 25, 27, 1877.

26. *Syracuse Morning Standard,* July 24, 27, 1877; *Syracuse Daily Courier,* July 26, 1877.

Chapter Five

1. *Proceedings of the Common Council of the City of Albany,* 1878, 105, 272.

2. *Proceedings of the Common Council of the City of Albany,* 1879, 124.

3. *Proceedings of the Common Council of the City of Albany,* 1879, 293.

4. *Proceedings of the Common Council of the City of Albany,* 1879, 549, 563–64. There is no record of this resolution coming to a vote in the council.

5. *Proceedings of the Common Council of the City of Albany,* 1882, 258–59.

6. *Proceedings of the Common Council of the City of Albany,* 1882, 334.

7. *Common Council Proceedings,* 1877, 308, 364; *Syracuse City Directory,* 1876–77.

8. *Common Council Proceedings,* 1878, 446.

9. *Common Council Proceedings,* 1877, 300–301, 329, 381; 1878, 258.

10. *Common Council Proceedings,* 1878, 395; 1879, 402; *Syracuse City Directory,* 1878–79.

11. *Proceedings of the Common Council of Buffalo,* 1877, 1046–47.

12. *Proceedings of the Common Council of Buffalo,* 1877, 1064; John Gorman cannot be positively identified in the city directories. If we can extrapolate from other cases in Buffalo, however, it is probable that Gorman was the saloon owner who resided on Fourth Street, one of the streets to be used by the proposed railroad; *Buffalo City Directory,* 1877, 1878.

13. *Proceedings of the Common Council of Buffalo,* 1877, 1116–17.

14. *Proceedings of the Common Council of Buffalo,* 1878, 318; *Buffalo Express,* April 30, 1878. On the retirement of Matthews from the *Commercial Advertiser,* see *Buffalo Daily Dispatch,* October 30, November 2, 1877.

15. *Buffalo Express,* May 2, 1878.

16. *Buffalo Express,* May 4, 1878.

17. *Buffalo Express,* October 1, 1875, May 7, 9, 10, 1878; *Buffalo Daily Courier,* May 10, 1878.

18. *Buffalo Express,* October 1, 1875, May 7, 9, 10, 1878; *Buffalo Daily Courier,* May 10, 1878. The crossing of the foot of Main Street by the Crosstown railroad must have been of enormous concern to the many retail and wholesale businesses on the lower part of Main, for Main Street was one of the principal thoroughfares of retail trade.

19. *Proceedings of the Common Council of Buffalo,* 1878, 368–69; *Buffalo Express,* May 14, 1878; *Buffalo Daily Courier,* May 14, 1878.

20. *Proceedings of the Common Council of Buffalo,* 1878, 368–69; *Buffalo City Directory,* 1877, 1878.

21. *Buffalo City Directory,* 1877, 1878; *Atlas of the City of Buffalo,* 1872. One petitioner lived and worked a considerable distance from the proposed route.

22. *Proceedings of the Common Council of Buffalo,* 1878, 384, 408; John Reynolds could not be positively identified.

23. *Buffalo Express,* May 23, 25, 1878; *Buffalo Daily Courier,* May 24, 1878.

24. *Proceedings of the Common Council of Buffalo,* 1878, 440; *Buffalo City Directory,* 1877, 1878; *Atlas of the City of Buffalo,* 1872.

25. *Proceedings of the Common Council of Buffalo,* 1878, 440, 478–79; *Buffalo Express,* May 28, 1878.

26. Mark S. Hubbell, ed., *History of the City of Buffalo with Biographies of Typical and Representative Citizens* (Buffalo, 1893), 296–97; Smith, ed., *History of the City of Buffalo and Erie County,* 4; *New York Supreme Court Reports,* 26:30–31; the conflict as it continued during 1878–82 can be followed in the *Proceedings* and the daily press.

27. *Proceedings of the Common Council of the City of Albany,* 1883, 330.

28. For Buffalo, see Robert B. Adam, "History of the Abolition of Railroad Grade Crossings in the City of Buffalo," in Severance, ed., *Publications of the Buffalo Historical Society,* 153–255; for Syracuse, see Chase, *Syracuse and Its Environs;* and the *Report on Grade Crossing Elimination in the City of Syracuse,* December 31, 1915 (Syracuse, 1917), in the Grade Crossing folder in the collections of the Onondaga Historical Association.

Conclusion

1. Duis, *The Saloon;* McShane, "Transforming the Use of Urban Space," 279–307; Stansell, *City of Women;* Bluestone, "'The Pushcart Evil,'" 68–92.

2. Hoffman, *Local Attachments,* 91–92, 101–2.

3. Bruce, *1877: Year of Violence,* 31.

4. "The Charge" is the title of chapter 1 in Bruce's *1877: Year of Violence.*

5. I am consciously using the term "scaffolding" from Sam Bass Warner, Jr., "If All the World Were Philadelphia," 26–43.

6. See, for example, Feldberg, *The Turbulent Era.*

7. Stromquist, *A Generation of Boomers,* 24.

8. The *Buffalo Express* of July 25, 1877, ran a column entitled "Riots of the Past," in which a series of riots ranging from 1812 to 1863 were listed as examples of "the mob spirit upon any great scale previous to the present deplorable railroad riots."

9. The most succinct exposition for this perspective on the bifurcated nature of urban working-class life is found in chapter 3 of Katznelson's *City Trenches.*

Selected Bibliography

Articles, Books, and Dissertations

Adam, Robert B. "History of the Abolition of Railroad Grade Crossings in the City of Buffalo." In Frank H. Severance, ed., *Publications of the Buffalo Historical Society.* Vol. 8. Buffalo: Buffalo Historical Society, 1905.

Alexander, E. P. *Iron Horses: American Locomotives, 1829–1900.* New York: W. W. Norton, 1941.

Anderson, Stanford, ed. *On Streets.* Cambridge, MA: MIT Press, 1978.

Archer, Melanie. "Small Capitalism and Middle-Class Formation in Industrializing Detroit, 1880–1900." *Journal of Urban History* 21, no. 2 (January 1995): 218–55.

Ashworth, John. *Slavery, Capitalism, and Politics in the Antebellum Republic: Commerce and Compromise, 1820–1850.* Cambridge: Cambridge University Press, 1995.

Beard, Charles A., and Mary R. Beard. *The Rise of American Civilization.* Vol. 2. New York: Macmillan Company, 1927.

Bedarida, Francois, and Anthony Sutcliffe. "The Street in the Structure and Life of the City: Reflections on Nineteenth-Century London and Paris." *Journal of Urban History* 6, no.4 (August 1980): 379–96.

Berger, Max. *The British Traveler in America, 1836–1860.* New York: Columbia University Press, 1943.

Berk, Gerald. *Alternative Tracks: The Constitution of American Industrial Order, 1865–1917.* Baltimore: Johns Hopkins University Press, 1994.

Bernstein, Iver. *The New York City Draft Riots: Their Significance for American Society and Politics in the Age of the Civil War.* New York: Oxford University Press, 1990.

Bluestone, Daniel M. "'The Pushcart Evil': Peddlers, Merchants, and New York City's Streets, 1890–1940." *Journal of Urban History* 18, no. 1 (November 1991): 68–92.

Brecher, Jeremy. *Strike.* San Francisco: Straight Arrow Books, 1972.

Bridges, Amy. *A City in the Republic: Antebellum New York and the Origins of Machine Politics.* New York: Cambridge University Press, 1984.

Brown, Josh, Steve Brier, and Nancy Musser. "The American Social History Project's '1877: The Grand Army of Starvation.'" New York: American Social History Productions, Inc., 1985.

Bruce, Dwight H., ed. *Onondaga's Centennial: Gleanings of a Century.* Boston: Boston History Co., 1896.

Bruce, Robert V. *1877: Year of Violence.* Chicago: Ivan R. Dee, 1989 [1959].

Burbank, David T. *Reign of the Rabble: The St. Louis General Strike of 1877.* New York: Augustus M. Kelley, 1966.

Carr, Edward Hallett. *What Is History?* New York: Vintage Books, 1961.

Caye, James Francis, Jr. "Crime and Violence in the Heterogeneous Urban Community: Pittsburgh, 1870–1889." Ph.D. dissertation, University of Pittsburgh, 1977.

Chandler, Alfred D., Jr., ed. *The Railroads: The Nation's First Big Business.* New York: Harcourt, Brace and World, 1965.

Chase, Franklin H. *Syracuse and Its Environs: A History.* New York: Lewis Historical Publishing Co., 1924.

Clayton, W. W. *History of Onondaga County, New York.* New Berlin, NY: Molly Yes Press, 1980 [1878].

Coffin, Charles Carleton. *The Story of the Great Fire, Boston, November 9–10, 1872.* Boston, 1872.

Couvares, Frances. *The Remaking of Pittsburgh: Class and Culture in an Industrializing City, 1877–1919.* Albany: SUNY Press, 1984.

Cronon, William. *Nature's Metropolis: Chicago and the Great West.* New York, 1991.

Dacus, J. A. *Annals of the Great Strike in the United States.* New York: Arno Press and The New York Times, 1969 [1877].

Davis, Susan G. *Parades and Power: Street Theater in Nineteenth-Century Philadelphia.* Philadelphia: Temple University Press, 1986.

Debouzy, Marianne. "Workers' Self-Organization and Resistance in the 1877 Strikes." In Dirk Hoerder, ed., *American Labor and Immigration History, 1877–1920: Recent European Research.* Chicago: University of Illinois Press, 1983.

Deverell, William. *Railroad Crossing: Californians and the Railroad, 1850–1910.* Berkeley: University of California Press, 1994.

Dickens, Charles. *American Notes for General Circulation.* Edited and with an introduction by John S. Whitley and Arnold Goldman. New York: Penguin Classics, 1985.

Dolan, William H., and Mark S. Hubbell. *Our Police and Our City: The Official History of the Buffalo Police Department from the Earliest Days to the Present Time and a History of the City of Buffalo with Biographies of Typical and Representative Citizens.* Buffalo: Bensler and Wesley, 1893.

Dublin, Thomas. *Women at Work: The Transformation of Work and Community in Lowell, Massachusetts, 1826–1860.* New York: Columbia University Press, 1979.

Duis, Perry R. *The Saloon: Public Drinking in Chicago and Boston, 1880–1920.* Chicago: University of Illinois Press, 1983.

Dunn, Walter S., Jr., ed. *History of Erie County, 1870–1970.* Buffalo: Buffalo and Erie County Historical Society, 1972.

Eggert, Gerald G. *Railroad Labor Disputes: The Beginnings of Federal Strike Policy.* Ann Arbor: University of Michigan Press, 1967.

1877: The Grand Army of Starvation. Film. New York: American Social History Project, 1985.

Ellis, David Maldwyn. "Rivalry between the New York Central and the Erie Canal." *New York History* 29, no. 3 (July 1948): 268–300.

Ellis, David M., James A. Frost, Harold C. Syrett, and Harry J. Carman. *A History of New York State.* Ithaca: Cornell University Press, 1967.

Feldberg, Michael. "The Crowd in Philadelphia History: A Comparative Perspective." *Labor History* 15, no. 3 (Summer 1974): 323–36.

———. *The Turbulent Era: Riot and Disorder in Jacksonian America.* New York: Oxford University Press, 1980.

Foner, Eric. *Reconstruction: America's Unfinished Revolution, 1863–1877.* New York: Harper and Row, 1988.

Foner, Philip S. *The Great Labor Uprising of 1877.* New York: Monad Press, 1977.

Franzosi, Roberto. "The Press as a Source of Socio-Historical Data: Issues in the Methodology of Data Collection from Newspapers." *Historical Methods* 20, no. 1 (Winter 1987): 5–16.

Freehling, William W. *Prelude to Civil War: The Nullification Controversy in South Carolina, 1816–1836.* Oxford: Oxford University Press, 1976.

Genovese, Eugene. *The Political Economy of Slavery: Studies in the Economy and Society of the Slave South.* New York: Pantheon, 1967.

Gerber, David A. *The Making of an American Pluralism: Buffalo, New York, 1825–1860.* Chicago: University of Illinois Press, 1989.

Gillette, Howard, Jr., and Zane L. Miller, eds. *American Urbanism: A Historiographical Review.* New York: Greenwood Press, 1987.

Glaab, Charles N. *Kansas City and the Railroads: Community Policy in the Growth of a Regional Metropolis.* Madison: State Historical Society of Wisconsin, 1962.

Glazier, Willard. *Peculiarities of American Cities.* Philadelphia: Hubbard Brothers, 1884.

Goldman, Mark. *High Hopes: The Rise and Decline of Buffalo, New York.* Albany: SUNY Press, 1983.

Goodrich, Carter. *Government Promotion of American Canals and Railroads, 1800–1890.* New York: Columbia University Press, 1960.

Goodwyn, Lawrence. *The Populist Moment: A Short History of the Agrarian Revolt in America.* New York: Oxford University Press, 1978.

Greenberg, Brian. *Worker and Community: Response to Industrialization in a Nineteenth-Century American City: Albany, New York, 1850–1884.* Albany: SUNY Press, 1985.

Grimstead, David. "Rioting in Its Jacksonian Setting." *American Historical Review* 77 (April 1972): 361–97.

Gutman, Herbert G. "Trouble on the Railroads in 1873–1874: Prelude to the 1877 Crisis?" In Gutman, *Work, Culture and Society in Industrializing America: Essays in American Working-Class and Social History.* New York: Knopf, 1976.

Hamlin, Mrs. Charles S. "Elk Street and Its Neighborhood." Manuscript, October 1926, Pruyn Library at the Albany Public Library.

Hammet, Theodore. "Two Mobs of Jacksonian Boston: Ideology and Interest." *Journal of American History* 62 (March 1976): 845–68.

Harrison, Mark. *Crowds and History: Mass Phenomena in English Towns, 1790–1835.* New York: Cambridge University Press, 1988.

Henry, Sarah M. "The Strikers and Their Sympathizers: Brooklyn in the Trolley Strike of 1895." *Labor History* 32, no. 3 (Summer 1991): 329–53.

Hershberg, Theodore. "The New Urban History: Toward an Interdisciplinary History of the City." *Journal of Urban History* 5, no. 1 (November 1978): 3–40.

———. *Philadelphia: Work, Space, Family, and Group Experience in the Nineteenth Century.* New York: Oxford University Press, 1981.

Hill, Henry Wayland, ed. *Municipality of Buffalo, New York: A History, 1720–1923.* New York: Lewis Historical Publishing Co., 1923.

Hoerder, Dirk. *Crowd Action in Revolutionary Massachusetts, 1765–1780.* New York, 1977.

———, ed. *American Labor and Immigration History, 1877–1920: Recent European Research.* Chicago: University of Illinois Press, 1983.

Hoffman, Alexander Von. *Local Attachments: The Making of an American Urban Neighborhood, 1850–1920.* Baltimore: Johns Hopkins University Press, 1994.

Horton, John Theodore, Edward T. Williams, and Harry S. Douglass, eds. *History of Northwestern New York.* New York: Lewis Historical Publishing Co., 1947.

Hubbell, Mark S., ed. *History of the City of Buffalo with Biographies of Typical and Representative Citizens.* Buffalo: Bensler and Wesley, 1893.

Joyaux, Georges J. "A Franc-Tireur in New York: The Observations of Auguste Foubert." *New York History* (October 1988): 441–70.

————. "The New York Peregrination of Armand Parrot-La Riviere." *New York History* (January 1988): 79–98.

Katznelson, Ira. *City Trenches: Urban Politics and the Patterning of Class in the United States*. New York: Pantheon, 1981.

Katznelson, Ira, and Aristide R. Zolberg, eds. *Working Class Formation: Nineenth-Century Patterns in Western Europe and the United States*. Princeton: Princeton University Press, 1986.

Kellett, John R. *The Impact of Railways on Victorian Cities*. London: Routledge and Kegan Paul, 1969.

Kent, Donald H. "The Erie War of the Gauges." *Pennsylvania History* 15, no. 4 (October 1948): 253–75.

Kimball, Francis P. *The Capital Region of New York State: Crossroads of Empire*. Vol. 2. New York: Lewis Historical Publishing Co., 1942.

Kolko, Gabriel. *Railroads and Regulation: 1877–1916*. Princeton: Princeton University Press, 1965.

————. *Main Currents in Modern American History*. New York: Pantheon Books, 1984.

Lane, Roger. *Violent Death in the City: Suicide, Accident, and Murder in Nineteenth-Century Philadelphia*. Cambridge, MA: Harvard University Press, 1979.

Larned, J. N. *A History of Buffalo*. New York: Progress of the Empire State Co., 1911.

Laurie, Bruce. *Artisans into Workers: Labor in Nineteenth-Century America*. Chicago: University of Illinois Press, 1997.

Leach, Eugene E. "Chaining the Tiger: The Mob Stigma and the Working Class, 1863–1894." *Labor History* 35, no. 2 (Spring 1994).

Levine, Bruce. *Half Slave and Half Free: The Roots of the Civil War*. New York: Hill and Wang, 1992.

Licht, Walter. *Working for the Railroad: The Organization of Work in the Nineteenth Century*. Princeton: Princeton University Press, 1983.

————. *Industrializing America: The Nineteenth Century*. Baltimore: Johns Hopkins University Press, 1995.

Mackey, Philip English. "Law and Order, 1877: Philadelphia's Response to the Railroad Riots." *Pennsylvania Magazine of History and Biography* 96, no. 2 (April 1972): 183–202.

Martin, Edward Winslow [James Dabney McCabe]. *The History of the Great Riots*. New York: Augustus M. Kelley Publishers, 1971 [1877].

Marx, Leo. *The Machine in the Garden: Technology and the Pastoral Ideal in America*. New York: Oxford University Press, 1964.

McPherson, James. *Battle Cry of Freedom: The Civil War Era*. New York: Oxford University Press, 1988.

McShane, Clay. *Technology and Reform: Street Railways and the Growth of Milwaukee, 1887–1900*. Madison, WI: Department of History, 1974.

————. "Transforming the Use of Urban Space: A Look at the Revolution in Street Pavements, 1880–1924." *Journal of Urban History* 5, no. 3 (May 1979): 279–307.

Molloy, Scott. *Trolley Wars: Streetcar Workers on the Line*. Washington, DC: Smithsonian Institution Press, 1996.

Monkkonen, Eric H. *Police in Urban America, 1860–1920*. Cambridge: Cambridge University Press, 1981.

Montgomery, David. "Strikes in Nineteenth-Century America." *Social Science History* 4, no. 1 (February 1980): 81–103.

————. *Citizen Worker: The Experience of Workers in the United States with Democracy and the Free Market during the Nineteenth Century*. Cambridge: Cambridge University Press, 1993.

North, Douglass C. *Growth and Welfare in the American Past: A New Economic History*. Englewood Cliffs: Prentice-Hall, 1974.

Oakes, James. *The Ruling Race: A History of American Slaveholders*. New York: Vintage Books, 1983.

Padover, Saul K., ed. *The Letters of Karl Marx*. Englewood Cliffs: Prentice-Hall, 1979.

Painter, Nell Irvin. *Standing at Armageddon: The United States, 1877–1919*. New York: W. W. Norton, 1987.

Pinkerton, Allan. *Strikers, Communists, Tramps and Detectives*. New York: G. W. Carleton and Co., 1878.

Rayback, Joseph. *A History of American Labor*. New York: Macmillan Co., 1963.

Reynolds, Cuyler. *Albany Chronicles: A History of the City Arranged Chronologically*. Albany, New York: J. B. Lyon Co., 1906.

Richards, Leonard L. *Gentlemen of Property and Standing: Anti-Abolition Mobs in Jacksonian America*. New York: Oxford University Press, 1970.

Ringenbach, Paul T. *Tramps and Reformers, 1873–1916: The Discovery of Unemployment in New York*. Westport: Greenwood Press, 1973.

Rock, Howard B. *Artisans of the New Republic: The Tradesmen of New York City in the Age of Jefferson*. New York: New York University Press, 1979.

Roediger, David R. "'Not Only the Ruling Classes to Overcome, But Also the So-Called Mob': Class, Skill and Community in the St. Louis General Strike of 1877." *Journal of Social History* (Winter 1985): 213–39.

Rosen, Christine Meisner. "Infrastructural Improvement in Nineteenth-Century Cities: A Conceptual Framework and Cases." *Journal of Urban History* 12, no. 3 (May 1986): 211–56.

———. *The Limits of Power: Great Fires and the Process of City Growth in America*. New York, 1986.

Rosenzweig, Roy. *Eight Hours for What We Will: Workers & Leisure in an Industrializing City, 1870–1920*. Cambridge: Cambridge University Press, 1985.

Rowley, William Esmond. "Albany: A Tale of Two Cities, 1820–1880." Ph.D. dissertation, Harvard University, 1967.

Rude, George. *The Crowd in History: A Study of Popular Disturbances in France and England, 1730–1848*. London: Lawrence and Wishart, 1981 [1964].

Salvatore, Nick. "Railroad Workers and the Great Strike of 1877: The View from a Small Midwest City." *Labor History* 21, no. 4 (Fall 1980): 522–45.

Sawislak, Karen. *Smoldering City: Chicagoans and the Great Fire, 1871–1874*. Chicago: University of Chicago Press, 1995.

Saxton, Alexander. *The Indispensable Enemy: Labor and the Anti-Chinese Movement in California*. Berkeley: University of California Press, 1971.

Schneirov, Richard. "Chicago's Great Upheaval of 1877." *Chicago History* (1980): 3–17.

Severance, Frank H., ed. *Publications of the Buffalo Historical Society*. Vol. 8. Buffalo: Buffalo Historical Society, 1905.

Shefter, Martin. "Trade Unions and Political Machines: The Organization and Disorganization of the American Working Class in the Late Nineteenth Century." In Ira Katznelson and Aristide R. Zolberg, eds., *Working Class Formation: Nineteenth-Century Patterns in Western Europe and the United States* (Princeton, 1986).

Shupe, Barbara, Janet Steins, and Jyoti Pandit, eds. *New York State Population, 1790–1980*. New York: Neal-Schuman Publishers, 1987.

Slaner, Philip A. "The Railroad Strikes of 1877." *Marxist Quarterly* 1, no. 2 (April–June 1937): 214–36.

Slotkin, Richard. *The Fatal Environment: The Myth of the Frontier in the Age of Industrialization, 1800–1890*. New York: Atheneum, 1985.

Smith, Barbara Clark. "Markets, Streets and Stores: Contested Terrain in Pre-Industrial Boston." In Elsie Marienstras and Barbara Karsky, eds., *Autre Temps, Autre Espace: An Other Time, An Other Space.* Nancy, France: University of Nancy Press, 1986.

Smith, Carl S. *Urban Disorder and the Shape of Belief: The Great Chicago Fire, the Haymarket Bomb, and the Model Town of Pullman.* Chicago: University of Chicago Press, 1995.

Smith, H. Perry. *History of the City of Buffalo and Erie County.* Syracuse: O. Mason and Co., 1884.

Stansell, Christine. "Women, Children and the Uses of the Streets: Class and Gender Conflict in New York City, 1850–1860." *Feminist Studies* 8, no. 2 (Summer 1982): 309–335.

———. *City of Women: Sex and Class in New York, 1789–1860.* Chicago: University of Illinois Press, 1987.

Stover, John F. *American Railroads.* Chicago: University of Chicago Press, 1961.

Stowell, David O. "Albany's Great Strike of 1877." *New York History* 76, no. 1 (January 1995): 31–55.

———. "'Small Property Holders' and the Great Strike of 1877: Railroads, City Streets, and the Middle Classes." *Journal of Urban History* 21, no. 6 (September 1995): 741–63.

Stromquist, Shelton. *A Generation of Boomers: The Pattern of Railroad Labor Conflict in Nineteenth-Century America.* Chicago: University of Illinois Press, 1987.

Sullivan, James, ed. *History of New York State, 1523–1927.* New York: Lewis Historical Publishing Co., 1927.

Sutcliffe, Anthony R. "Urban History in the Eighties: Reflections on the H. J. Dyos Memorial Conference." *Journal of Urban History* 10, no. 2 (February 1984): 123–44.

Talcott, S. V. "Docks, Wharves, and Basin of Albany, with Many Historic Events and Reminiscences of Olden Times" (n.d.). In *Old Albany.* Vol. 3 (n.d.). Albany: Privately printed by Morris Gerber; in The Morris Gerber Collection, 1970.

Tarr, Joel A., and Josef W. Konritz. "Patterns in the Development of the Urban Infrastructure." In Howard Gillette, Jr., and Zanel L. Miller. eds., *American Urbanism: A Historiographical Review.* New York: Greenwood Press, 1987.

Taylor, George Rogers, and Irene D. Neu. *The American Railroad Network, 1861–1890.* Cambridge, MA: Harvard University Press, 1956.

Tenney, Jonathan. "History of the City of Albany" (n.d.). In *Old Albany* (n.d.). Albany: Privately printed by Morris Gerber; in The Morris Gerber Collection, 1970.

Thelen, David. *Paths of Resistance: Tradition and Dignity in Industrializing Missouri.* New York: Oxford University Press, 1986.

Trachtenberg, Alan. *The Incorporation of America: Culture & Society in the Gilded Age.* New York: Hill and Wang, 1982.

Van Zandt, Roland, ed. *Chronicles of the Hudson: Three Centuries of Travelers' Accounts.* New Brunswick: Rutgers University Press, 1971.

Vidler, Anthony. "The Scenes of the Street: Transformations in Ideal and Reality, 1750–1871." In Stanford Anderson, ed., *On Streets.* Cambridge, MA: MIT Press, 1978.

Walter, Francis Joseph. "A Social and Cultural History of Buffalo, New York, 1865–1901." Ph.D. dissertation, Western Reserve University, 1958.

Ward, James A. *Railroads and the Character of America, 1820–1887.* Knoxville: University of Tennessee Press, 1986.

Warner, Sam Bass, Jr. "If All the World Were Philadelphia: A Scaffolding for Urban History, 1774–1930." *American Historical Review* 74 (October 1968): 26–43.

Weaver, Bill L. "Louisville's Labor Disturbance, July, 1877." *Filson Club Historical Quarterly* 48, no. 2 (April 1974): 177–86.

Webster, Noah, ed. *An American Dictionary of the English Language.* Springfield, MA: George and Charles Merriam, 1859.

White, John H., Jr. *American Locomotives: An Engineering History, 1830–1880*. Baltimore: Johns Hopkins University Press, 1968.

Wiebe, Robert H. *The Search for Order, 1877–1920*. New York: Hill and Wang, 1967.

Wilner, Merton. *Niagara Frontier: A Narrative and Documentary History*. Chicago: S. J. Clarke Publishing Co., 1931.

Woodward, C. Vann. *Reunion and Reaction: The Compromise of 1877 and the End of Reconstruction*. Boston: Little, Brown, 1951.

Yearley, Clifton K., Jr. "The Baltimore and Ohio Railroad Strike of 1877." *Maryland Historical Magazine* 51, no. 3 (September 1956): 188–211.

Newpapers and Magazines
Buffalo
Buffalo Commercial Advertiser
Buffalo Daily Courier
Buffalo Daily Dispatch
Buffalo Express
Buffalo Sunday Morning News
Buffalo Weekly Courier
Christian Advocate
Every Saturday

Albany
Albany Argus
Albany Evening Journal
Albany Evening Times
Albany Express
The Albany Handbook for 1881
The New Albany
Troy Daily Times

Syracuse
Syracuse Daily Courier
Syracuse Daily Journal
Syracuse Morning Standard

Common Council Records
Proceedings of the Common Council of Buffalo
Proceedings of the Common Council of the City of Albany
Common Council Proceedings [Syracuse]

City Directories
Albany City Directory
Buffalo City Directory
Syracuse City Directory

Maps
City of Syracuse and Village of Geddes (H. Wadsworth Clarke, 1874)
Map of the City of Syracuse (H. Wadsworth Clarke, 1873)
Map of the City of Syracuse (Andrew Boyd, 1884)
Beer's Atlas of Onondaga County (F. W. Beers and Co., New York, 1874)
Map of the City of Albany (Sprague and Co., 1857)

New Topographical Atlas of the Counties of Albany and Schenectady, New York (Philadelphia: Stone and Stewart, 1866)
City Atlas of Albany, New York (G.M. Hopkins, 1876)
Atlas of the City of Buffalo, Erie Co., New York (G.M. Hopkins, 1872)
The Courier Company's Map of Buffalo (Buffalo: The Courier Co., 1876)

New York State
Documents of the Assembly of the State of New York

U.S. Census Data
1860 U.S. Census. *Population of the United States in 1860*
1870 U.S. Census. *The Statistics of the Population of the United States*
1880 U.S. Census. *Statistics of the Population of the United States*
1880 U.S. Census. *Report on the Social Statistics of Cities*
1880 U.S. Census. *Report on the Manufactures of the United States*

Index